ATLAS
OF
AMERICAN
WOMEN

To my daughters, Amy and Kate

ATLAS OF AMERICAN WOMEN

Barbara Gimla Shortridge
University of Kansas

MACMILLAN PUBLISHING COMPANY
NEW YORK

Collier Macmillan Publishers
LONDON

Macmillan Publishing Company
866 Third Avenue, New York, N.Y. 10022

Collier Macmillan Canada, Inc.

Library of Congress Catalog Card Number: 86–675054

Printed in the United States of America

printing number
1   2   3   4   5   6   7   8   9   10

Library of Congress Cataloging-in-Publication Data

Shortridge, Barbara Gimla.
   Atlas of American women.

   Much of the atlas based on the 1980 U.S. census in
addition to other sources.
   Bibliography: p.
   1. Women—United States—Maps.   2. Women—United
States—Economic conditions—Maps.   3. Women—United
States—Social conditions—Maps.   4. Women—United
States—Statistics.   I. Title.
G1201.E1S5   1986   912′.13054′0973   86–675054
ISBN 0–02–929120–8

CONTENTS

GRAPHICS LIST

CHAPTER FIVE—EDUCATION

Maps

Tables

CHAPTER SIX—SPORTS

Maps

Table

CHAPTER SEVEN—RELATIONSHIPS

Maps

Table

CHAPTER EIGHT—PREGNANCY

Maps

CHAPTER NINE—HEALTH

Maps

CHAPTER TEN—CRIME

Maps

CHAPTER ELEVEN—POLITICS

Maps

PREFACE

American women have made tremendous strides in recent years toward being accepted as equal members of society. Their accomplishments are well documented. Women have not progressed at the same rate everywhere, however. These variations are the focus of this atlas. Women are compared spatially over a variety of issues related to birth, death, and everything in between. The geography of women provides basic information about what women do. In addition, it is a valuable approach to discrimination issues. Knowing where women are especially low in a particular socioeconomic variable provides needed information for policymakers. Examination of historical trends over space or gender comparison, other approaches to discussing women, are used sparingly and where appropriate throughout the atlas.

Women do not go to the voting booth, the workplace, or their death beds at the same rate everywhere in the United States. For those who rely upon national-level statistics for information about women, the regional variations and ranges between high and low values for the variables in this atlas will come as a surprise. Even though journalists like to emphasize the homogenization of American culture, strong state-to-state variations exist in descriptive measures of that culture. The women of California, for example, are just not the same as the women of Mississippi.

All of our perceptions of reality are cloudy, some more than others. If you see more female doctors and lawyers in your city, perhaps you assume that women are doing all right in your state. But your sample is limited and so is your knowledge about conditions in the neighboring state, let alone a state a thousand miles away. It is not until someone does the data processing and data presentation that objective comparisons can be made. This atlas does that for you—128 maps plus graphs and tables that detail women's participation in the labor force, earnings, jobs, education, athletic endeavors, relationships with other people, childbearing, health, criminal victimization, voter participation, and legislative representation. An opening section on demographics sets the stage and discusses women by age, by residence, and by race.

An attempt has been made to map topics of common interest using the latest data available. Half of the maps in this atlas are based on data from the 1980 U.S. census; the remainder are from various government and private sources. The census is one of the few data-collection agencies that provide extensive state data by sex. Even with underreporting problems of minority racial/ethnic groups, it remains the best source for population, social, and economic data. Data on some topics are just not available at the state level for the entire country; lesbians, contraceptive use, and prostitution are three examples. Other topics, including suicide or inmates of mental institutions, were not included because they involve few women and the variation among states was small.

The classification system used in the choropleth maps (shaded states) in the atlas is based on the United States average for women. The average value for a particular variable runs through the middle of the middle class. The remaining classes, usually two above and two below, are subdivided based on distance of data values from the mean. In general, one may interpret the sequence of boxes to mean very low, low, average, high, and very high.

Because comparisons among women are the emphasis in this atlas, most variables are presented as a percentage of the female population of a state. In some cases a special group of women is used to derive the comparison measure as, for example, females 18 years and over are used to calculate voter-participation rates. Mapping total numbers is meaningless unless one wants to see California, New York, and Texas (the states with the largest number of women) always at the top. Hence the extensive use of percentages that control for the effects of total population. Occasionally absolute numbers have been presented in tabular form to aid the reader in interpretation.

CHAPTER ONE

DEMOGRAPHICS

INTRODUCTION

Women, like men, are not the same throughout the United States. Even in regard to such basic issues as age structure or racial composition significant variations exist from one region of this country to another. This chapter of the atlas presents some of this basic information about women; it is the foundation upon which subsequent chapters build. Take a good look at these maps, for their patterns help to explain many of the regional variations shown throughout the atlas. This is what geography is all about—attempts to explain the spatial variation of a phenomenon. Knowing about other related phenomena makes the process easier.

A basic demographic consideration is where women actually are. As is the case for the population in general, they are spread very unevenly over the surface of our 50 states. California, New York, and Texas, for example, account for 24% of the female population. Although comparison of the sexes is not a focus of this atlas, male/female ratios are presented because the ratio is pertinent to other issues. Maps portray both the overall ratios and those for nonmarried adults aged 20 to 39 years.

Age structure of a population is an important descriptive measure that helps to explain many socioeconomic variables. Median age of women, a standard measure, is presented. Two specific age groups of women are also singled out for mapping: older women over 65 and those 85 and older. The percentage of women in this latter age group is increasing dramatically.

Rural women, those living in settlements of fewer than 2,500 people or in dispersed residences, are the subject of another map. Since women are primarily grouped in metropolitan areas, those parts of the country with more than the average percentage of rural women reveal important information about alternative economic activity. A recent rural renaissance provides interesting cultural and demographic factors.

Mapping increases or decreases from 1970 to 1980 indicates the growth areas where the economy is booming, at least temporarily, and permanent residents have to adjust to the new influx of women. A related issue, population stability, is also mapped by calculating the percentage of women

who lived in the same county in 1980 as they did in 1975.

Although one's religious affiliation (or lack of affiliation) is an important determinant of various attitudes and values, data for church membership by gender are unavailable. Instead, a generalized map of leading denominations by state is presented for the entire population. Racial and ethnic composition of the American population has had important historical implications in the development and vitality of our diverse culture. Since birthrates are high among recent immigrant groups and their children, the racial composition of women in the future will likely be altered. Maps are presented for white, black, Asian and Pacific islanders, and American Indians, Eskimo, and Aleut women. In addition, foreign-born women and women of Hispanic origin are mapped and discussed.

POPULATION

The population distribution of women in the United States affects many of the issues discussed subsequently in this atlas and is an important consideration in understanding the geography of women. Each state's female population is portrayed in Map 1.1 as a circle proportinate in size to the number living in the state. This provides comparisons but since it is difficult for a reader to assign numerical values with this mapping technique, the 1980 female population of each state is also presented (Table 1.1).

The population in this country is unevenly distributed. It would tilt toward the Northeast if a proportional weight were attached to each circle. Not even the counterweight of our most populous state of California, home to 12,001,417 women, manages to destroy this visual effect. If people mean power, as measured, for example, with votes or money generated by industry, jobs, and federal payments to states, then the Northeast controls the country.

If one mentally dissects each of the circles that overhang a state border and then reassembles the parts within the state border, one has an indication of relative population density among women. For many states, of course, there is no need to even disturb the circle, for it falls well within the limits.

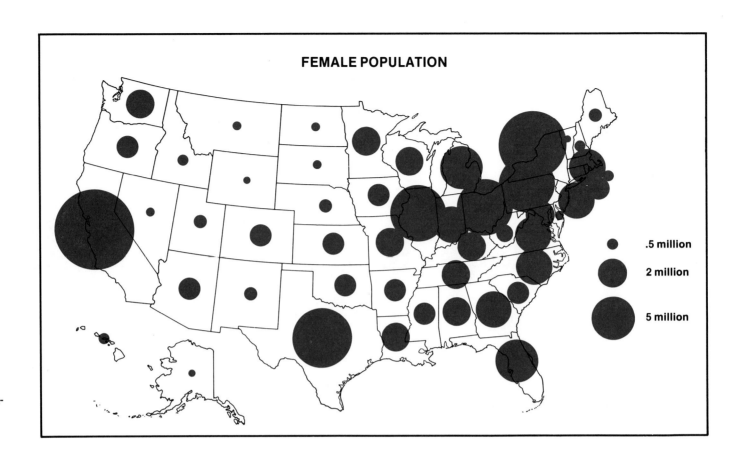

FEMALE POPULATION

.5 million

2 million

5 million

Map 1.1   Female popula-
tion—1980. Total is
116,492,644 women.

TABLE 1.1 FEMALE POPULATION BY STATE					
UNITED STATES	116,492,644				
Alabama	2,022,354	Louisiana	2,166,006	Ohio	5,580,493
Alaska	188,810	Maine	578,425	Oklahoma	1,548,585
Arizona	1,380,273	Maryland	2,174,165	Oregon	1,336,539
Arkansas	1,181,747	Massachusetts	3,006,144	Pennsylvania	6,181,305
California	12,001,417	Michigan	4,745,889	Rhode Island	495,903
Colorado	1,455,671	Minnesota	2,078,144	South Carolina	1,603,807
Connecticut	1,609,571	Mississippi	1,306,760	South Dakota	350,085
Delaware	307,739	Missouri	2,551,199	Tennessee	2,374,520
Florida	5,070,698	Montana	394,065	Texas	7,230,468
Georgia	2,822,660	Nebraska	803,931	Utah	736,536
Hawaii	470,008	Nevada	395,433	Vermont	262,376
Idaho	472,780	New Hampshire	472,148	Virginia	2,728,508
Illinois	5,888,981	New Jersey	3,831,811	Washington	2,079,849
Indiana	2,824,399	New Mexico	660,737	West Virginia	1,004,236
Iowa	1,497,418	New York	9,218,650	Wisconsin	2,400,340
Kansas	1,206,738	North Carolina	3,026,381	Wyoming	228,997
Kentucky	1,871,738	North Dakota	324,291		

Alaska, for example, has a population density of .33 women per square mile. Wyoming, with 2.36 women per square mile, ranks second, and Montana is third with 2.71. New Jersey is at the other extreme, with 513.10. Rhode Island (470.05), Massachusetts (384.22), and Connecticut (330.37) follow.

Even with the well-publicized population shift to the Sun Belt, a lot of women remain in the Northeast. Recent efforts to rejuvenate industry and diversify this Frost Belt are proof of its viability as a region. Note the densely settled metropolitan corridor from Massachusetts to Maryland. If the female population of Connecticut, Maryland, Massachusetts, New Jersey, New York, Pennsylvania, and Rhode Island were added together, the number of women would be 2.2 times the population of California, over a roughly equivalent land area.

Comparisons between males and females are a minor aspect of this atlas. The male/female ratio, however, is particularly germane to subsequent discussions. The number of males per 100 females for each state is presented in Map 1.2. It should come as no surprise that women outnumber men in this country: 116,492,644 versus 110,053,161 in 1980. Where men predominate and at what ages are the intriguing issues.

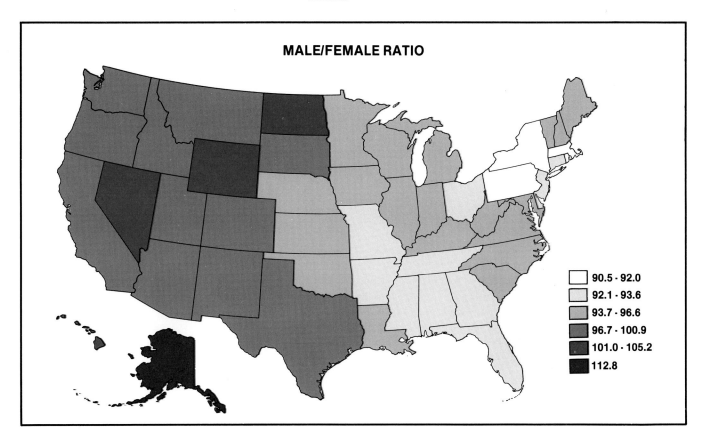

MALE/FEMALE RATIO

☐	90.5 - 92.0
☐	92.1 - 93.6
☐	93.7 - 96.6
☐	96.7 - 100.9
☐	101.0 - 105.2
■	112.8

Map 1.2 Male/female ratio—males per 100 females, 1980. U.S. Average is 94.5.

The ratio of 112.8 men for each 100 women in Alaska is remarkable and merits its own category in the map. Only 47% of Alaska's population is female, compared with the U.S. average of 51.4%. Other states with more males than females, the anomalous situation, are Hawaii, Nevada, North Dakota, and Wyoming. All of the above states are in the western half of the country. Why should this area attract and/or retain more men? Much of the land is harsh and characterized by energy extraction, fishing, forestry, mining and other occupational groupings that have traditionally not included many women. Job opportunities for women, therefore, are largely restricted to subsidiary service occupations. In addition, population in the western half of the country is young, and since American males actually outnumber females in the young age groups, this produces the unexpected gender reversals.

States with exceptionally low male/female ratios are found in the Northeast. New York, with 90.5 males per 100 females, is the lowest. Translated into percentages this means that 52.5% of the state's population is female. Massachusetts and Rhode Island follow with ratios of 90.8 and 91 respectively. Florida, New Jersey, and Pennsylvania are next. One explanation for the extreme dominance of females over males in these parts of the East is the older age structure there. Women simply outlive men. Another factor is that women have a tendency to reside in urban areas and the East is heavily urbanized. In New York, for example, the ratio for urban areas is only 88.9.

Sex ratios change with age. Slightly more boys than girls are born in this country and for children under 5 the ratio is 104.7. From this age onward the ratio declines until in the 25- to 29-year-old cohort women finally outnumber the men (98.9 ratio). Early deaths because of war, accidents, and disease contribute to this change in balance. From the age of 25 on, ratios steadily decline until old age. At 65 to 69 years, the ratio is 80; at 95 to 99, it is 36.4. There is an upward swing only in the 100-and-over category, where the sex ratio is 47.1. Age structure of a population, therefore, is significant in explaining regional differences in sex ratios.

In explaining international differences in sex ratios, culture enters the picture as well. Selective infanticide and maternal deaths during childbirth are important factors. Males outnumber females, on the average, throughout the world (sex ratio 101). Males especially exceed females in South Asia (105) and East Asia (103) whereas females predominate in North America and Europe (95).

Sex ratios for young unmarried males and females are quite different than for the population as a whole. In fact, they are in the women's favor in all 50 states when the number of unmarried males (single, widowed, or divorced) from age 20 to 39 is compared with the number of females in the same categories (Map 1.3). The ratio for all 50 states is 117 eligible males per 100 eligible females. Wyoming represents the best husband-hunting territory with 169.3 males for every 100 females. Alaska is next with a ratio of 161.8. North Dakota and Hawaii follow with ratios of 153.2 and 144.8 respectively. In general, intermontane areas of the West plus South Dakota, Alaska, Hawaii, and Kansas present the best odds. Although there are still more unmarried males between the ages of 20 and 39 in all other parts of the country than unmarried females, the odds deteriorate in parts of the Northeast and the South. New York has the lowest ratio with 106.2, but Massachusetts (107.8) and Georgia (109.8) also have low ratios. Alabama, Delaware, Mississippi, and New Jersey are similar.

How can the sex ratio be in a woman's favor when there are more women than men in this country? Sex ratios for adults in the 20-to-24 bracket are 99.9, for example, whereas those in the 35-to-39 bracket are 96.5. Looking only at marriage-eligible males and females makes the difference. Obviously some women in this age category are married to older men. The "best" sex ratios exist between single males and single females, where the ratio is 136.4. For the 8,992,030 single women, there are 12,261,739 single men. If for some reason a widow would be intent upon finding a widower, then the chances decrease considerably; the ratio is only 21.2. The odds of a divorced woman finding a divorced man are quite a bit better, but still not good; the ratio is 70.3.

AGE

Median age (Map 1.4) is a standard descriptive measure of a population. Half of the female population of a state is younger than the median value, half is older. In 1980 the median age for females in the United States was 31.2 years. Is was slightly higher in urban areas (31.3 years) than in rural areas (31.0). The median age for white women (32.5) is significantly higher than that for black women (26.1) or women of Hispanic origin (23.8). Within each of these racial/ethnic groups the median age for women is higher than that for men. Overall the median male age is 28.8.

Florida has the highest median age for females at 36.6, reflecting the retirement mecca image for that state. In Charlotte County, north of Fort Myers, the median age among females reaches an astounding 57.8 years. Pennsylvania follows Florida at 33.6, with New Jersey next at 33.4. The particular northeastern concentration of higher median ages will be discussed later in this chapter.

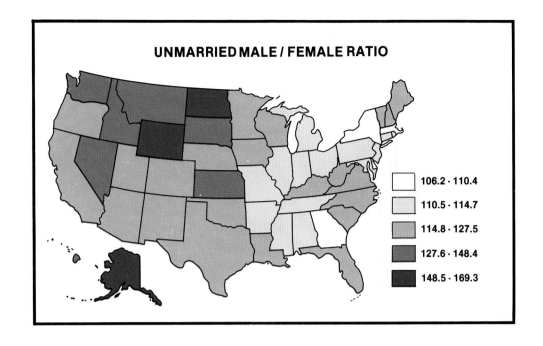

Map 1.3 Unmarried male/female ratio—ratio of single, widowed, and divorced adults, 20 to 39 years of age, 1980. U.S. average is 117.0.

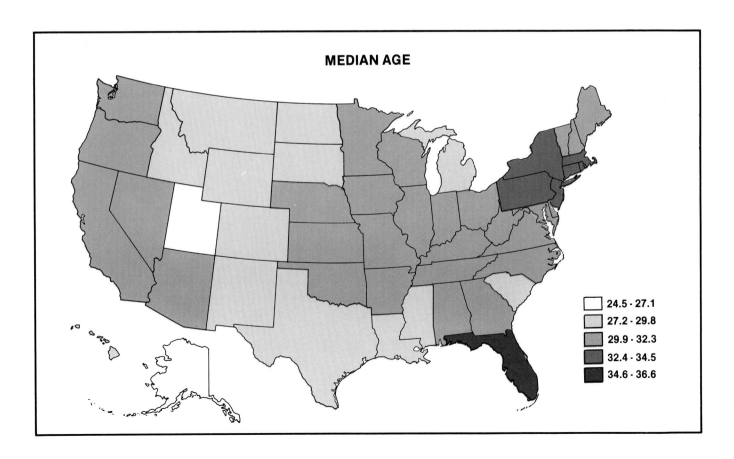

Map 1.4 Median age—1980. U.S. median age for females is 31.2 years.

The lowest median age among women belongs to Utah (24.5 years). Recent growth of this state because of in-migration combined with a high birthrate tends to bring the median age down. Alaska with a median of 25.7 displays a similar youthful profile with similar explanations for its existence. The birthrate for Utah in 1979 was 29.0 per 1,000 residents; for Alaska it was 22.5. These are the two highest birthrates in the United States. In the past, Alaska, with its long and harsh winters, was not a particularly attractive place for older people, but interest in wilderness areas and natural living may change this tendency in the future. Other low median-age values exist throughout the interior West plus the Plains states of North and South Dakota. The tendency toward low median age is also found in parts of the South, Michigan, and Hawaii. In general, the western half of the country is much younger than the eastern half.

A population pyramid of 5-year age groups for both sexes is presented in Figure 1.1. The shape of the charted ages gives demographers descriptive information about a population and allows comparisons across space or through time. Pro-jections of future age structures are also possible. Although called generically a pyramid, the U.S. version has bulges in the midyears and an indentation at the base to ruin the geometrical shape. The constriction at younger ages indicates a sharp decline in birthrates since 1970. Those people too young or too old to work (the percentage of people from birth to 15 years and then those over 65), compared with the remainder of the population in their productive years, creates a dependency ratio. In the United States children do not create as great a financial burden to society as they do in some countries with uncontrolled birthrates. The projected increase in older people, however, will tax the financial resources of the country. Still, middle-aged women outnumber dependent women. Girls up to 14 constitute 21.53% of the female population whereas women 65 and older represent 13.09%. The remainder, from 15 to 64, total 65.41%.

To aid in understanding the generalized information just presented, two age-specific groups of women are mapped. Older women are singled out because of their unique position in society. Those 65 and older constituted only 13.09% of all women in 1980, but their proportion is increasing. What to do with the dependent group is a leading social problem of the future. These questions are even more acute for the second group mapped, the elderly 85 and older.

As a cohort group, older women are increasing proportionally because of improvements in life expectancy and a decline in the birthrate. In 1950 older women represented 8.6% of all females. By 1960 this figure had reached 10.0% and in 1970 it was 11.2. Projections for 1990 are 14.9% with proportions reaching 20.0% by 2020. Both life expectancy and birthrate vary geographically (see health and pregnancy chapters) and thus spatial variation in the proportion of older women is to be expected. Migration to retirement areas also contributes to geographical variation. The effect of large proportions of older women upon local economies is mixed: transfer payments such as social security represent regional income, but social-service costs may stretch the local governmental budget.

Of the 15,235,818 women over 65 in 1980, 6.65% were single, 37.45% married, and 4.18% divorced, but the majority, 51.71%, were widowed. These figures become even more striking when the situation of the nation's 10,262,568 older men is examined. Of them, 5.49% were single, 76.29% were married, 3.64% were divorced, but only 14.57% were widowed. Thus men often have the advantage of approaching the years of increasing physical infirmity with a caring partner; women do not. Not many marriageable men exist for these women. The male/female ratio for persons 65 and over is 67.6—the men have died off.

Figure 1.1
Population pyramid.

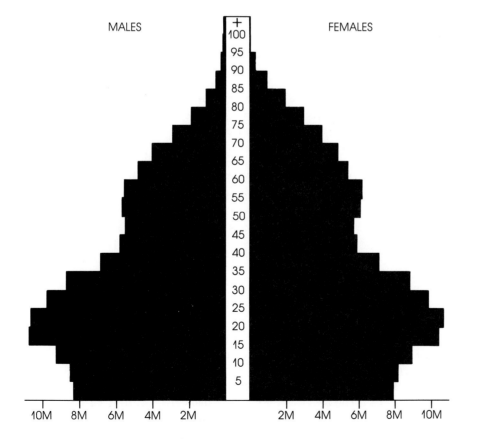

MALES   FEMALES

10M 8M 6M 4M 2M   2M 4M 6M 8M 10M

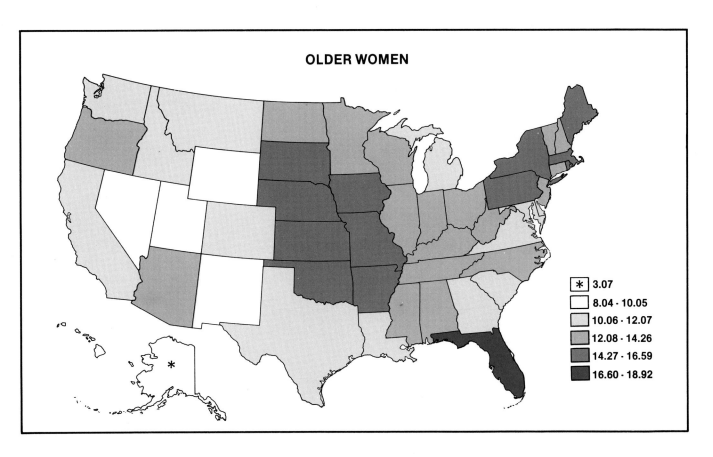

OLDER WOMEN

*	3.07
	8.04 - 10.05
	10.06 - 12.07
	12.08 - 14.26
	14.27 - 16.59
	16.60 - 18.92

Map 1.5 Older women—women 65 years and older as a percentage of all women, 1980. U.S. average is 13.09 percent.

Adequate income is a continuing concern of older women. Some of the income worries of the past have been alleviated by employment retirement plans and increased social-security payments, but for a great number of older women poverty still is just around the corner. Mean annual income for those women with income who were 65 years and older in 1979 was $5,601; for all adult women this figure was $6,928. Except for women 15 to 19 years, whose annual income was $2,313, the dollar amount for older women is the lowest of any age category. In contrast, mean income for men in the older age category was $10,682. The plight of older women is further dramatized by the high percentage whose income in 1979 was below the poverty level. The poverty threshold for a single person 65 and older was $3,479 in 1979. Of all women 65 and older, 17.6%, or 2,510,107, were poor. Again this is the greatest concentration of female poverty in any age group.

The pattern displayed in the map of older women (Map 1.5) represents a complex series of forces. Florida, as expected on the basis of median age data, has the greatest percentage of older women in its population: 18.92%. This high concen-

tration is a result of in-migration by older women in search of a warm climate and other amenities. Charlotte, Pasco, Pinellas, and Sarasota counties in peninsular (West coast Florida) have especially high proportions of older women (above 30%). Other states attractive to retirees, such as Texas, California, the Pacific Northwest, and the Phoenix/Sun City complex in Arizona, have high in-migrations of younger people as well and, therefore, do not show up on a map of older women. The three Ozark states of Arkansas, Missouri, and Oklahoma, however, do show a concentration. Mild winters plus water-based recreational opportunities have led to recent retirement growth in these states.

The remaining two areas of above-average concentrations in the Great Plains and parts of the Northeast are in large part the result of selective out-migration of young adult women. The remaining female population simply stays behind and "ages in place." This tendency is especially prominent in nonmetropolitan areas of these states.

Alaska has the lowest precentage of older women; only 3.07%. Utah is the second lowest, at 8.04%, and similar values are present throughout the youthful West. Low proportions

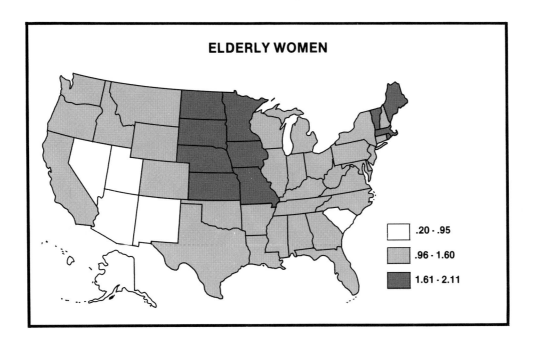

ELDERLY WOMEN

.20 - .95

.96 - 1.60

1.61 - 2.11

Map 1.6   Elderly women—women 85 years and older as a percentage of all women, 1980. U.S. average is 1.34 percent.

of older women are also found in Michigan, selected parts of the South, and Delaware, Maryland, and Virginia. Government-oriented jobs in the Washington, D.C., area account for part of the youth-dominated age structure of these last-mentioned states.

There are proportionally more women over 65 in Europe than in the United States. Especially high rates are found in Western and Northern Europe with Sweden the highest at 19%. In contrast, older women in Africa, South Asia, and the Middle East constitute small shares of the female population because of low life expectancies in these areas. Proportions are especially low in the Ivory Coast, Kuwait, Libya, Mauritania, and Yemen (2%).

Claiming that all women over 65 represent a dependent, nonproducing sector of the population clearly is a bit presumptuous. Many of these women are still working, though often on a part-time or self-employment basis. The dependency claim comes much closer to the truth for those 85 or older. This group is growing rapidly (a 60.9% increase from 1970 to 1980), thanks to the miracles of modern medicine, and we need to reconsider our thinking about how they can be usefully integrated into our society. These women constitute only 1.3% of all women now, but by the year 2000 they are projected to represent 3.5%.

Elderly (85 or older) women are concentrated in the Midwest (Map 1.6). New England forms a secondary high node. Iowa has the highest percentage of elderly women with 2.11%.

Nebraska and South Dakota follow with 2.03% and 2.00%. The residential persistence of elderly women in these areas contributes to part of the explanation; longevity for women in these states is another factor.

Alaska has the lowest percentage of elderly women (.20% of all women). Again, the precedent for elderly women to consider Alaska a possible retirement area does not exist. Recent migrants have not had the opportunity to age in place and decide whether making it through the winter is possible for someone with poor blood circulation. Nevada, Hawaii, and Utah, all youth-oriented states, also have low values of elderly women (.62%, .76%, and .79% respectively).

RURAL/URBAN

An important distinction among women is whether they reside in a rural area or an urban area. Residential setting influences attitudes about many issues such as voting patterns, amount of crime, job opportunities, income limitations, and educational background. For purposes of classification the census divides women into rural and urban categories based on the size of their residential place. If a woman lives in an urbanized area, including central city and urban fringe, or in any place of 2,500 population or more, she is, for official purposes, an urban creature. If she lives in any settlement of fewer than 2,500 or in an area of dispersed population, she is classified as rural. Rural women constitute only 25.52% of the female population, despite the past agrarian reputation of the United States and the vastness of our territorial extent. Central cities contain 30.6% of the women, the urban fringe of large cities 31.83%, places of 10,000 or more 6.04%, and places of 2,500 to 10,000, 6.47%.

California has the lowest percentage of rural women with only 8.29% (Map 1.7). Although California has the most women of any state, numbers of rural women in Georgia, Michigan, New York, North Carolina, Ohio, Pennsylvania, and Texas are greater. Pennsylvania, for example, has 1.8 times the number of rural women as has California, but California has 1.9 times the female population of Pennsylvania. California could be put forward as the ultimate urban environment.

Other states with particularly low percentages of rural women are New Jersey (10.64%), Rhode Island (12.52%), and Hawaii (13.25%). All three states are dominated by urban areas with relatively little empty space left. Greater Providence, for example, accounts for 89.87% of the female population of Rhode Island. More than 78% of women in Hawaii live in Honolulu, and 85.80% of women in New Jersey are in the New Jersey part of New York–Newark–Jersey City and Philadelphia–Wilmington–Trenton.

Parts of the upper Midwest, intermontane states, upper New England, and the South have high proportions of rural women. Vermont with 64.83% has the highest. The villages here, in fact, epitomize the nonfarm country life. West Virginia follows with 62.50%; South Dakota is next.

Standard Metropolitan Statistical Areas (SMSAs) are census-designated agglomerations of counties that form major urban areas. People within them have good access to the cultural events, variety in job opportunities, specialized medical care, shopping facilities, and other amenities associated with cities. In the United States 74.99% of women live in areas falling in this class. California leads with 95.03% of its women living in SMSAs—never far from a shopping center. In Rhode Island, New Jersey, and New York, the figures are 92.47%, 91.46%, and 90.42%, respectively. Wyoming has the lowest proportion of women within SMSAs: 15.41%. South Dakota has 16.31%, whereas Idaho has 18.59%. Other low states include Mississippi, Montana, and Vermont.

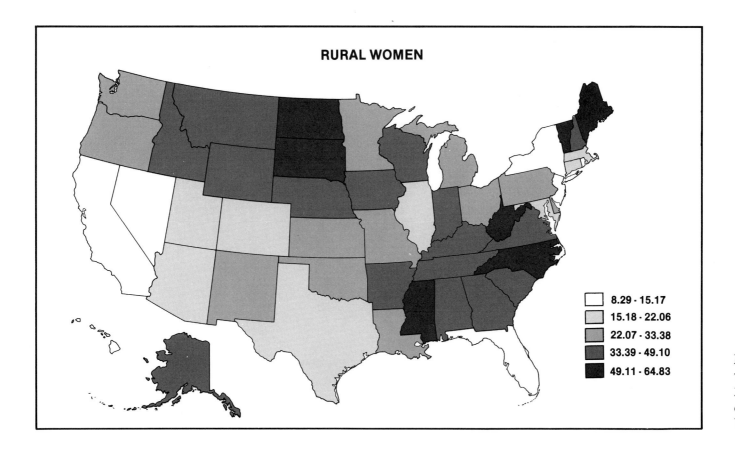

RURAL WOMEN

☐	8.29 - 15.17
☐	15.18 - 22.06
☐	22.07 - 33.38
☐	33.39 - 49.10
☐	49.11 - 64.83

Map 1.7 Rural women— women who live in places with 2,500 or fewer people as a percentage of all women, 1980. U.S. average is 25.52 percent.

MIGRATION

The female population in this country is in a constant flux. Every day some move coast to coast to assume new jobs, others move across town as a move up, relocate from city to suburb, and make the migration to mild winters upon retirement. Often changes in residence correspond with changes in the life-cycle. Marriage, birth of children, attaining business success, retirement, and death of a spouse are a few occasions that may prompt a move.

Two interrelated issues are discussed. First the percentage increase or decrease from 1970 to 1980 in a state's female population is presented (Map 1.8). Two aspects of natural increase—death and birthrates—account for some of the geographical variation in population growth, but in-migration is another significant factor. Next, areas of residential persistence are highlighted (Map 1.9), stable population areas where not many new women are coming in and those that are already there are staying put.

Nevada leads the nation with the greatest percentage increase in women from 1970 to 1980 (64.12%). Arizona follows with 53.38%; Florida has 44.31%. Above-average percentage increases occur within a diagonal strip from Oregon to Arizona to Texas to Wyoming. Alaska and Hawaii are also included. Anomalies in the eastern half of the country include New Hampshire and Florida. Florida's attractiveness is evident, but not that of New Hampshire. Low state-income taxes may be one attractive factor, country life style may be another. Recent relocation of formerly Boston-based industries in the southern half of New Hampshire certainly is a source of new jobs. If one considers absolute increases in female population instead of percentage increases, the leaders are California, Florida, and Texas. Together these three states accounted for 40.5% of all growth in the female population. After the three blockbuster states (increases from 1.5 to 1.9 million women), there is a significant fall-off to the next states of Arizona, Georgia, and North Carolina (all increases in the 400,000 range).

New York was the only state with a decrease in female population between 1970 and 1980; its loss of 302,978 women amounted to a 3.18% decrease. States with very low increases include Pennsylvania (.86%), Massachusetts (1.22%), and Ohio (1.67%). Rhode Island, Illinois, Connecticut, and Iowa represent the next round. A critical planning issue for these northeastern states is precisely which groups of women are leaving these states and which groups are remaining. If all the movers are young professional women with critical job skills, there should be concern. If the stayers are welfare recipients, there also should be concern.

Demographers explain population mobility by using a set of "push/pull" factors. In the case of population increase, the western states may be seen as attractive because of new jobs (energy-related in part, but others associated with service industries in a booming economy), open spaces, a more casual and natural life-style, and a move to the sun. Examples of push factors, those that make the northeastern states no longer attractive, are bad economic conditions, cold winters, and a perception that an area of the country is falling behind the mainstream.

At the opposite end of the residential migration spectrum from growth areas are those parts of the country where women display residential persistence. Stayers, for purposes of Map 1.9, are defined as those women who were in the same house in 1980 as they were in 1975, plus those women who changed homes during the time period, but remained in the same county. Local moves, such as from a city to a suburb, most likely would still qualify a woman as a stayer. By expanding the category in this way, intraurban moves are largely eliminated from consideration and interstate or long-distance moves are the focus.

Of all females 5 years and older in the United States, 79.6% lived in the same county in 1980 as they did in 1975. In a society known for its footlooseness, this figure should come as a shock: We still are a residentially stable people. As expected from the previous map, considerable geographical variation exists in stability. The women of Pennsylvania displayed the greatest residential stability with 87.5% remaining in the same county. Rhode Island and Ohio also had high values (85.2% for both). Connecticut, Illinois, Massachusetts, New York, and West Virginia follow. The stayers are concentrated in older parts of the country, especially in old manufacturing and coal-mining areas. A regional exception occurs in the Virginia–Maryland Area, the hinterland for Washington, D.C., employment. Recent Sun Belt moves to Florida and Georgia reduced the stayer percentage in these two southern states. A rural renaissance in Vermont had a similar effect.

The parts of the country that belong to the movers, women who made an out-of-the-county move between 1975 and 1980, correspond roughly with the growth areas shown on the previous map. The most mobile state is Alaska with only 60.7% of its women remaining in the same county from one time period to the next. Nevada, Wyoming, and Colorado follow with 63.2%, 63.6%, and 64.0% stability, respectively. These rapidly growing areas of the country have lots of mobile homes and high numbers of rental properties, both indicators of a transient population.

Socioeconomic variables are related to stability. High income, education, and a professional occupation contribute to a propensity to migrate. So does being young. Women

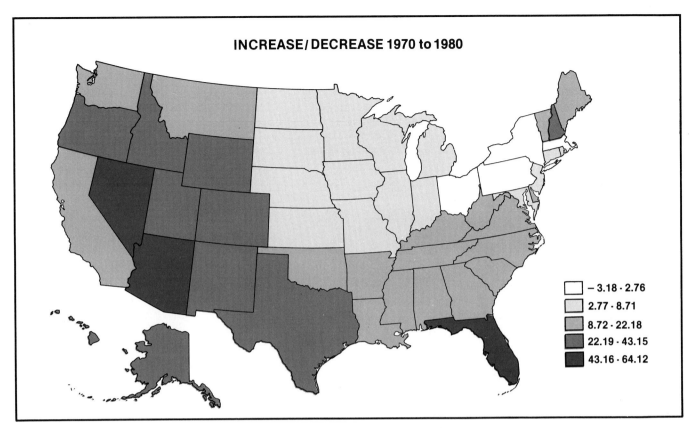

INCREASE/DECREASE 1970 to 1980

- − 3.18 - 2.76
- 2.77 - 8.71
- 8.72 - 22.18
- 22.19 - 43.15
- 43.16 - 64.12

Map 1.8 Increase/decrease in female population 1970 to 1980—the number of women in the U.S. increased 11.69 percent between 1970 and 1980.

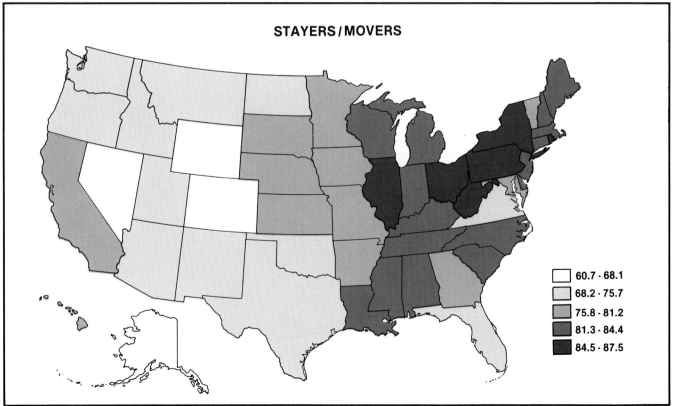

STAYERS/MOVERS

- 60.7 - 68.1
- 68.2 - 75.7
- 75.8 - 81.2
- 81.3 - 84.4
- 84.5 - 87.5

Map 1.9 Stayers/Movers— percentage of females 5 years and older who lived in the same county in 1975 and 1980. U.S. average is 79.6 percent.

who are passing points in the life-cycle such as career advancement, marriage, and/or first child show considerable mobility. After age 30 when stable women represent 71.4% of their cohorts, the degree of stability increases progressively with age. Older women from 70 to 74 are the most geographically stable group of all (91.23%). Widows are more stable than other women. Among racial groups, black women are the most stable with 87.54% remaining within a county. Asians and Pacific islanders have the lowest stability of any racial group (57.11%) whereas white women (79.04%), American Indian–Eskimo–Aleut women (77.04%) and Hispanic women (78.16%) come close to the overall average (79.63%).

C Catholic Church

B Southern Baptist Convention

M United Methodist Church

LDS Church of Jesus Christ of Latter-Day Saints

L American Lutheran Church

() Denomination less than 10 percent

C High religious intensity (greater than 60 percent of population are adherents)

* Low religious intensity (less than 40 percent of population are adherents)

RELIGION

Religion is an important part of the lives of more than half of the women in this country, and religious affiliation, in turn, has direct bearing upon social attitudes, voting patterns, and the like. Religious affiliation also may indicate socioeconomic status. Small-scale surveys reveal that more women than men attend church regularly and that women are considered more religious than men, but no national data set exists that divides major denominational groups both by state and by gender. As a result, Map 1.10 is the only map in this atlas that is based upon the entire population, not just women. Data are from a 1980 survey sponsored by the

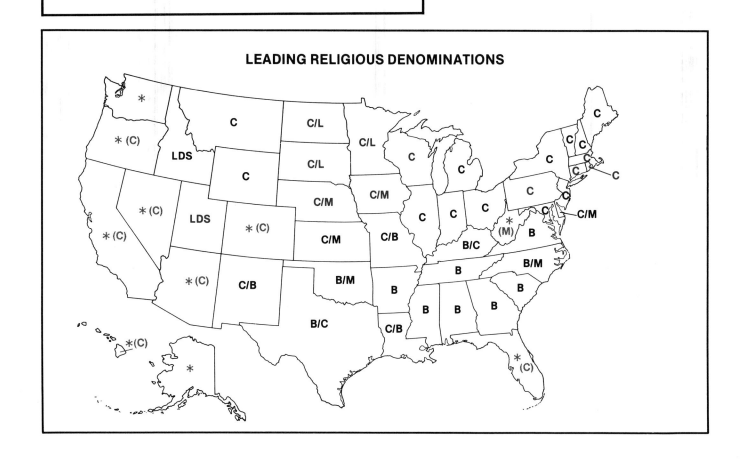

LEADING RELIGIOUS DENOMINATIONS

National Council of the Churches of Christ and other research organizations, and are limited to church bodies identified as Judeo-Christian. Independent churches with no connection to a major denomination also are not included.

Religious involvement as measured by the percentage of the population that adheres to any denomination is one variable indicated on the map. States with less than 40% of their population belonging to a church are singled out; so are those with more than 60%. Low-intensity states include Alaska, Arizona, California, Colorado, Florida, Hawaii, Oregon, Nevada, Washington, and West Virginia. The inclusion of Buddhism in Hawaii's total would increase that state's religious involvement. Similarly, West Virginia is low because it has many local autonomous groups not affiliated with a reporting denomination. Other low-value states, however, are genuinely low in religious involvement. They represent areas of high in-migration where people often go to escape traditional lifestyles, including organized religion. Percentages are as low as 29.3 in Nevada, 30.8 in Alaska, and 31.0 in Washington.

Highly religious states are located in a northeast cluster of Connecticut, Massachusetts, Pennsylvania, and Rhode Island, as well as Utah in the West and an upper midwestern cluster of Iowa, Nebraska, Minnesota, North Dakota, South Dakota, and Wisconsin. Church participation rates are as high as 75.5% in Rhode Island and 75.2% in Utah.

Leading religious denominations is the other variable indicated on the map. In order to be included, a denomination had to represent at least 10% of the population of a state. If more than one church qualified, the one with the most adherents is listed first. Even with this low threshold, only five denominations met the criterion.

Catholicism is the largest American church, both in terms of numbers (47,502,152 adherents or 21.0% of the population) and geographical extent. Catholics are rare only in parts of the South, and the church dominates in French Louisiana and Hispanic areas of the Southwest. On a state basis, Rhode Island has the highest percentage of Catholics with 63.7%. Massachusetts (53.0%) and Connecticut (44.7%) follow. Even though they are labeled Catholics, many attitudes—for example, toward birth-control practices and activism within the church—vary greatly between the East-coast liberal Catholic and the more traditional variety found in the Hispanic borderlands and Louisiana.

The Southern Baptist Convention, the largest Protestant denomination and a conservative one, claims 16,281,692 members or 7.2% of the American population. Located primarily in the South, but extending as far west as eastern New Mexico, Baptist dominance stops at the Kansas border, but oozes over into southern Illinois and Indiana. North Floridians are Southern Baptists, but there are not enough of them to pull the state out of its low-ranking religious category. As states, Alabama (30.4% of population) and Mississippi (30.2%) have the highest concentrations of Baptists.

The United Methodist Church, one of the moderate Protestant groups, has 11,552,111 members and 5.1% of the population. On the map it does not dominate in any one state, but shares status with Baptists or Catholics in the Iowa, Kansas, Nebraska, and Oklahoma cluster and in Delaware and North Carolina. The denomination is present nationally, and shows its greatest concentration in West Virginia, with 11.3% of the population. Kansas at 11.1% has the next highest value. Unlike the other Protestant denominations discussed, Methodists are not a regional institution but belong to almost all of America.

The Church of Jesus Christ of Latter-day Saints is intensely conservative and regionalized. It represents only 1.2% of the total American population, but 67.4% of Utah's population. Idaho is 25.5% Mormon and Wyoming 8.6%. The church has 2,684,744 members, and its strength clearly is in the western half of the country.

The American Lutheran Church, another moderate Protestant group, represents 2,361,845 members (1.0% of the population). It is primarily concentrated in the upper Midwest, with occasional enclaves asociated with ethnic groups in other parts of the country. North Dakota has the greatest concentration with 25.1% of its population belonging to this Lutheran body. South Dakota (16.0%) and Minnesota (12.0%) follow.

Together, these five denominations account for 35.5% of the American population. Another 14.2% are dispersed among the other 106 denominations of the survey. Truly this fact alone reveals our religious diversity. The remaining 50.3% of Americans do not belong to any of the surveyed denominations.

RACE/ETHNICITY

Determining the race of a person can be a sensitive and complex issue. Underreporting of some racial groups became one of the more controversial aspects of the 1980 census following publication of preliminary tabulations. Question 4 asked respondents to self-report their race by checking one of the following: White; black; American Indian, Eskimo, or Aleut; Asian and Pacific islander; or an "other" category. Some people find it difficult to determine their race, and self-classification can be expected to provoke many problems. Census officials undertook several reviews of the issue. Following are the general rules established for classification purposes.

If a person could not provide a single response to the

race question, the race of a person's mother was used. If this provided problems as well, then the first race reported was assigned. Each racial category includes those checking the box plus some additional options. White, for example, includes those people who indicated an identity in the "other" category with a country having a predominantly white population such as Canada or Poland. Women specifying such groups as Jamacian, black Puerto Rican, West Indian, Haitian, or Nigerian were assigned black. American Indian, Eskimo, or Aluet includes people who gave the name of a specific tribe. The Asian and Pacific islander category included specific check areas for race as Chinese, Filipino, Japanese, Asian Indian, Korean, Vietnamese, Hawaiian, Samoan, or Guamanian as well as write-in entries for Cambodian, Laotian, Pakistani, or Fijian under the "other" category. The "other," or not elsewhere classified, category is not mapped in this atlas because its contents are confounded. It includes people calling themselves Cuban, Puerto Rican, Mexican, or Dominican, people who specified Spanish origin, and write-in entries such as Eurasian, "cosmopolitan," or interracial. The biggest change from the 1970 census was in the reporting

of people of Spanish or Hispanic origin. In 1970, 93% of these peoples were self-classified as white; in 1980 only 58% opted for the white category, perhaps as a result of a growing consciousness among people of this origin.

The following maps present the spatial distribution of four racial groups of women based on their percentage of the total female population. Although some people would prefer that Americans abolish such racial distinctions as discriminatory, others point to the benefits gained by having detailed socioeconomic information divided by race. Seen by enlightened legislators and other policymakers, inequalities among races could result in direct aid to the disadvantaged group.

White women constitute the largest racial group among women in the United States (Map 1.11). In 1980 they represented 83.0% of the female population, a total of 96,686,289 women. The highest concentrations were found in the north central Plains and Mountain states, plus New England and West Virginia. Vermont had the highest value with 99.12%. New Hampshire and Maine followed with 98.92% and 98.76% respectively.

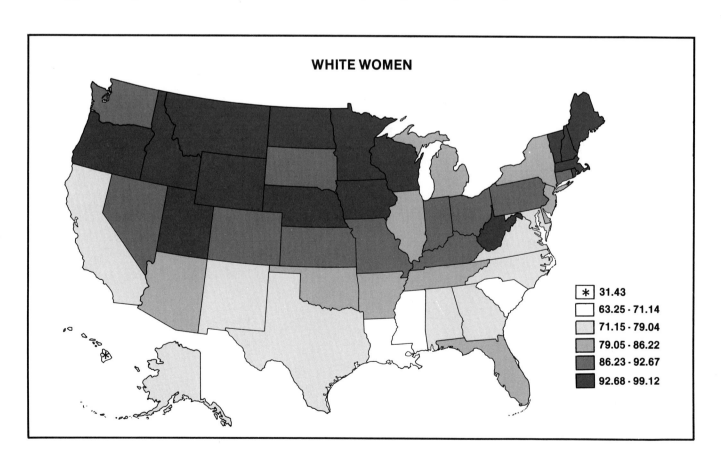

WHITE WOMEN

✳	31.43
	63.25 - 71.14
	71.15 - 79.04
	79.05 - 86.22
	86.23 - 92.67
	92.68 - 99.12

Map 1.11 White women—as a percentage of all women, 1980. U.S. average is 83.00 percent.

TABLE 1.2 SOCIOECONOMIC VARIABLES BY RACE AND HISPANIC ORIGIN

	HIGH SCHOOL[a]	BRAINS[b]	FERTILITY RATE[c]	LABOR FORCE[d]	UNEMPLOYED[e]	MEDIAN INCOME[f]	POVERTY LEVEL[g]	STAYERS[h]	SINGLE[i]	MARRIED[j]	SEPARATED[k]	WIDOWED[l]	DIVORCED[m]	URBAN[n]
All Women	63.6	11.0	1302	49.9	6.5	$5514	13.8	79.6	23.0	54.8	2.7	12.4	7.2	74.5
White	65.9	11.5	1246	49.4	5.7	$5612	10.6	79.0	21.2	57.4	1.8	12.6	7.0	72.1
Black	51.0	6.7	1576	53.3	11.3	$4863	32.5	87.5	34.4	35.1	8.8	12.8	9.1	85.9
American Indian, Aleut, Eskimo	50.8	4.7	1687	48.1	11.9	$4552	29.4	77.0	28.9	48.0	4.1	8.9	10.1	54.5
Asian and Pacific Islander	68.9	22.9	1194	57.7	5.2	$6908	12.9	57.1	25.0	61.7	1.7	7.6	4.0	92.7
Hispanic Origin	42.1	4.8	1591	49.3	9.6	$4943	25.2	78.2	27.6	52.8	5.0	7.2	7.5	90.4

[a] Percentage of women fifteen years and older who were high school graduates, 1980.
[b] Percentage of women fifteen years and older who had completed more than four years of college, 1980.
[c] Children ever born per 1000 women age 15 to 44, 1980.
[d] Percentage of women sixteen years and older in labor force in 1980.
[e] Percentage of women sixteen years and older unemployed in 1980.
[f] Median income of women eighteen years and older in 1980.
[g] Percentage of women below poverty level in 1979.
[h] Percentage of women five years and older who stayed in the same county from 1975 to 1980.
[i] Percentage of women fifteen years and older who were single, 1980.
[j] Percentage of women fifteen years and older who were married, 1980.
[k] Percentage of women fifteen years and older who were separated, 1980.
[l] Percentage of women fifteen years and older who were widowed, 1980.
[m] Percentage of women fifteen years and older who were divorced, 1980.
[n] Percentage of women who lived in an urban environment in 1980.

The New England states, a destination of early European settlers, have retained their largely white racial composition through time. French-Canadians have been the most recent and distinguishable immigrant group there, assuming low-paying jobs. Many of the midcontinental states were destinations for whites from older eastern states and various northern European peoples, especially Germans, Scandinavians, and various Slavic groups. The most southerly state to be included in the exceptionally high category is Utah. An environmental ordering is suggested by the north–south pattern. Certainly the slavery heritage is a factor, but perhaps also women of other races may consider the cold winters of the North an abomination.

Areas of low concentration of white women extend across the extreme southern states of the country and part way up the East coast. Arizona and Florida both form exceptions to the generalization, mostly because they have been migration destinations for whites from the North. The lowest value belongs to Hawaii; here the 31.43% white is so low that the state merits a separate category. Asian and native groups in Hawaii have always been predominant. Mississippi also has a low value (63.25%), followed by South Carolina, Louisiana, Georgia, Alabama, Maryland, and New Mexico. In all of these states except New Mexico black women form the second leading racial group. In New Mexico the "other" category is prominent, referring here to the approximately 14.5% in this state who are of Hispanic origin and have elected not to include themselves in the white category. A third-level group in New Mexico is the 8.3% who are American Indians.

White women, of course, display the same internal diversity as any of the racial groups covered here. Just because they have light-colored skin does not mean they agree on all other attributes. Nevertheless, several summary statistics for white women as well as the other racial groups plus women of Hispanic origin are presented in Table 1.2. Many of these same variables are presented by state in other parts of this atlas, but not by race.

Black women have endured double discrimination in our

society. Though individually they have made great strides, as a group they are hampered by poverty. These women constitute 12.0% of the American female population. Most are concentrated in the South (46.3% in 12 states), but New York has the largest number with 1,307,696. California, Illinois, and Texas follow in that order.

The present distribution of black women displayed in Map 1.12 is best explained by looking at the past migration patterns in this country. Blacks were originally imported to be an agricultural labor source for tropical and subtropical crops such as tobacco, rice, cotton, and indigo. Since these crops were grown in the South, the slaves of African origin entered through southern ports and then spread to nearby hinterlands. Early areas of forced settlement centered on the Chesapeake Bay area and coastal South Carolina. From there slaves were traded and spread to the cotton-producing areas in Alabama, Mississippi, Louisiana, and Texas. At the time of the Civil War the extent of blacks approximated that of the Confederacy.

After emancipation, small numbers of blacks went to Kansas and several northeastern states. Large migrations, however, did not take place until World War I. Wartime labor shortages in northern manufacturing cities were accentuated when the European immigrant flow stopped during the war. Some blacks took advantage of the circumstances and moved to middle Atlantic and Great Lakes states. South-to-north movement of blacks continued in the interwar period with a combination of rural poverty and urban job opportunities being the chief motivating factors. Chicago, Cleveland, and Detroit were early centers; Cincinnati, Indianapolis, New York, Philadelphia, and St. Louis followed. Because blacks were not readily assimilated into the dominant white culture in these cities, they settled in ghettos. During World War II, industrial opportunities encouraged even greater black movement to urban centers and Boston, Buffalo, Los Angeles, Milwaukee, Rochester, and San Francisco joined the list of favored destinations. Very recently a countermigration of educated and skilled northern blacks back to the South has begun, following poor economic conditions in the North. The blacks left behind in northern ghettos are often poor and now compete with newly arrived Hispanics and Asians for lower-rung jobs.

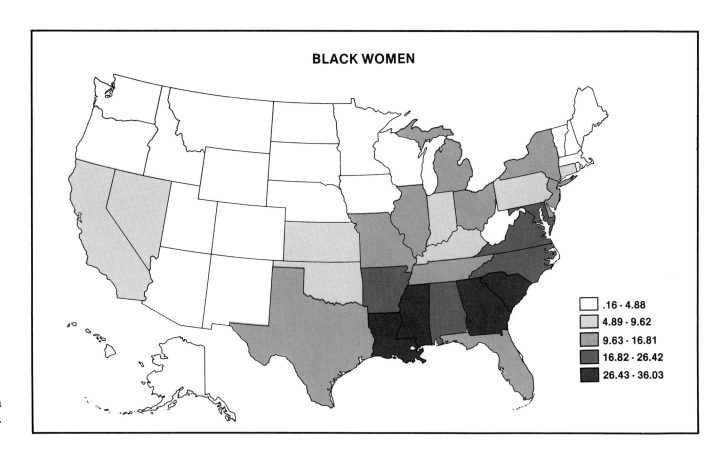

BLACK WOMEN

.16 - 4.88
4.89 - 9.62
9.63 - 16.81
16.82 - 26.42
26.43 - 36.03

Map 1.12   Black women—as a percentage of all women, 1980. U.S. average is 12.00 percent.

TABLE 1.3 BLACK WOMEN IN SMSAs

LOCATION	%
Anaheim–Santa Ana–Garden Grove, Calif.	1.19
Atlanta, Ga.	25.45
Baltimore, Md.	26.22
Boston, Mass.	5.86
Buffalo, N.Y.	9.38
Chicago, Ill.	20.85
Cincinnati, Ohio-Ky.-Ind.	12.77
Cleveland, Ohio	18.73
Columbus, Ohio	12.51
Dallas–Fort Worth, Tex.	14.57
Denver-Boulder, Colo.	4.78
Detroit, Mich.	21.03
Fort Lauderdale–Hollywood, Fla.	11.07
Houston, Tex.	18.90
Indianapolis, Ind.	13.77
Kansas City, Mo.-Ks.	13.37
Los Angeles–Long Beach, Calif.	12.98
Miami, Fla.	17.22
Milwaukee, Wis.	11.09
Minneapolis–St. Paul, Minn.-Wis.	2.29
Nassau-Suffolk, N.Y.	6.47
New Orleans, La.	33.67
New York, N.Y.-N.J.	21.97
Newark, N.J.	21.90
Philadelphia, Pa.-N.J.	19.34
Phoenix, Ariz.	3.09
Pittsburgh, Pa.	7.96
Portland, Oreg.-Wash.	2.62
Riverside–San Bernardino–Ontario, Calif.	4.87
Sacramento, Calif.	5.94
St. Louis, Mo.-Ill.	17.88
San Antonio, Tex.	6.87
San Diego, Calif.	5.19
San Francisco–Oakland, Calif.	12.19
San Jose, Calif.	3.29
Seattle-Everett, Wash.	3.50
Tampa–St. Petersburg, Fla.	9.37
Washington, D.C.-Md.-Va.	28.59

Louisiana to South Carolina in 1980, the same areas of intense plantation agriculture and slavery outlined earlier. Mississippi has the highest percentage of blacks among its women: 36.03%. South Carolina and Louisiana follow with 31.23% and 30.36% respectively. The northern states containing those urban centers mentioned previously fall within the average category.

Small numbers of black women reside in parts of the mountain West, upper Midwest, New England, Alaska, Hawaii, and West Virginia. Although this latter state provides a distinctive gap spatially, West Virginia has neither large cities nor heavy industry to attract blacks. Montana has the lowest percentage of black women (.16%); Vermont is next with .19%. Other especially small percentages are found in Idaho, Maine, New Hampshire, North Dakota, and South Dakota. None of these states have any attracting factors; they lack metropolitan areas and established settlements of blacks.

At the SMSA level the current distribution of black women reflects past migration patterns (Table 1.3). New Orleans has the highest concentration with 33.67% of its women in this racial category; it is followed in order by Washington, D.C., Baltimore, and Atlanta. Anaheim-Santa Ana-Garden Grove has the lowest percentage of black women (1.19%); Minneapolis-St.Paul, Phoenix, Portland, San Jose, and Seattle-Everett also have low proportions.

To group all Asian-origin women in one category undoubtedly hides many interesting map patterns (Map 1.13). To add in Pacific islanders only compounds the problem. In defense, the total number of Asian and Pacific islander women in this country is small in a relative sense, only 1.55% of all women. Filipinos, the single largest group, constitutes only .34% of all women.

Chinese and Japanese women in the United States are largely second-generation or older. Filipino, Korean, and Vietnamese women, however, have immigrated more recently. Immigrants from 1970 to 1980 account for 46.39% of all Filipino women, 69.61% of Korean women, and 84.87% of Vietnamese women.

Hawaii has the highest concentration of Asian and Pacific islanders: 62.80% of its women classified themselves as belonging to this racial category. California has the next highest percentage with 5.33%, followed by Washington with 2.60% and Alaska with 2.22%. This West-coast dominance reflects the ports of entry for these immigrants. Average values of Asian women are found in Illinois and three eastern Seaboard states, all places with at least one large metropolitan area. Many states have an insignificant Asian presence among their women. Alabama and West Virginia have the lowest values with .28%; Maine, South Dakota, and Vermont follow.

Filipino women, 400,461 in number, are largely based

What has been sketched above is the historical migration of all blacks; little specific information exists on paths of black women and thus we must assume (perhaps erroneously) that they followed their families. The geography of black women, as with other double minorities, has been lost in the geography of blacks and the geography of women. At any rate, black women were concentrated in the lower southern states of

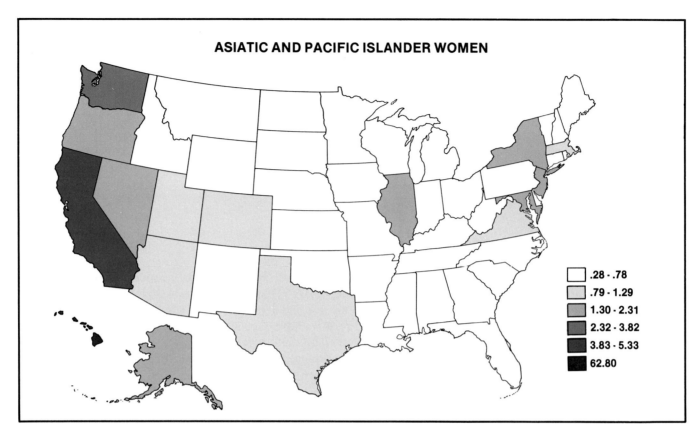

ASIATIC AND PACIFIC ISLANDER WOMEN

☐	.28 - .78
	.79 - 1.29
	1.30 - 2.31
	2.32 - 3.82
	3.83 - 5.33
■	62.80

Map 1.13 Asiatic and Pacific islander women—as a percentage of all women, 1980. U.S. average is 1.55 percent.

AMERICAN INDIAN, ESKIMO, AND ALEUT WOMEN

☐	.08 - .28
	.29 - .50
	.51 - 2.16
	2.17 - 5.25
	5.26 - 8.34
■	16.72

Map 1.14 American Indian, Eskimo, and Aleut women—as a percentage of all women, 1980. U.S. average is .62 percent.

in California (42.28%) and Hawaii (16.01%) with a secondary concentration in Illinois (6.08%). Chinese women, the next minority group with 398,496 members, are also based in California (40.52%), but New York is the next preferred location (18.10%). Hawaii ranks third (7.13%). The 380,033 Japanese women are highly urbanized with Los Angeles and Honolulu the favorite locales. California claims 36.85% of these women and Hawaii 32.57%. A smaller number, 3.95%, reside in Washington. The 206,768 Korean women show more variation in their locational choice but California remains in first place (27.30%). New York (8.98%), Illinois (6.33%), and Hawaii (5.06%) are other leading locations. Asian Indian women, who total 174,448, show a similar dispersed pattern: 16.56% of them live in New York, 15.70% in California, and 9.51% in Illinois. Finally, the 126,089 Vietnamese women show the most scattered pattern, a surprising finding for recent immigrants, but one explained by a deliberate governmental policy of dispersed settlement. Secondary migrations to ethnic enclaves in large cities may alter this pattern. California is a favorite state for Vietnamese women (34.11%), but Texas (10.91%), Virginia (4.12%), and Louisiana (4.11%) are also highly ranked.

American Indian, Eskimo, and Aleut women are truly a minority in this country as they represented only 718,172 women in 1980, .62% of all women (Map 1.14). The American Indian population today is approximately at the same size as it was 500 years ago. Population growth is now the rule, however. High birthrates, increased medical care, better sanitary conditions, and improved diet all contribute.

Eskimo and Aleut women constitute only a small portion of the mapped variable, 2.87% and .98% respectively of the women in the category. Of the 20,637 Eskimo women, 81.12% are located in Alaska. The next largest groups are in California (3.86%) and Washington (3.2%). Aleut women are a bit more dispersed, although Alaska still accounts for the majority (56.58%) of the 7,019 women. California is home to 10.7% and Washington to 10.5%.

American Indian women are concentrated in the western half of the country. Some reside on reservations but more live in urban settings along with non-Indians. Los Angeles, Oklahoma City, Phoenix, San Francisco, and Tulsa are the most popular locations. The western pattern in part reflects past relocation policies that forced Indians out of the East into what was thought to be worthless land in the West. Mineral production on some of these reservations has been an unexpected bonus to tribes. Cherokees in North Carolina remain one of the few tribes of any number left in the East.

Alaska has an exceptionally high percentage of American Indian, Eskimo, and Aleut women in its female population and thus garners a special category. New Mexico has the most intense concentration of the coterminous states (8.34%). South Dakota follows with 6.56%. In terms of total numbers, California leads with 101,931 or 14.19% of all American Indian women. Oklahoma (86,604) and Arizona (78,348) also represent large numbers, as do New Mexico (55,087), North Carolina (32,582), and Alaska (31,561).

Minuscule proportions of American Indian women are present throughout most of the East plus Texas. Small percentages in Arkansas, Maine, Michigan, Minnesota, North Carolina, Rhode Island, and Wisconsin are, in part, explained by the presence of still-active tribes, reservations, or, in the case of Arkansas, a spillover effect from Oklahoma. Pennsylvania and West Virginia have the lowest percentage of native American women in their populations (.08%), but Kentucky, New Jersey, Ohio, and Tennessee follow close behind.

A major focus of the 1980 census was to identify people of Hispanic origin. Respondents who identified themselves to be of Spanish or Hispanic origin or descent were asked to place themselves in categories of Mexican, Puerto Rican, Cuban, Spanish or other Hispanic origin. The latter two categories include women from Spain and Spanish-speaking countries of Central or South America, as well as those who labeled themselves Spanish-American, Hispano, or Latino. Data collected in 1980 for people of Spanish origin are not comparable with those collected in 1970; a different question design was used.

The 7,328,842 women of Hispanic origin reported in 1980 constituted 6.29% of all women in the United States (Map 1.15). As with the previous racial groups, distinct settlement clusters exist. New Mexico, with an exceptionally high 36.53%, deserves a separate category. Texas (20.73%) and California (18.71%) are the next leading states with Arizona following (15.97%). Highest concentrations of Hispanic women, therefore, exist in a core group of four southwestern states along the borderlands with Mexico. Secondary concentrations are found in Colorado and New York.

Many other parts of the United States contain almost no women of Hispanic origin. This is true for large sections of the Northwest, Midwest, South, and the Northeast. Florida, Illinois, New Jersey, and New York form the regional exceptions to this large void. In Maine the percentage of Hispanic origin women is as low as .41%. In South Dakota it is .55% New Hampshire, North Dakota, Vermont, and West Virginia have similar lows.

Metropolitan residences for Hispanic women duplicate the pattern for states (Table 1.4). These women are concentrated in southwestern cities with San Antonio having the highest percentage among its female population (45.12%). Miami and Los Angeles also have exceptionally high values.

Women of Mexican origin, with 4,297,798 members, are

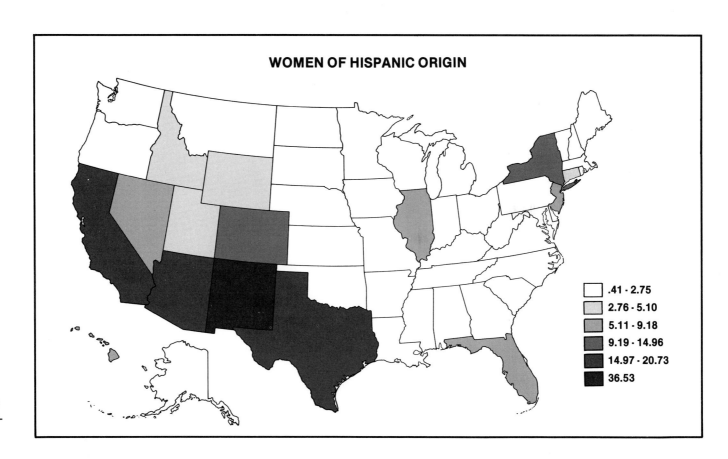

WOMEN OF HISPANIC ORIGIN

.41 - 2.75
2.76 - 5.10
5.11 - 9.18
9.19 - 14.96
14.97 - 20.73
36.53

Map 1.15 Women of Hispanic origin—as a percentage of all women, 1980. U.S. average is 6.29 percent.

TABLE 1.4 WOMEN OF HISPANIC ORIGIN IN SMSAs

LOCATION	%	LOCATION	%
Anaheim–Santa Ana–Garden Grove, Calif.	14.15	Minneapolis–St. Paul, Minn.-Wis.	1.01
Atlanta, Ga.	1.13	Nassau-Suffolk, N.Y.	3.90
Baltimore, Md.	.94	New Orleans, La.	4.05
Boston, Mass.	2.36	New York, N.Y.-N.J.	16.33
Buffalo, N.Y.	1.25	Newark, N.J.	6.60
Chicago, Ill.	7.57	Philadelphia, Pa.-N.J.	2.38
Cincinnati, Ohio-Ky.-Ind.	.55	Phoenix, Ariz.	12.80
Cleveland, Ohio	1.31	Pittsburgh, Pa.	.51
Columbus, Ohio	.67	Portland, Oreg.-Wash.	1.82
Dallas–Fort Worth, Tex.	7.80	Riverside–San Bernardino–Ontario, Calif.	18.10
Denver-Boulder, Colo.	10.57	Sacramento, Calif.	9.68
Detroit, Mich.	1.59	St. Louis, Mo.-Ill.	.92
Fort Lauderdale–Hollywood, Fla.	3.85	San Antonio, Tex.	45.12
Houston, Tex.	13.89	San Diego, Calif.	14.80
Indianapolis, Ind.	.72	San Francisco–Oakland, Calif.	10.62
Kansas City, Mo.-Ks.	2.34	San Jose, Calif.	17.34
Los Angeles–Long Beach, Calif.	26.93	Seattle-Everett, Wash.	1.92
Miami, Fla.	35.90	Tampa–St. Petersburg, Fla.	4.93
Milwaukee, Wis.	2.32	Washington, D.C.-Md.-Va.	3.13

the dominant group among women of Hispanic origin (58.64% of such women). Located primarily in the Southwest and West, these women have their greatest numbers in California and Texas (73.47% of the total). Much smaller numbers of Mexican-origin women are found in Arizona, Ilinois, New Mexico, and Colorado, in that order. The Mexican-American population is more urban than rural, and major centers include Chicago, El Paso, Houston, Los Angeles, and San Antonio. Regional inertia has kept these people in the borderland region, with only a short northward diffusion. Illinois, and particularly Chicago, is the only exception. Readers may wonder why New Mexico is so low on the list. After all, it is New Mexico. Ambiguity in labeling here becomes important. Only 48.15% of Hispanic women in this state claim to be of Mexican origin; the majority place themselves in the "other" category, thereby indicating their older heritage that predates even Mexican independence.

The number of legal Mexican entrants was restricted, starting in 1964, but illegal immigration has continued and is viewed by many as a problem. The availability of jobs in the Southwest is understandably tempting to the underemployed labor force in Mexico. Recent Mexican immigrants are young and tend to have large families. If immigration continues at its rapid pace and the birthrate remains high, Mexican-Americans soon will exceed blacks as America's largest ethnic minority.

Women of Puerto Rican origin total 1,031,625 and are 14.08% of the female Hispanics. The greatest number live in New York, home to 50.52% of the mainland female Puerto Rican population. New Jersey has 12.12% and Illinois 6.28%. Because Puerto Ricans are American citizens, they are allowed to move freely between island and mainland. The mainland population is young, has a high fertility rate, and a low education level. More women than men are present in the mainland population because of the kinds of jobs available. Assimilation of Puerto Rican women has been slow because they are concentrated in tight urban colonies and a constant influx of new immigrants reinforces ties to the island.

Women of Cuban origin are the most distinctive among Hispanic women. With only 420,906 members, (5.74% of Hispanic women), their influence is slight except in Miami, New Jersey, and New York City. Florida is home to 59.18% of Cuban-origin women. New Jersey accounts for 10.08%, New York for 9.61%, and California for 7.51%. Most Cuban-Americans are political refugees who arrived intermittently between 1959 and 1980. They are mostly middle-class women, older, and with lower birthrates than other ethnic groups. Many have professions or skills. They have become well assimilated into American culture as measured by intermarriage rates, use of the English language by the third generation, and suburban residential pattern.

FOREIGN-BORN WOMEN

The United States has gone through several stages of racial composition over its history. An original dominance of American Indians was followed by ascendancy to majority status of immigrant white Anglo-Saxon Protestants. Then came a growing minority proportion of blacks arriving by forced immigration, and a wide variety of European peoples. In all stages but the first, white women of European background have dominated the population of women. A new stage is about to begin: recent female immigrants are largely of Asian, Hispanic, and Caribbean origins. Of the 2,755,907 foreign-born women arriving in this country between 1970 and 1980, 37.92% originated in Canada and Central America, 32.44% were from Asia, 13.73% from Europe, 5.92% percent from South America, and 1.86% from Africa. Mexico accounted for 20.85% of the total.

National-origins quotas and restrictions against Asians, originally established in the 1920s and reaffirmed in 1952, have slowly been lifted since 1965. Newer preference systems have favored immigrants with skills and refugees. Interestingly, 53.26% of the foreign-born in 1980 were women.

Social scientists once viewed America as the melting-pot society, a place where the races would mix through intermarriage to form a new breed of American. This utopian idea was discarded when it became obvious that racial and ethnic minorities were not being assimilated. The new model is cultural pluralism. Minority groups are encouraged to retain their identity and maintain their culture while at the same time participating in the dominant society. Cultural retention is most effectively accomplished within ethnic enclaves and thus the self-creation of spatially separate islands of ethnicity, especially in large metropolitan areas. These neighborhoods are especially important to new arrivals.

The spatial distribution of immigrant women shows remarkable unevenness (Map 1.16). Although the average for the country is 6.44%, a large part of the interior and South have percentages below three. Mississippi has the lowest mark at 1.02%, followed by Arkansas and Kentucky. Alabama and Tennessee also have exceptionally low values. If one lives in one of these states, the chances of knowing a woman born in another country are small. Bilingualism, for example, does not concern you. If you live in Hawaii, California, or New York, however, language problems as well as other aspects of assimilation become more critical to you, your school board, and community groups. Hawaii has 15.78% of its female population foreign-born. In California it is 15.25% and in New York it is 14.14%. Florida and New Jersey also have

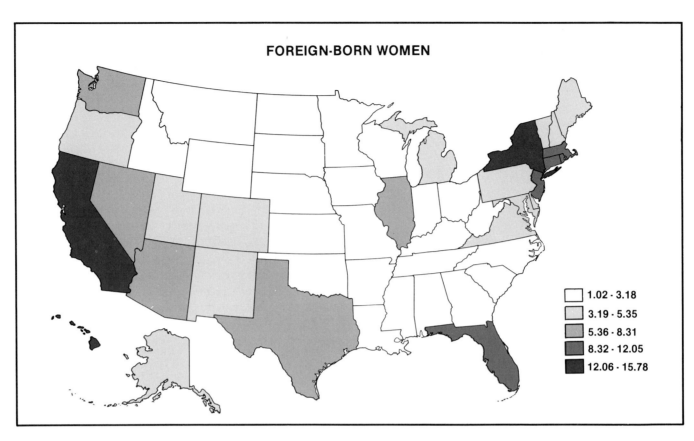

FOREIGN-BORN WOMEN

Legend:
- 1.02 - 3.18
- 3.19 - 5.35
- 5.36 - 8.31
- 8.32 - 12.05
- 12.06 - 15.78

Map 1.16 Foreign-born women—as a percentage of all women, 1980. U.S. average is 6.44 percent.

high values. The four leading entry points for immigrants (Honolulu, Los Angeles, Miami, and New York) are in the same states with high numbers of foreign-born women. Ethnic colonies in these port cities act as attractions to the next wave of migrants.

If women who immigrated from 1970 to 1980 are considered as a percentage of all foreign-born women, some interesting patterns emerge. Hawaii, for example, has had more women immigrate in recent years than all of those immigrating prior to 1970 who were still alive in 1980 (53.26% of all female immigrants are recent). Most of the recent Hawaiian immigrants are from Asia (82.83%), particularly from the Philippines (16,790 women or 42.5% of recent immigrants). Other states with recent immigrants accounting for 45 to 50% of all immigrants are California, Oklahoma, Texas, and Virginia. Kansas, Louisiana, Maryland, Mississippi, and New Mexico have high percentages as well. In California, New Mexico, and Texas the largest group of women come from North and Central America: Mexicans account for 40.4%, 56.0%, and 50.9% of recent immigrant totals in each state. In the remaining six states Asians constitute the largest group. Korea was the leading country of origin for Kansas, Mary-

land, and Virginia; in Louisiana, Mississippi, and Oklahoma women from Vietnam were the single largest group. Although Mexican immigrants dominate the immigration picture in Texas, 11,201 Vietnamese women form the second leading group. Vietnamese refugees have chosen Gulf coast locations, in part, for climate and the fishing industry.

One controversy arising through cultural pluralism is the degree to which a native language should be retained and English learned; hence the debates regarding bilingualism in the public-school system. Food, clothing, and religion are personal matters, but language is a public one. Most American women speak only English at home (88.85%), and in some parts of the country this percentage reaches as high as 98% (Alabama, Arkansas, Kentucky, Mississippi, North Carolina, Tennessee, and West Virginia). Other parts of the country are very different, however. Only 62.23% of New Mexicans speak only English; there Spanish (77.87% of other languages) and American Indian languages (16.88%) represent other cultural traditions. In Hawaii 71.64% speak only English; Japanese (38.45%) and Filipino languages (26.41%) are alternatives. In Arizona, California, New York, and Texas, Spanish is a dominant second language.

CHAPTER TWO

LABOR FORCE

INTRODUCTION

Women are working in greater numbers than ever before. They constitute more than two-fifths of the total labor force, they are working full-time as well as part-time, and they are working even though they have small children. This chapter examines some of these employment topics geographically. Maps begin with the proportion of the labor force that is female, a measure that reflects the proportion of females in a state's population, but also other important socioeconomic variables. The next four maps represent sectors of this female labor force: full-time employment, voluntary part-time employment, enforced part-time employment, and unemployment. The participation rate in the labor force for women forms the basis for another unit. What proportion of women choose to work out of the potential pool of female workers is followed by participation rates for women who have children under 6 years and women who have children from 6 to 17. The chapter closes with a map of nursery-school enrollment, a surrogate measure of the availability of child-care facilities for working mothers.

FEMALE LABOR FORCE

Times are changing. In 1940, 27.4% of women in the United States worked, versus 50.0% in 1980. Total female participation in the labor force has climbed from 13,840,000 women in 1940 to 43,963,000 women in 1980 (Figure 2.1). The most dramatic change has been among married women whose husband is present—14.7% of these women worked in 1940 whereas 50.2% did in 1980. Delayed childbearing, smaller families, increased child-care facilities, and changing sentiments toward working mothers have all influenced this increase. A large part of the change, however, can be traced to the women themselves. Dissatisfaction with the traditional housewife role and the need for accomplishment and creativity have led many women to "dual careers" combining work, household duties, and sometimes motherhood.

The number of women in the civilian labor force (full-time, part-time, and unemployed) totaled 47,755,000 by 1982 (Table 2.1). The states with the most women, California and

New York, had the most female workers whereas Alaska and Wyoming, representing the other end of the population spectrum, had the least.

The proportion of the 1982 labor force that is female, another way of analyzing these same data, reveals distinct regional patterns when mapped (Map 2.1). West Virginia at 38.8% represents the lowest proportion whereas South Carolina at 46.4% represents the highest. High proportions of women workers are evident along the East coast from Massachusetts to Florida, in Mississippi, Arkansas, Hawaii, and the midwestern states of Nebraska, Minnesota, and Wisconsin. Both West Virginia and Louisiana have exceptionally low rates while more modest lows can be found in sections of

Figure 2.1   Female labor force.

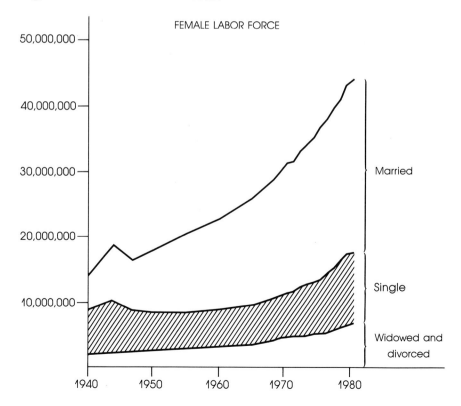

TABLE 2.1	NUMBER OF WOMEN IN THE LABOR FORCE
	(In thousands)
UNITED STATES	47,755
Alabama	744
Alaska	90
Arizona	572
Arkansas	455
California	5,335
Colorado	669
Connecticut	710
Delaware	134
Florida	2,115
Georgia	1,198
Hawaii	212
Idaho	186
Illinois	2,409
Indiana	1,127
Iowa	603
Kansas	516
Kentucky	710
Louisiana	746
Maine	221
Maryland	969
Massachusetts	1,341
Michigan	1,813
Minnesota	960
Mississippi	466
Missouri	1,002
Montana	159
Nebraska	351
Nevada	211
New Hampshire	212
New Jersey	1,562
New Mexico	248
New York	3,466
North Carolina	1,325
North Dakota	129
Ohio	2,176
Oklahoma	620
Oregon	553
Pennsylvania	2,331
Rhode Island	215
South Carolina	689
South Dakota	140
Tennessee	931
Texas	3,047
Utah	272
Vermont	116
Virginia	1,212
Washington	853
West Virginia	299
Wisconsin	1,085
Wyoming	104

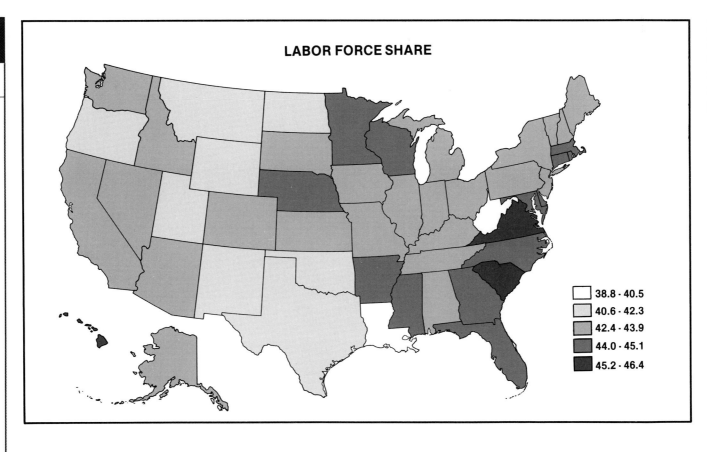

LABOR FORCE SHARE

Legend:
- 38.8 - 40.5
- 40.6 - 42.3
- 42.4 - 43.9
- 44.0 - 45.1
- 45.2 - 46.4

Map 2.1 Labor force share—percentage of labor force that is female, 1982. U.S. average is 43.3%.

the intermontane West. In no state does the percentage of women in the labor force exceed that of men (Table 2.2).

If the phenomenon of labor-force proportion were strictly related to male/female population ratios, a positive relationship of the values in Map 2.1 with female population proportion in a state could be expected. Both Hawaii and Alaska, however, have more women in the labor force than expected. These states are followed by South Carolina and Virginia. In turn, there are fewer working women than expected in West Virginia and Louisiana, followed by Utah and Pennsylvania. In some cases, therefore, other factors are operating.

Working women in Washington, D.C., represent the largest share of a metropolitan labor force with 47.01% (Table 2.2). Denver-Boulder ranks a close second (46.33%). In contrast, women in Houston, Nassau-Suffolk, and Pittsburgh have the smallest shares of metropolitan labor forces.

Regional imbalances such as those that can be seen on Map 2.1 may raise the specter of discrimination in the labor market. The factors behind the patterns on the map, however, are complex. They represent a melange of economic condi-

tions, age structures, ethnic compositions of the population, numbers of single mothers, employment opportunities, educational levels, and societal attitudes toward labor-force participation by women. To say that hiring practices in West Virginia and Louisiana are biased against women is clearly unfounded at the information level available here.

U.S. female labor force share is above the average for the world, but even higher proportions exist in Eastern Europe, U.S.S.R., and parts of Africa. In Botswana the share is as high as 52%, in the U.S.S.R. it is 49%, and in the Central African Republic, Mali, and Rwanda it is 48%. Much lower rates are found in the Arab countries with, for example, Iraq, Mauritania, and Saudi Arabia at 4%.

EMPLOYMENT/ UNEMPLOYMENT

The following four maps represent mutually exclusive segments of the total female labor force: workers who are full-time, part-time (voluntary and enforced), and unem-

TABLE 2.2 LABOR FORCE SHARE IN SMSAs

LOCATION	%
Anaheim–Santa Ana–Garden Grove, Calif.	43.41
Atlanta, Ga.	45.04
Baltimore, Md.	43.66
Boston, Mass.	45.65
Buffalo, N.Y.	42.96
Chicago, Ill.	44.10
Cincinnati, Ohio-Ky.-Ind.	44.48
Cleveland, Ohio	42.90
Dallas–Fort Worth, Tex.	42.32
Denver-Boulder, Colo.	46.33
Detroit, Mich.	43.77
Houston, Tex.	40.77
Indianapolis, Ind.	43.33
Kansas City, Mo.-Ks.	43.56
Los Angeles–Long Beach, Calif.	43.83
Miami, Fla.	45.01
Milwaukee, Wis.	43.64
Minneapolis–St. Paul, Minn.-Wis.	45.46
Nassau-Suffolk, N.Y.	41.53
New York, N.Y.-N.J.	44.44
Newark, N.J.	44.53
Philadelphia, Pa.-N.J.	44.04
Pittsburgh, Pa.	41.41
Riverside–San Bernardino–Ontario, Calif.	42.41
St. Louis, Mo.-Ill.	43.85
San Diego, Calif.	44.24
San Francisco–Oakland, Calif.	44.93
San Jose, Calif.	42.51
Seattle-Everett, Wash.	43.30
Washington, D.C.-Md.-Va.	47.01

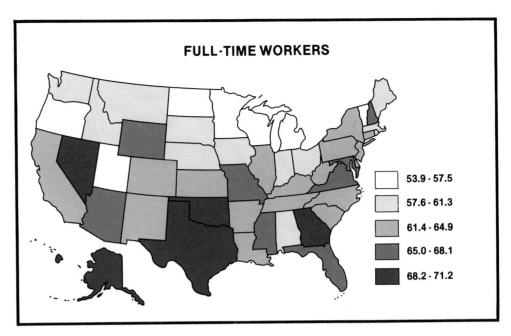

Map 2.2   Full-time workers—percentage of female labor force, 1982. U.S. average is 63.3%.

Map 2.3   Voluntary part-time workers—percentage of female labor force, 1982. U.S. average is 20.7%.

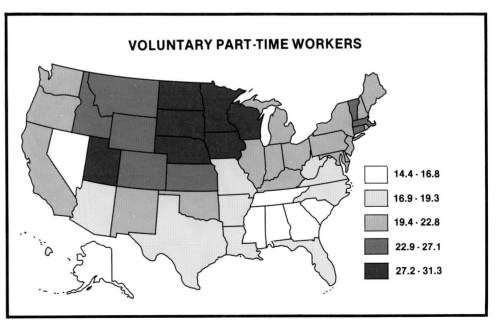

ployed but actively seeking employment. The data represent an annual average for 1982 and describe the labor status of the civilian noninstitutional population 16 years and over. Part-time employment is described by the Bureau of Labor Statistics as between 1 and 34 hours per week. Full-time employment is 35 hours or more.

Women employed on full-time schedules (Map 2.2) represent 63.3% of the total female labor force. Wisconsin had the lowest proportion of full-time workers at 53.9% whereas Texas had the highest at 71.2%. In general, there are smaller proportions of full-time workers in the northern tier of states and a greater-than-average concentration of full-time workers in parts of the Sun Belt, plus Alaska. Alabama, however, is

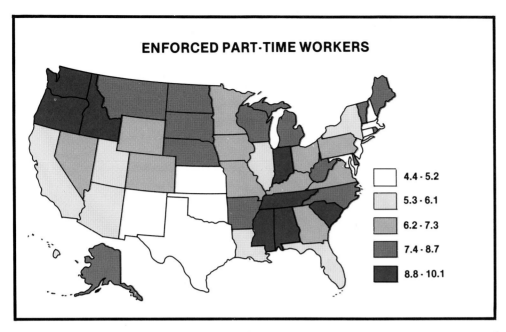

ENFORCED PART-TIME WORKERS

	4.4 - 5.2
	5.3 - 6.1
	6.2 - 7.3
	7.4 - 8.7
	8.8 - 10.1

Map 2.4   Enforced part-time workers—for economic reasons, percentage of female labor force, 1982. U.S. average is 6.6%.

Map 2.5   Unemployment—percentage of female labor force, 1982. U.S. average is 9.4%.

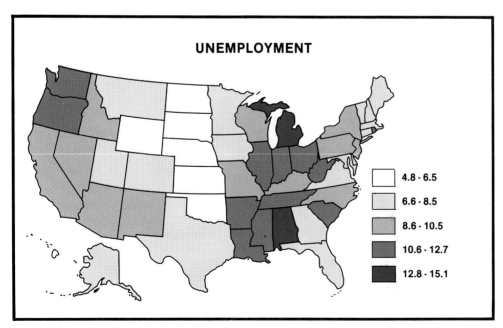

UNEMPLOYMENT

	4.8 - 6.5
	6.6 - 8.5
	8.6 - 10.5
	10.6 - 12.7
	12.8 - 15.1

a contradiction to the rosy southern picture. In addition, New Hampshire and Wyoming have higher proportions than expected based on their surrounding states. Full-time participation in the labor force appears to be a reflection of the general economic health of a state.

Part-time employment may usefully be divided into two categories: voluntary (20.7% of the female labor force) and enforced part-time employment as a response to poor economic conditions (6.6%). Voluntary part-time workers (Map 2.3) are those women who have elected to work an abbreviated schedule, perhaps to allow time with their children, perhaps in response to enlightened company policies that encourage flexible time schedules, job sharing, and reduced hours. They may be working for personal satisfaction rather than economic necessity in many cases. There is a remarkable concentration of these workers in the upper Midwest and Mountain states. Utah is the highest with 31.3% of its female labor force voluntarily employed part-time. A lesser concentration of such workers can be seen in parts of New England. In contrast, there are relatively few part-time workers in the South, Nevada, Alaska, and Hawaii. Alaska represents the lowest proportion at 14.4%. Surely this is a map of enlightened hiring practice and exercise of choice on the part of the worker rather than a map of discrimination.

Women who are forced to work part-time for economic reasons (Map 2.4), on the other hand, probably are disillusioned workers. They would prefer to be working full-time but, for one reason or another, have been forced onto a part-time schedule by their firms. Economic reasons could include slack work, material shortages, repairs to plant or equipment, inability to find full-time work, labor disputes, bad weather, illness, and/or seasonal employment. This enforced reduction in work hours, of course, reflects the faltering economic conditions of the early 1980s. Underemployed workers are evident in high proportions in the northwestern states and parts of the South. Oregon, with 10.1% of its female labor force in this category, leads the nation. This form of cutting back is virtually unheard of in parts of the Southwest and northern Atlantic coastal states. Massachusetts is the low at 4.4%.

Unemployed workers, including those who have been laid off as well as those actively seeking employment for the first time or returning to the labor force, form a distribution pattern similar to that of enforced part-time workers (Map 2.5). The unemployment rate for women in the United States in 1982 was 9.4%. Unemployment for women was lowest in the middle of the country plus New England, Alaska, and Hawaii. Oklahoma at 4.8% represented the healthiest situation with Wyoming close behind at 5.0%. Unemployment was high in

Washington and Oregon, parts of the South, and the eastern part of the Midwest. Michigan led the country with a rate of 15.1% with Alabama right behind at 14.9%.

When the female labor force is disaggregated racially, a distressing picture arises for minorities. The U.S. unemployment rate for white women in 1982, according to the Bureau of Labor Statistics, was 8.3%, but for black women it was 17.6%, and for Hispanic women it was 14.1%. Only in Hawaii does the unemployment rate for white women exceed that of the state average. In all other cases, unemployment for black women and Hispanic women exceeds the state rate for all women. Unemployment for black women ranges as high as 30.5% in Michigan, followed by 26.7% in Alabama and 26.2% in Tennessee with lower, but still substantial rates of 24.2% in Indiana, 23.4% in Illinois, and 22.7% in Ohio. These rates may help to explain why the northward migration of blacks is reversing with a return to the South. Among Hispanic women the unemployment rate is as high as 19.0% in Illinois, followed by 18.0% in Arizona and 17.3% in New Jersey.

No discussion of women's employment patterns would be complete without a comparison with that of men. In all states the proportion of men in the labor force who are employed in full-time schedules exceeds the proportion for women in 1982. Whereas 78.3% of the males were full-time, only 63.3% of the females were. The discrepancy between these proportions was greatest in Alaska, the Dakotas, and Vermont. Men's and women's full-time employment percentages were closest in Hawaii and Nevada. Voluntary part-time employment was higher for women than for men in all states, with nationwide proportions of 20.7% and 7.0% respectively. This relationship is, of course, expected based on the traditional role of the male as breadwinner. The greatest proportions of men employed part-time were in Utah, Minnesota, and Arkansas. Enforced part-time employment (for economic reasons) also claims higher proportions of the female labor force than of the male labor force, but with a smaller difference—6.6% for females compared with 4.9% for males. Unemployment for men (9.9%) exceeds that for women (9.4%) nationally, but regional exceptions occur. The southern states of Alabama, Arkansas, Florida, Georgia, Louisiana, Mississippi, North Carolina, South Carolina, Tennessee, and Virginia all have higher unemployment rates for women. New Mexico and Texas extend this trend farther west. In addition, the industrial states of New Hampshire, New Jersey, New York, and Rhode Island exhibit this pattern, as do the rural Dakotas.

Because employment/unemployment is a dynamic variable and subject to rapid change with economic conditions, these four maps should be viewed only as a snapshot in time. For example, between 1980 and 1982 women employed full-time dropped from 66.1% of the labor force to 63.3%, a direct result of the poor economy in the United States at the time. Such a snapshot, however, has utility and, if nothing else, will serve as a useful reference point for future comparisons. In 1982 Alabama was not an especially good place for a working woman to move to with its high rates of unemployment, enforced part-time work, and low proportion of full-time workers. Michigan was almost as bad. Oklahoma, on the other hand, represented one of the best deals going.

PARTICIPATION RATES

Labor-force participation is a measure of how many women work and, conversely, how many stay home. Specifically, Map 2.6 shows the percentage of noninstitutionalized women 16 years and older who were in the labor force in 1980. Women in the armed forces are included. This category encompasses women who are currently employed on a full-time or part-time basis plus those who are temporarily unemployed. It excludes "discouraged" workers who are not looking for work because they do not think they can find a job (age, lack of education, job market factors).

The range of female participation in the U.S. was from 36.6% in West Virginia to 60.6% in Nevada and 60.4% in Alaska. At first glance these statistics perpetuate images of "barefoot and pregnant in the kitchen" in West Virginia and of the vibrant pioneer woman in Alaska and Nevada, the last of the American frontier areas. More likely the numbers reflect varying labor-market opportunities in these three states. High work involvement can be seen in southern portions of the eastern Seaboard, New England, Minnesota/Wisconsin, Colorado, the far Southwest, West coast, Alaska, and Hawaii. Low participation is evident in parts of Appalachia and the Gulf coast as well as New Mexico. Traditional low labor-force participation among women of Hispanic, American Indian, and French background partly account for lows in New Mexico, Louisiana, and elsewhere.

It is too simplistic to attribute the regional groupings of participation rate to attitudes toward women's roles in each of these areas. Poverty, incidence of single women, educational level, and job opportunities are additional explainers.

The participation rate among women varies with marital status and presence of children (Figure 2.2). Not surprisingly, it is the divorced woman with children 6 to 17 years of age who participates at the highest rate, followed by the divorced woman with no children; these are participation rates spurred

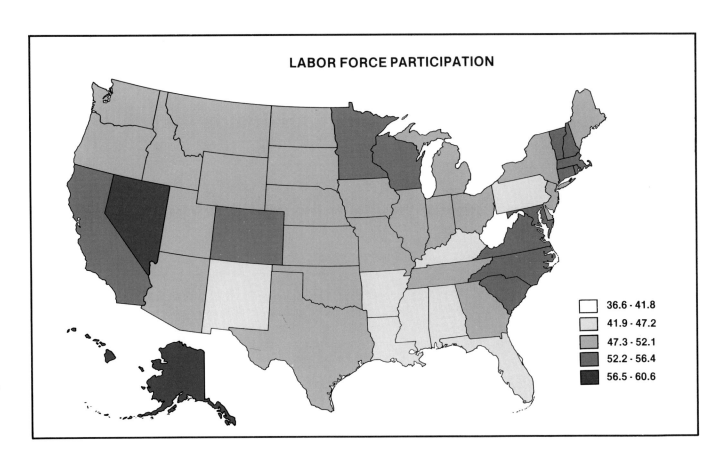

LABOR FORCE PARTICIPATION

☐	36.6 - 41.8
▨	41.9 - 47.2
▨	47.3 - 52.1
▨	52.2 - 56.4
■	56.5 - 60.6

Map 2.6   Labor-force participation—percentage of females 16 years and older in labor force, 1980. U.S. average is 50.0%.

Figure 2.2
Participation rate, 1980.

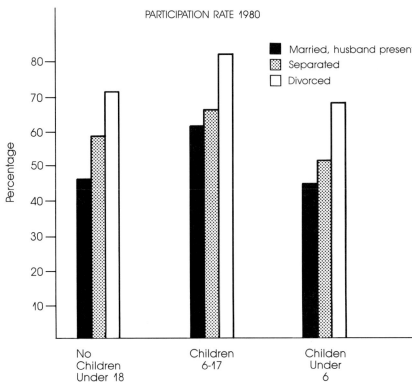

PARTICIPATION RATE 1980

■ Married, husband present
▨ Separated
☐ Divorced

by economic necessity. The participation rate is lowest for those women who are married with husband present and have children under 6 years of age.

Map 2.7 portrays the percentage of women with own children under 6 who participated in the labor force in 1980. "Own" in this case includes stepchildren and adopted children as well as natural children. In 1980 there were 6,220,525 women in this category, 13.9% of the total female labor force. The participation rate for women with young children ranged from 32.3% in West Virginia to 59.0% in North Carolina. The pattern of working mothers is remarkably low in the Northeast where Catholicism is a dominant religion. Large family size is not compatible with labor-force participation. An intense concentration of working mothers is evident in the southeastern states with the exception of Louisiana. Lesser proportions are in the middle Plains states, Nevada, and Hawaii. Southern black women who customarily have withdrawn from the labor force for only a short time during childbearing years are responsible for some of the southeastern concentration.

Map 2.8 shows the percentage of women with children 6 to 17 years of age who participated in the labor force in 1980. The low state in this category is again West Virginia at 46.9% with North Carolina high at 71.7%. A total of 10,726,125 women are in this group, 23.9% of the total female labor force. High proportions of working women are evident in the southeastern states, parts of New England, the central Plains area, portions of the west, plus Alaska and Hawaii. Low proportions occur in the Northeast, New Mexico, and Louisiana.

School-age children are cared for through our school systems, but only for part of the working day and part of the working year. Nevertheless, having a child matriculate in the first grade has long been viewed as a liberating influence on mothers in regards to their out-of-the-home activities. Consequently, participation in the labor force increases nationwide as one's children reach school age. The average percentage of mothers with children under 6 who work is 45.8%. That percentage climbs to 63.2% for mothers with children 6 to 17.

Comparison of Maps 2.7 and 2.8 shows a dramatic increase in participation in Utah and Wyoming (differences of 27.7 and 26.7% respectively). Utah's case can be partly explained by the large Mormon population who believe a mother's place is in the home, at least during the children's formative years. Mormon influence is also a factor in Wyoming. Changes in participation rates also take place in the northeastern states of Connecticut, Massachusetts, New Hampshire, New Jersey, New York, Pennsylvania, Rhode Island, and Vermont, where the percentage difference in labor-force participation between the two children's age groups ranges between 19.8 and 25.8%. A dedication to mothering in the preschool years is one interpretation of the data. Another is slower acceptance of the employment-cycle changes taking place in other parts of the country. In contrast, the difference between maps is low (9.1 to 13.4%) in Alabama, Arkansas, Georgia, Mississippi, North Carlina, South Carolina, Tennessee, and Virginia, areas where women with younger children are already participating at a high rate.

The traditional pattern of female employment has been to work after leaving school, to withdraw from the labor force after marriage or the birth of the first child, and then, occasionally, to return when the last child reaches school age. This cycle is changing. Higher proportions of women are returning to work after the last child, temporarily withdrawing for shorter periods during the childbearing years, and having fewer children. Work commitment is becoming more than an alternative to family and child rearing; for an increasing proportion of American women it is complementary to family life.

Something needs to be said about women who do not work outside the home. After all, 50% of the women in this country over 16 are "nonparticipants." Because they are en-

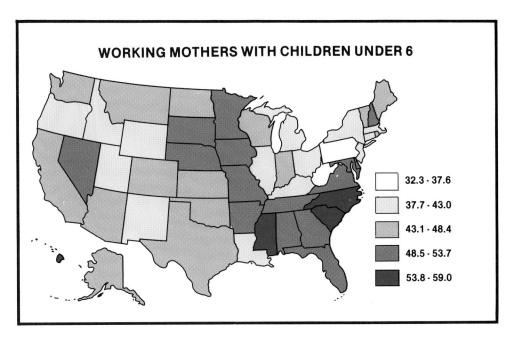

Map 2.7   Working mothers with children under 6—percentage of mothers with young children who work, 1980. U.S. average is 45.8%.

Map 2.8   Working mothers with children 6 to 17—percentage of mothers with school-age children who work, 1980. U.S. average is 63.2%.

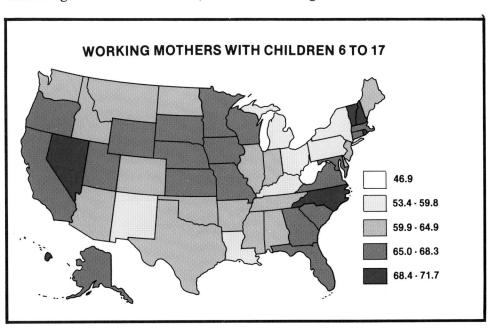

gaged in amorphous activities that normally are not counted by those who collect data, their activities cannot be mapped, even though these 44.7 million women are contributing members of society. Of the women who do not work, 7.4 million have children under 6 years of age and 6.3 million have children 6 to 17 years of age (some overlap occurs between these two groups). Many of these nonworking women are engaged in volunteer activities.

Why do these women not work? According to a 1979 survey, 5.5% of the women who said they did not want a job were ill or disabled, 75.4% had home responsibilities, 7.8% were going to school, 6.4% were retired, and 4.9% had other reasons. Other nonparticipants fall in the category of "discouraged" workers who have stopped looking for employment because they thought they would be unable to find a job. Because these women have not actively sought employment in the month prior to the survey, they are not officially classified with the unemployed. Discouraged workers cite age, lack of education, or job-market factors as reasons for their status.

CHILD CARE

Describing the patchwork of child-care arrangements used by working mothers is difficult. The arrangements are uniquely individual, often involving family members or unlicensed day care in the home of a nonrelative. As a result, child-care data are elusive, based on estimates, and not available at the state level. One small segment of group care available from census data, however, is represented in Map 2.9. Children 3 and 4 years old enrolled in nursery school (if the school included instruction as an important integral phase of its program) are counted. Head Start programs and similar pre-primary education programs are included, but custodial day care is not. Nursery schools, however, account for only 5.6% of the total child-care arrangements for employed mothers with youngest child under 5 years. The map portrays current availability and demand for this facility.

The highest percentage of children enrolled in nursery schools is in Connecticut (47.7%), followed by Florida (44.7%) and Maryland (43.8%). North Dakota (14.1%), West Virginia (14.8%), and South Dakota (14.9%) have the lowest percentages enrolled. This form of child care is not used in the less densely populated areas of the intermontane West and northern Plains. Although there may be interest in preprimary educational programs, the logistics of distance make it an unviable solution for parents who must do the daily chauffeuring and for nursery-school owners who must rely upon a certain size of population within a given radius to survive. Kentucky and West Virginia, states with rough topography, also have low percentages of 3- and 4-year-olds enrolled in nursery school. Accessibility, as measured through driving time, is possibly a limiting factor in these two states. Nursery schools, thus, are largely a phenomenon of urban America.

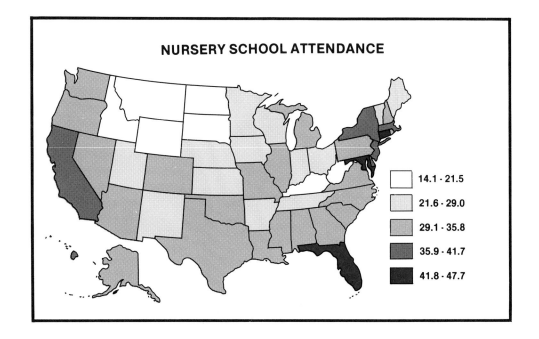

NURSERY SCHOOL ATTENDANCE

14.1 - 21.5
21.6 - 29.0
29.1 - 35.8
35.9 - 41.7
41.8 - 47.7

Map 2.9 Nursery school attendance—percentage of 3- and 4-year-olds enrolled in school, 1980. U.S. average is 32.8%.

Nursery-school participation increased in the United States from 21% of 3- and 4-year-olds in 1970 to 37% in 1980. The greatest increases were in some of the same states that now have high enrollments—Connecticut, Florida, Maryland, Massachusetts, New Jersey, and South Carolina. The leading church-related nursery-school enrollments are in Tennessee, Hawaii, and North Carolina (38.9 to 40.7% of the enrollment); leading public-school enrollments, including Head Start, are in Alaska (60.3%), South Dakota (52.8%), and Michigan (50.6%); and private schools dominate in New Hampshire (62.7%), Utah (52.0%), Massachusetts (51.1%), Rhode Island (51.0%), and Vermont (50.4%), some of the same states that rely upon private secondary education to a large degree.

In-home child care by relatives still remains the primary arrangement among working women. Paternal child care is used more frequently by women in blue-collar or service occupations because shift work allows for a sharing of responsibilities. Among unmarried mothers, grandparents or other relatives often have assumed responsibility for child care. In-home care is the usual case for children under 3.

Child-care arrangements for young children with working mothers is a national issue related both to the effect on children and the effect on equal-employment opportunities for women. We should all be concerned about the .2% of children whose mothers use "other arrangements" (child taking care of self), presumably because they cannot find or afford alternate arrangements. But we should be equally concerned about the mothers who drop out of school, leave the labor force, and turn down jobs or promotions because they cannot arrange for satisfactory care for their children. This includes women who need to work (often single parents) and those who prefer to work. Flexible or part-time positions solves part of the problem; more day-care facilities at the place of employment is another partial solution.

CHAPTER THREE

EARNINGS/INCOME

INTRODUCTION

Much has been written about the "earnings gap." In 1980 for every dollar a man made as a full-time, year-round worker, a woman made only $.60. Major contributing factors to this discrepancy are occupational segregation and tenure. Pooling of women in "pink-collar" occupations through choice, convention, or training has led to overcrowding in these occupations and, consequently, lower wages and limited potential for advancement. Income generated by the female labor force concentrated in low-paying occupations such as secretary, waitress, cashier, nursing aide, or hairdresser cannot compete, therefore, on the average, with income derived by men in higher paying jobs. Components of tenure—attachment to the labor force and seniority—are two additional factors related to the earnings gap. Women's family responsibilities have led to breaks in work history and less work experience, measures of labor-force attachment. Because of the recentness of women's mass entry into the labor force, women generally have lower seniority than men. Even after controls for such variables as occupational segregation and tenure, however, there is still an unexplained portion of unequal wages that can be attributed to nothing but discrimination. One way to approach this problem has been the concept of equal pay for equal work. The concept has recently been replaced by equal pay for comparable worth, a comparison across occupations.

The atlas first addresses median income of females to develop geographical comparisons. Next income of males and females are compared and earnings gap data by states are examined. This is followed by earnings differentials for equivalent work for 70 metropolitan areas and three broad occupational classifications. The chapter ends with a discussion of wealthy women. The percentage of women whose annual earnings exceed $50,000 is mapped, along with the homes of women in the *Forbes* list of the 400 wealthiest Americans.

INCOME

Median income data are for women 15 years and older who are year-round, full-time workers. In addition to earnings from wages and salary or self-employment, income also includes interest, dividends, royalties, rental income, social security, and welfare payments. Alaska clearly stands as a world apart on this measure (Map 3.1). Median income for women living in Alaska is more than $5,000 higher than the national average of $10,380 and about $4,000 more than the next leading state (California at $11,788). Beyond this phenomenon, income tends to be high in states with large cities: California, Illinois, Maryland, Michigan, New Jersey, New York, and Washington. Only Texas and Florida do not follow this urban generalization.

Mississippi is last in the income race with both rural ($7,680) and urban ($8,605) parts of the state included. South Dakota joins this low list along with Arkansas. Incomes are generally low throughout the South, but not to the same degree in Virginia with its strong economic ties to Washington, D.C. Persistence of women in low-paying "female" occupations may account for low incomes among southern women.

Urban women have a higher median income than rural women in all states except Connecticut, New Hampshire, and Rhode Island. The unusual exurban settlement pattern in these states sets them apart. Living in the country is desirable, even prestigious, in this part of New England and the proliferation of transportation alternatives give these commuters ready access to the major cities of the Northeast, the location of employment opportunities. Therefore, women who claim a rural residence actually may work in an urban setting where the higher income jobs exist.

Women in Washington, D.C., have the highest median income among SMSAs with $13,375 (Table 3.1). San Francisco-Oakland and San Jose women follow with $12,958 and $12,761 respectively. The lower median incomes, including San Antonio's $9,243, are still much higher than their state averages.

EARNINGS GAP

Earnings gap is that popularly quoted ratio comparing women's income with that of men (Map 3.2). Data again are for persons 15 years and older who are employed full-time, year-round. Income includes the supplementary sources of

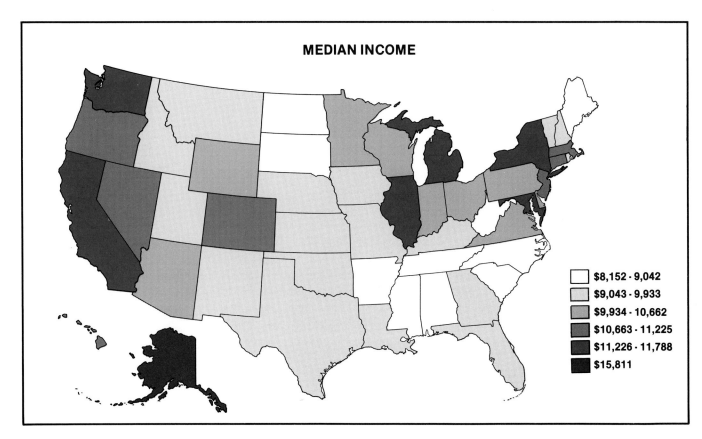

MEDIAN INCOME

$8,152 - 9,042
$9,043 - 9,933
$9,934 - 10,662
$10,663 - 11,225
$11,226 - 11,788
$15,811

Map 3.1 Median income of females 15 years and older who are year-round full-time workers, 1979. U.S. average is $10,380.

TABLE 3.1 MEDIAN INCOME IN SMSAs			
LOCATION	%	LOCATION	%
Anaheim–Santa Ana–Garden Grove, Calif.	$11,970	Minneapolis–St. Paul, Minn.-Wis.	$11,460
Atlanta, Ga.	$10,827	Nassau-Suffolk, N.Y.	$11,607
Baltimore, Md.	$11,106	New Orleans, La.	$ 9,688
Boston, Mass.	$11,500	New York, N.Y.-N.J.	$12,151
Buffalo, N.Y.	$10,262	Newark, N.J.	$11,596
Chicago, Ill.	$11,916	Philadelphia, Pa.-N.J.	$10,932
Cincinnati, Ohio-Ky.-Ind.	$10,742	Phoenix, Ariz.	$10,411
Cleveland, Ohio	$11.092	Pittsburgh, Pa.	$10,593
Columbus, Ohio	$10,832	Portland, Oreg.-Wash.	$11,488
Dallas–Fort Worth, Tex.	$10,540	Riverside–San Bernardino–Ontario, Calif.	$10,971
Denver-Boulder, Colo.	$11,614	Sacramento, Calif.	$11,764
Detroit, Mich.	$12,481	St. Louis, Mo.-Ill.	$10,557
Fort Lauderdale–Hollywood, Fla.	$10,241	San Antonio, Tex.	$ 9,243
Houston, Tex.	$11,493	San Diego, Calif.	$10,908
Indianapolis, Ind.	$10,581	San Francisco–Oakland, Calif.	$12,958
Kansas City, Mo.-Ks.	$10,855	San Jose, Calif.	$12,761
Los Angeles–Long Beach, Calif.	$11,830	Seattle-Everett, Wash.	$12,374
Miami, Fla.	$ 9,853	Tampa–St. Petersburg, Fla.	$ 9,272
Milwaukee, Wis.	$11,462	Washington, D.C.-Md.-Va.	$13,375

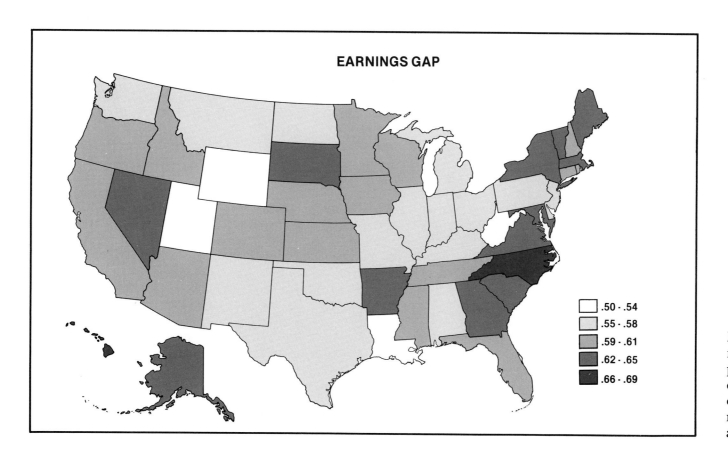

EARNINGS GAP

□	.50 - .54
▨	.55 - .58
▨	.59 - .61
▨	.62 - .65
■	.66 - .69

Map 3.2 Earnings gap—female median income compared with male median income for workers 15 years and older who are employed year-round and full-time, 1979. U.S. average is $.60.

money listed above in addition to money earned as a direct result of employment. Remember that the earnings gap is an average and includes all occupations—it is a gross generalization but one that has journalistic shock value.

Earnings gaps for individual states range from $.50 in Wyoming to $.69 in Hawaii. More precisely, the smallest gap in the country may be found in rural Hawaii, where women make $.70 for every dollar made by a man. Other relatively small gaps are found in urban Hawaii ($.69), rural and urban North Carolina ($.66), rural Vermont ($.66), and urban Alaska ($.66). The largest gap in the country is in rural Wyoming and rural West Virginia ($.50), followed by urban Wyoming and rural Louisiana ($.51), urban West Virginia, rural Illinois, and rural Utah ($.52), and rural Texas ($.53).

The rural/urban difference in comparative salaries is especially pronounced in certain states. For example, the earnings gap for urban women and men in South Dakota is $.56 (the gap for rural men and women there is $.65, and the state average is $.62). Rural women bring home closer to the same amount of bacon in South Dakota, primarily because the rural male there does not bring home much bacon (male

median income of $11,705, the lowest in the nation).

A reverse statistical aberration is found in Connecticut, Illinois, Massachusetts, and Texas. Urban comparisons in these states are $.61, $.57, $.64, and $.59; rural comparisons are $.54, $52, $.58, and $.53. Rural males in Connecticut make a lot of money; average median income of $20,554, or the second largest state income in the U.S. after Alaska. Urban males, in contrast, have a median income of $17,887, much closer to their female coworkers' figures of $10,857. In this case, therefore, the magnitude of the income of men who live in affluent rural Connecticut dwarfs that of female workers. A similar pattern exists in Massachusetts. In Illinois and Texas the rural female just does not make much money, and this accounts for the larger rural earnings gap. In all four states, averaging the urban and rural components of the population puts the state earnings gap in the middle; $.59 for Connecticut, $.57 for Illinois, $.63 for Massachusetts, and $.58 for Texas.

Women looking for fair treatment regarding the amount of money they bring home versus that of male workers should go to Hawaii. In contrast, Wyoming and West Virginia have

Earnings/Income

problems, but Louisiana and Utah are not much better. Male-dominated economies in these states (such occupations as ranching and mining) force women into lower-paying jobs in industries using cheap female labor or the traditional waitress/secretary syndrome. Occupational segregation, therefore, accounts for part of the gap. Discrimination may be responsible for another part. These particular four states might be good places to conduct wage-discrimination surveys and public-consciousness raising.

The earnings gap figure of $.60 loses some of its sting when earnings for equivalent jobs are compared for males and females. The Bureau of Labor Statistics regularly conducts wage surveys in 70 major metropolitan areas for a list of specific occupations. For some of these occupations BLS collects either hourly wages or weekly salaries for both males and females. By comparing gender figures, therefore, for the same general work classification demanding similar degrees of responsibility and skills, a more specific pattern for earnings gaps can be determined.

Earnings gaps for specific occupations are generally much smaller than the $.60 average. The largest gap from the BLS data is for order fillers at $.78. For every dollar that a male makes as an order filler, a female makes $.78. Earnings for this occupation has geographical variation with a range from $.54 in Baltimore to $1.04 in Denver. Hence, women, on the average, are making more money as order fillers in Denver than their male coworkers. The smallest "gap" to be found in these data is for the occupation of drafter II (level two indicates greater independence and skill than level one) where the average ratio of earnings is $1.04. The gap ranges from $.95 in Kansas City to $1.15 in Miami. Some of the precise manual skills involved in drafting are especially suited to the dexterity and patience of women and, therefore, they are apparently in turn rewarded with a higher salary.

Some office jobs, such as file clerks, secretaries, stenographers, and typists, have traditionally been held by women, but there is increasing integration as males move into this job market. Some office jobs, of course, have long been male-dominated—accountants, auditors, directors of personnel. Among specific office occupations the largest earnings gap is for order clerk II at $.81. The gap for this occupation ranges from $.67 in Philadelphia to $.95 in Newark. The smallest "gap" is for messengers, where women earn $1.02 for every $1.00 a man earns, with $.78 in Pittsburgh representing one end of the spectrum and $1.21 in Kansas City representing the other.

The largest gap among professional and technical occupations is for a computer programmer III with a gap of $.92 and regional gaps from $.77 in San Diego to $1.01 in Washington, D.C. The smallest "gap" at $1.04 is for drafter II, as detailed above. Many occupations in this broad professional and technical category are either high-technology related and/or recently created jobs. Because of the timing, therefore, women entered the job market at the same time as men and with the same job skills and preparation. Tenure at these jobs, therefore, should not be a dominant factor in salary determination.

Among material-movement and custodial occupations the largest gap is for order fillers at $.78 (see above). The smallest gap, on the other hand, is for guards I at $.99. Variation is from $.77 in Richmond, Va., to $1.39 in Gary, Ind. Larger gaps among these blue-collar workers might have been expected, but employers and unions seem to be doing their part to provide equal pay for equal work.

Maps 3.3 through 3.5 represent earnings gap averages for specific occupations in each of three broad categories—office occupations, professional and technical occupations, and material-movement and custodial occupations. Data are not available for all cities in all three categories and, therefore, each map contains a different selection of points. In addition, average values for a city can represent anywhere from 1 to 11 occupations, depending upon the classification system and availability of data differentiated by female/male earnings. Despite these limitations the maps allow us to examine a synthesized earnings-gap variable in a geographical context.

The average earnings gap for office occupations (file clerk, messenger, order clerk, accounting clerk, payroll clerk, and key entry operator) is $.88 (Map 3.3). Particularly high gaps are scattered throughout the country with the most inequitable value in Green Bay at $.56. Cities with no earnings gap for this category of occupations are located in the midcontinent area (Denver, Minneapolis, Omaha, San Antonio, and Kansas City) and on both coasts (New York, Nassau/Suffolk, Washington, D.C., and San Francisco). The lowest gap is in Nassau/Suffolk (suburban New York City), where women make $1.07 for each $1.00 made by a male.

Similar data for professional and technical occupations (computer systems analyst, computer programmer, computer operator, and drafter) form a $.91 average for the country as a whole (Map 3.4). The only particularly high gap is the $.74 in Saginaw, Mich. No gap is evident at scattered locations throughout the midsection of the country, with Denver the most favorable ratio at $1.10. Again, occupations in this category are ones to which women have had equal access.

The earnings gap for material-movement and custodial occupations (order fillers; shipping packers; janitors, porters, and cleaners; material-handling laborers; guards; receivers; warehousemen; forklift operators; truck drivers; shippers; and shippers and receivers) is $.91 (Map 3.5). Large gaps

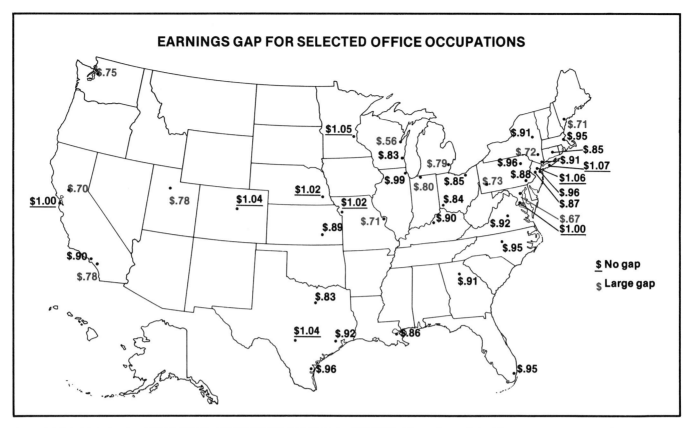

EARNINGS GAP FOR SELECTED OFFICE OCCUPATIONS

$.75

$1.05
$.56
$.83
$.79
$.91
$.71
$.95
$.85
$.72
$.91
$1.07
$.96
$.88
$1.06
$.96
$.87
$.70
$.78
$1.04
$1.02
$1.02
$.99
$.80
$.85
$.73
$1.00
$.84
$.67
$1.00
$.89
$.71
$.90
$.92
$.90
$.95
$.78
$.91
$.83
$1.04
$.92
$.86
$.96
$.95

$ No gap
$ Large gap

Map 3.3   Earnings gap for selected office occupations—comparison of female and male weekly salaries, 1982–83. U.S. average is $.88.

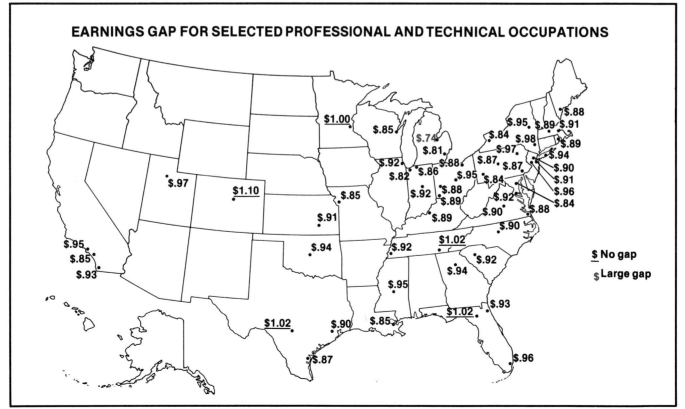

EARNINGS GAP FOR SELECTED PROFESSIONAL AND TECHNICAL OCCUPATIONS

$1.00
$.85
$.74
$.81
$.88
$.95
$.89
$.91
$.84
$.98
$.89
$.97
$.94
$.92
$.86
$.88
$.87
$.87
$.90
$.82
$.95
$.84
$.91
$.97
$1.10
$.88
$.96
$.85
$.92
$.89
$.92
$.84
$.91
$.89
$.90
$.95
$.94
$.90
$1.02
$.85
$.92
$.92
$.94
$.93
$.95
$.85
$1.02

$ No gap
$ Large gap

$1.02
$.90
$.87
$.96

Map 3.4   Earnings gap for selected professional and technical occupations—comparison of female and male weekly salaries, 1982–83. U.S. average is $.91.

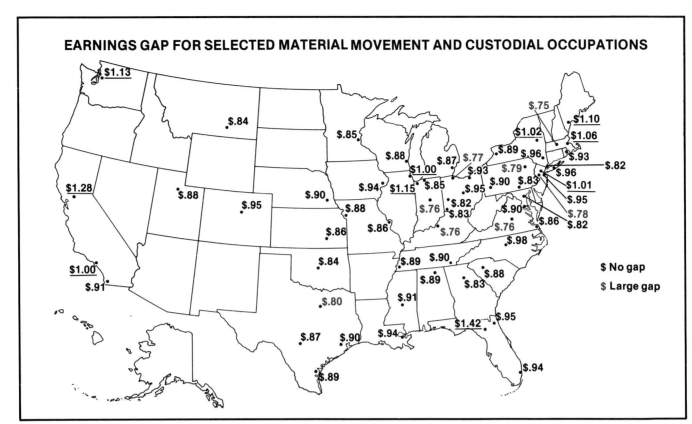

EARNINGS GAP FOR SELECTED MATERIAL MOVEMENT AND CUSTODIAL OCCUPATIONS

$ No gap

$ Large gap

Map 3.5   Earnings gap for selected material-movement and custodial occupations—comparison of male and female hourly wages, 1982–83. U.S. average is $.91.

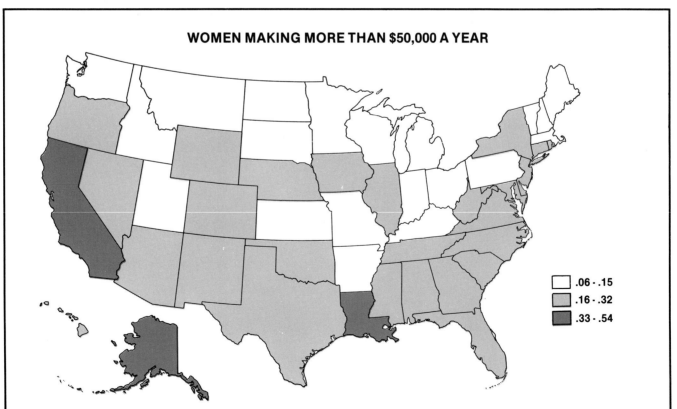

WOMEN MAKING MORE THAN $50,000 A YEAR

.06 - .15
.16 - .32
.33 - .54

Map 3.6   Women making more than $50,000 a year—as a percentage of all women 16 years and older with earnings, 1979. U.S. average is .21%.

are concentrated in parts of the Northeast, with Dallas a regional anomaly. Worcester, Mass., has the most unequal value of $.75. Cities with no earnings gap can be found along the West coast, around Chicago, in parts of the Northeast, plus that extreme value of $1.42 in Gainesville, Fla. Average hourly wages for female janitors, porters, and cleaners in Gainesville is $6.00, whereas that for males is $4.24.

WEALTHY WOMEN

The well-paid American woman is unusual. Setting an arbitrary figure of $50,000 or more per year, the percentage of working women in each state who had earnings in this category is presented in Map 3.6. In 1980 there were 86,526 women in the United States earning more than $50,000 in the previous year. This sounds like a lot, but these women constituted only .21% of women 16 years and older with earnings. Remember this definition does not include income from sources other than employment. Including all income would increase the total number of wealthy women to 182,100, but would only raise the percentage to .26% of all women with income. The wealthy woman is truly an exception in this society.

The well-paid working woman is relatively absent in the states of South Dakota and Maine where they constitute only .06 and .08% of women with earnings. Low-value areas are scattered throughout the northern half of the country with New England and the upper Midwest presenting the lowest pockets.

Women earning $50,000 or more per year present an exceptional case in Alaska at .54%. Both California and Louisiana provide the next highest values at .33% followed by Florida at .31%. The pattern on this map defies explanation on commonsense grounds. Monetarily successful women are so rare and the reasons for their success so individualized that any attempt at explanation may be inadequate.

A look at industry classifications of wealthy women provides some insight to their financial situation. For the United States as a whole, 28.8% of the women making $50,000 or more are engaged in professional and related services, 16.0% in retail trade, 14.5% in manufacturing, and 13.5% in finance, insurance, and real estate. Business and repair services produce 5.4% of wealthy women, followed by 4.3% from both personal services and wholesale trade. The remaining eight broad industrial classifications provide minor percentages of wealthy women. At a more specific level, 18.0% of women making $50,000 are in health services, with approximately

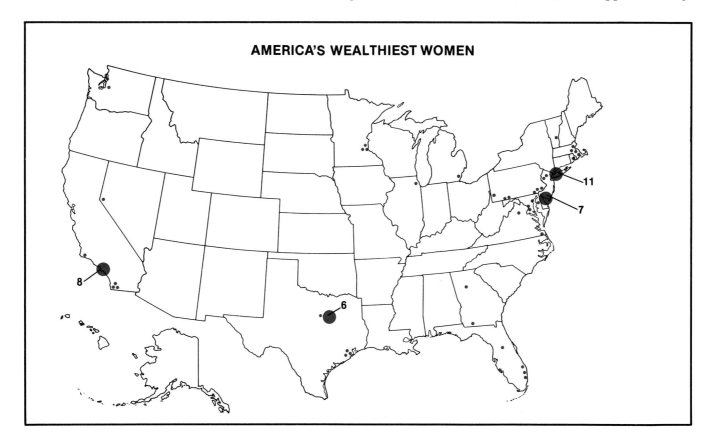

Map 3.7 America's wealthiest women—from the Forbes 400 list, 1984.

half of these in hospitals. One may assume that most of the remaining half are physicians in private practice. Real estate forms the second most lucrative occupation with 9.3% of wealthy women, followed by nondurable manufacturing with, 8.1% (apparel and finished textile products being the most popular), durable manufacturing (6.0%), with machinery and electrical machinery, equipment, and supplies providing the highest proportions; and educational services (5.6%). Remarkably, 65% of the highly paid women in educational services are in elementary and secondary schools, most likely in administrative positions. Eating and drinking places provide earnings for 4.1% of the women, whereas legal, engineering, and other professional services together account for 3.3%.

Regional variation in these percentages is, of course, to be expected. Looking at those four states with the highest percentages of women making $50,000 confirms some spatial quirks in the industries to which these women belong. For example, Alaska has a larger proportion of these women in retail trade (27.1%) than any of the other four states. Women in professional and related services form a much lower-than-average percentage (18.8) with health services being particularly low. Legal and engineering services are higher than expected. Manufacturing provides little high income to the Alaskan woman (or man either). California women, in contrast, are making their money in real estate with 17.8% of wealthy women in the state engaged in this industry. As expected, high-earning women in the entertainment-and-recreation services category are anomalously prominent in the California

picture (4.8% of wealthy women). Women of Florida have diversified sources of exceptional earnings with their participation in wholesale trade (5.0% of women earning $50,000 or more) being the only nonaverage industrial category. Louisiana women overwhelmingly derive their high earnings from professional and related services with educational services alone providing 13.7%. Banking and public administration are other activities that differentiate well-paid Louisiana women from other women.

If we turn our attention to 69 women who are very rich, the residential pattern is somewhat different. Because of their extreme wealth (all over $150 million in assets), these women have the opportunity to locate anywhere, but have chosen the locales plotted on Map 3.7. Multiple residences are included. Information comes from the *Forbes* 1984 list of 400. Published annually, this magazine uses a complicated series of estimates to ascertain net wealth. Most of the women on the list inherited their fortunes, but there are some who are actively making money in their own corporations.

These wealthy women are concentrated in the Northeast with other distinct nodes in Texas and California, the states claiming the greatest number of wealthy women along with New York. Many of the women have retained family ties by locating in the same region as their extended families; for example, the du Pont focus in Delaware. Notice the complete void of wealthy women in the middle of the country as well as their absence in Denver and San Francisco.

CHAPTER FOUR

OCCUPATIONS

INTRODUCTION

Occupations reveal a lot about women's position in our economic society. Women dominate the service-producing sector with 80.5% of female employment in this category. In many cases women thus are perpetuating the domestic functions associated with the homemaker role, such as the caring and nurturing of teacher or nurse, or the assistance function of a secretary. In some cases, however, women have broken out of their traditional roles and are integrating themselves into occupations that have long been male-dominated.

Of women 18 years and over who worked 35 or more hours per week in 1979 (full-time) 80.5% were high-school graduates, but only 16.1% had 4 years or more of college. A higher-education degree often provides the credentials for jobs with good pay, career ladders, decision making, variety, opportunity to learn, and interaction with people. These creative occupations belong to very few among our working women. Many women, in contrast, have jobs that are just that—labor in exchange for monetary payment. For these women their leisure time may be their passion.

Maps in this chapter first address the industrial sectors to which employed women belong. The percentage of women in professional and related services; retail trade; manufacturing; and finance, insurance, and real estate are reported. Together these top four sectors account for 75.8% of all female employment. In addition, the unusual patterns formed by women who are employed in entertainment and recreational services are described.

Switching from broad industrial categories to specific occupations, a set of selected female-dominated occupations are mapped: secretaries, elementary teachers, cashiers, nurses, and waitresses. Although all 5 of these occupations are among the top 10 occupations for women in terms of total numbers, together they account for only 22.5% of employed women. In addition, women who are employed in private households as cleaners or servants, possibly a vanishing occupation in its traditional sense, are mapped.

Next, the states are given a "grade" based on the integration of women into a set of 10 highly male-dominated occupations. Increased participation in these occupations by women can be seen as a surrogate for the success of the women's liberation movement. The acutal number of female physicians, lawyers, or whatever, is still very small, partly because some of these occupations require enormous investments of time and money; success depends upon career persistence.

Finally a cultural index for women in the arts is presented. Numbers of female authors, musicians, actors, painters, and dancers are compared with the resident population of a state to determine women's visibility as professionals in the arts. Women's participation as amateurs or patrons of the arts is inestimable and, unfortunately, unmappable because of a lack of data.

ECONOMIC SECTORS

Women are not represented in the same proportion as men in the various sectors of the American economic structure. Analysis of these differences between sexes offers insights into some of the labor-force participation problems that plague women. Analysis also allows us to see how women contribute to our economy.

The government and its data-collection agencies have divided economic activity into the 14 broad categories listed in Table 4.1. Based on the Standard Industrial Classification (SIC), workers are assigned an industry sector regardless of their function in that industry. Both secretaries and welders for a construction firm, for example, would receive the industrial classification of construction. The sector of public administration is limited to legislative, judicial, and adminstrative functions as well as regulatory activities of local, state, and federal governments. Other government run organizations, such as schools, hospitals, and transport, are classified by industry, such as teachers in the professional category. Since the following maps are based on 1980 census data, workers are counted at their residence, not place of work. In addition, dual jobholders are assigned a sector for only their major job. The percentage of employed females and males belonging to each of these sectors is presented in Table 4.1 along with actual numbers of employees for comparative purposes. The number of employed men is still far greater than the number of employed women, even with women's increased participation in the labor force.

TABLE 4.1 ECONOMIC SECTOR EMPLOYMENT

ECONOMIC SECTOR	% OF LABOR FORCE		NUMBER OF	
	FEMALE	MALE	FEMALES	MALES
Agriculture	1.19	4.05	493,658	2,266,555
Forestry and Fisheries	.07	.22	28,392	124,984
Mining	.30	1.61	124,173	904,005
Construction	1.15	9.39	479,766	5,259,832
Manufacturing	16.80	26.64	6,995,805	14,918,949
Transportation, Communications, and Other Public Utilities	4.21	9.53	1,752,965	5,334,490
Wholesale Trade	2.72	5.51	1,133,761	3,083,471
Retail Trade	19.22	13.77	8,004,399	7,712,295
Finance, Insurance, and Real Estate	8.22	4.42	3,421,717	2,476,342
Business and Repair Services	3.31	4.82	1,380,020	2,701,657
Personal Services	5.20	1.63	2,165,306	910,458
Entertainment and Recreation	.98	1.07	407,324	599,746
Professional and Related	31.57	11.90	13,144,812	6,667,007
Public Administration	5.05	5.44	2,102,567	3,044,899

Although the top three employment sectors are the same for both men and women, the ordering differs. For men the greatest source of employment is the manufacturing sector, almost twice the total for the second category of retail trade. Professional and related services follow. For women the professional and related services sector is the most important source of employment, followed by retail trade, and then manufacturing. Finance, insurance, and real estate is in a more distant fourth place. In only four categories does the number of women outnumber that of men—retail trade; finance, insurance, and real estate; personal services; and professional and related services.

When the 14 broad industrial categories are further collapsed into the three traditional economic sectors, even more distinct differentiation exists between the sexes. Agriculture (represented by the first 2 categories) accounts for only 1.26% of female employment and 4.27% of male employment. Women have little impact on this sector of the economy. Goods-producing activities (the next 3 categories) account for 18.25% of female employment and 37.64% of male employment. Here women play a more prominent role although their activities are essentially restricted to manufacturing rather than mining or construction. It is when the remaining 9 categories are merged into one service-producing sector that the real economic function of women is evident. Services account for 80.48% of female employment, but only 58.09% of male employment. As we shall see later in this chapter, most of the occupations employing large numbers of women fall in the service sector, including some office workers, pink-collar workers, and public employees such as nurses and teachers.

As the labor force has expanded in recent years along with the increased participation of women, it is the services sector that has been augmented to accommodate the new workers. Women's first jobs are most likely to be in the services (83.2% of first jobs). Since three-fourths of all new employees are women, we can see how important women are to this part of the economy.

The top four employment sectors for women (professional and related services; retail trade; manufacturing; and finance, insurance, and real estate) are presented in map form in order to examine the regional variation. Together these four sectors account for 75.81% of female employment. Not all women are doing the same thing throughout this country even when it comes down to basic pursuits. The variation, of course, provides the spice.

Women in professional and related services (Map 4.1) represent 31.57% of employed women. Of these 42.0% come from the health services (the majority of which are hospital-based) and 41.4% from educational services, with elementary and secondary schools being the primary employers. An additional 10.0% of women in the professions is provided by those women employed by social services, religious, and member-

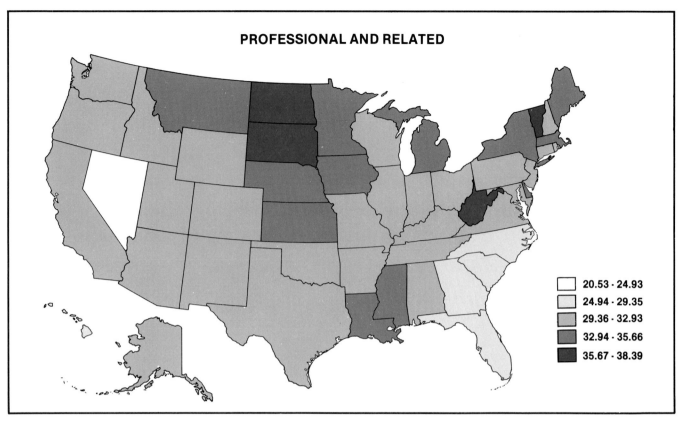

PROFESSIONAL AND RELATED

	20.53 - 24.93
	24.94 - 29.35
	29.36 - 32.93
	32.94 - 35.66
	35.67 - 38.39

Map 4.1 Professional and related—percentage of employed women belonging to this sector, 1980. U.S. average is 31.57%.

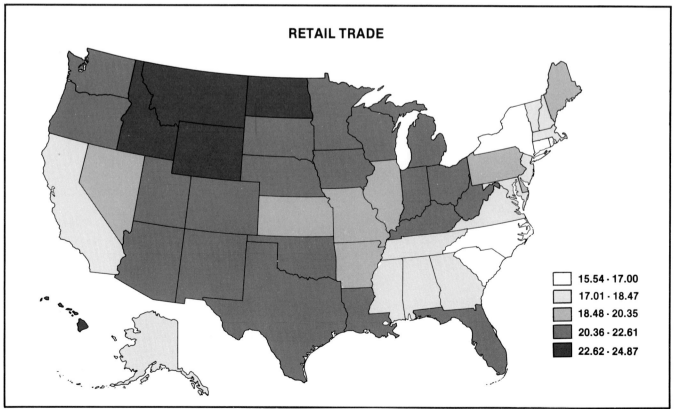

RETAIL TRADE

	15.54 - 17.00
	17.01 - 18.47
	18.48 - 20.35
	20.36 - 22.61
	22.62 - 24.87

Map 4.2 Retail trade—percentage of employed women belonging to this sector, 1980. U.S. average is 19.22%.

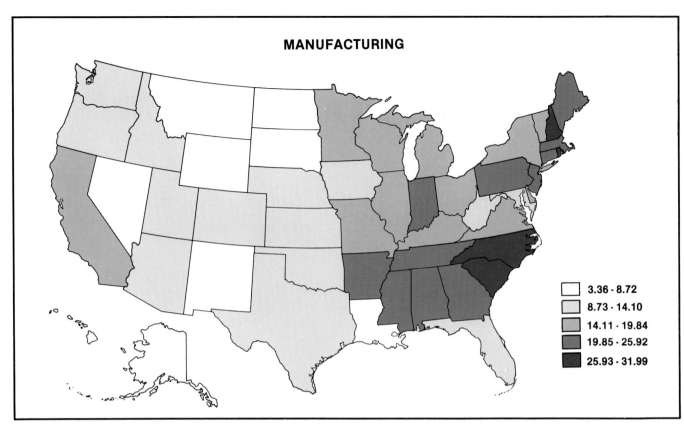

MANUFACTURING

3.36 - 8.72
8.73 - 14.10
14.11 - 19.84
19.85 - 25.92
25.93 - 31.99

Map 4.3 Manufacturing—percentage of employed women belonging to this sector, 1980. U.S. average is 16.80%.

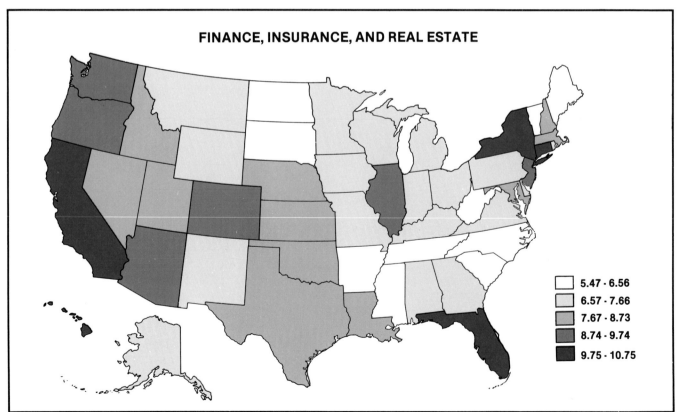

FINANCE, INSURANCE, AND REAL ESTATE

5.47 - 6.56
6.57 - 7.66
7.67 - 8.73
8.74 - 9.74
9.75 - 10.75

Map 4.4 Finance, insurance, and real estate—percentage of employed women belonging to this sector, 1980. U.S. average is 8.22%.

ship organizations. Only 6.5% come from such professional services as the legal or engineering fields. Women in professional and related services are concentrated in two sections of the northern part of this country. One is based on the Dakota core in the upper Great Plains where North Dakota has the highest percentage in the country (38.39). Another concentration is evident in scattered states of the Northeast with Vermont and West Virginia representing the more intense states. A minor outlier is present in Mississippi and Louisiana.

The lowest value belongs to Nevada with only 20.53% of its women belonging to the professional-services sector. Keep an eye on this state throughout this discussion of occupations; it is our most anomalous state in this regard. Hawaii follows at 25.14%. Another low area can be found in the southeastern corner of the country.

Retail trade is an important sector for women, as it employs 19.22% of women, the second highest employment sector (Map 4.2). In the northern intermontane West and Hawaii it becomes especially important. North Dakota has the highest value at 24.87% of its employed women belonging to this sector. It is followed closely by Hawaii and Montana. Actually, above-average values are present throughout large portions of the country with the exception of California, the Southeast, and the Northeast. The lowest values belong to New York at 15.54% and North Carolina at 15.74%.

Of the women in retail trade 31.1% are associated with eating and drinking places whereas 18.3% are with general merchandise stores and 14.3% with food, bakery, and dairy stores. Only small percentages are employed in service stations (1.3%), hardware and building-material retailing (2.0%), and automotive dealers and auto-supply stores (2.8%). Employment in apparel and accessory stores (7.8%), furniture, home furnishings, and appliance stores (3.5%), and drugstores (3.7%) employ more, but still minor, numbers of women.

Manufacturing, the third leading sector for women, provided the workplace for 16.80% of employed females in 1980 (Map 4.3). Among these women the most common source of employment was in the manufacture of apparel and other finished textile products. This industry employed 14.5% of women belonging to the manufacturing sector. Since operating sewing machines is the ninth ranking occupation for women, their high participation in this particular sector of manufacturing comes as no surprise. Some would say that these women are just being paid for a domestic task associated with being female. The second leading manufacturing sector employer is electrical machinery, equipment, and supplies, which involves 13.4% of the female manufacturing labor force. Over a quarter of these women manufacture radio, television, and communication equipment. All are jobs well suited to traditional female stereotypes of nimble fingers and patience. Printing, publishing, and allied industries employ 8.9% of the women in manufacturing whereas 8.5% are involved in the manufacture of nonelectrical machinery, and 5.0% are concerned with chemicals and allied products.

The pattern on Map 4.3 is one of the most striking in this set for what it says about the shift of manufacturing in this country. The old manufacturing belt was composed of the northeastern states from Wisconsin and Illinois east to the coast. Although some of these states still employ high numbers of women (New Hampshire and Rhode Island, for example), there has been a definite southward shift of the belt. North Carolina and South Carolina (leading the country with the high percentages of 31.99 and 28.87% of employed women, respectively) form the core of this new southern concentration. The shift has occurred as a response to the cheaper labor force available in the South as well as lower overhead costs involved with building construction and maintenance. A beneficial tax structure could be another factor. Manufacturing, therefore, shows two concentrations, one in the South and another in New England, plus Pennsylvania and New Jersey. Indiana is an outlier.

The lowest participation in manufacturing among women is in Montana with only 3.36% of its employed women belonging to this sector. Similar low values can be found in Alaska, North Dakota, and Wyoming. The upper Mountain states form but a center of low participation that extends throughout the West with the only average state represented by California.

Manufacturing has the greatest range of participation among any of the industrial sectors, and thus serves well to illustrate how different the country is from region to region. Some women have next to no opportunity to be employed in manufacturing because there are no plants in their area. They must, therefore, turn to other avenues for gainful employment.

Finance, insurance, and real estate represent the fourth leading sector as an employer of women (Map 4.4). In the United States 8.22% of employed women belong to these industries. State values range from 5.47% in South Carolina to 10.75% in Connecticut. The map pattern has distinct high-value nodes associated with the centers of financial power in the metropolitan areas of New York, Chicago, Los Angeles, and San Francisco. Since the data represent residence rather than place of employment, the inclusion of Connecticut and New Jersey is partly explained by commuting patterns. National headquarters of insurance companies and other institutions in these two states, however, explain another part of the pattern. Opportunity, therefore, becomes an explainer of this distribution. Opportunity carries over to the real-estate market as well. The more active the turnover in property (as governed by growth and in-migration), the happier the real-estate dealer. Women are especially active in this occupation in Arizona, California, Colorado, and Florida. Of the 3,421,717 women employed in this general category, 45.0% are associated with banking and credit agencies, 31.5% with insurance, and 23.4% with other finance and real estate.

South Carolina has the lowest participation in the country with 5.47% of its employed women. Mississippi, North Carolina, and West Virginia display similar low involvements. Low values in this sector can be seen throughout the upper Midwest, the South, and parts of New England. Whether these low values can be attributed to low opportunity or low inclination of women in these states to pursue careers associated with this particular industrial sector remains an unanswered question.

Entertainment and recreation is the final economic sector represented in this set of maps (Map 4.5). Although only .98% of employed women in the United States belong to this sector (it ranks twelfth among 14 sectors), it is nevertheless included because of what it says about American life and one state in particular. Nevada's participation at 9.67% is so significantly above all other state values that it warrants a separate

class of its own. More women in this state are involved in entertainment and recreation than in manufacturing or finance, insurance, and real estate, for example. Obviously a large number of these 16,571 women are connected with Las Vegas and Reno entertainment enterprises. Prostitutes, however, do not belong to this industry sector, but to personal services.

Other states with high values in entertainment and recreation include Florida, California, and Hawaii, all states where tourism is a major component of economic activity. Florida, with the second highest value of 1.61%, is an isolated node, as is New York. California and Hawaii are part of a larger western concentration of states with ski resorts, summer recreational areas, and spectacular scenery.

The general category of entertainment and recreation services includes those people connected with theaters and motion pictures (everything from actors to videotape production, including such diverse jobs as agents, magicians, and theater ticket agents), those employed in bowling alleys, billiard and pool parlors, as well as a large miscellaneous category. Miscellaneous is diverse, to put it mildly, and could include such jobs as bookies, dance studio operators, hunting guides, rodeo performers, and professional sports instructors.

SPECIFIC OCCUPATIONS

Secretaries and elementary teachers are obvious first guesses for inclusion on a list of the top 10 occupations for women (Table 4.2). After that, the list includes bookkeepers, general office clerks, registered nurses, nurses aides, textile sewing-machine operators, assemblers, waitresses, and cashiers. All of these occupations, with the possible exception of the two manufacturing jobs, are ubiquitous and are basic to making our society run. In fact, continuing down the list through cooks, typists, child-care workers, receptionists, secondary teachers, hairdressers, maids, janitors, bank tellers, and licensed practical nurses yields the same basic societal functions. Any reader could name a friend or acquaintance who does each of these jobs. Still, even though these jobs are common, they are not participated in at the same level everywhere in this country. The geographical variation gives us insights into the conomic character of regions.

The government identified 482 occupations derived from census questions asking respondents to name the company where he or she worked and to describe the type of work done. Those who were employed at one or more jobs were to list only the one at which they worked the greatest number of hours.

Occupations selected for mapping (secretaries, elemen-

Map 4.5 Entertainment and recreation—percentage of employed women belonging to this sector, 1980. U.S. average is .98%.

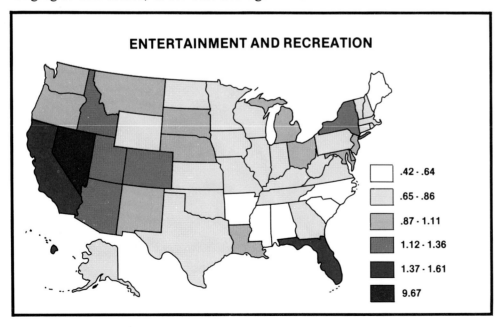

ENTERTAINMENT AND RECREATION

.42 - .64
.65 - .86
.87 - 1.11
1.12 - 1.36
1.37 - 1.61
9.67

tary teachers, cashiers, registered nurses, and waitresses) all come from the list of the top 10. They were selected mainly because they represent large numbers of ignored women. If you ask 10-year old girls today what they plan to be when they grow up, not very many will list one of these five occupations (with the possible exception of teacher or nurse) because the jobs lack glamour. Girls these days are going for the veterinarian–architect–policeman image together with the traditional model–actress–dancer syndrome. Many of these same girls, however, will still opt for one of these five jobs when they grow up because of their probable discontinuous participation in the labor force. All of these jobs have easy in-and-out access and, furthermore, are not tied to one locale. Because of the interruptions caused by child rearing and other reasons, only relatively few women are so career-oriented and committed as to maintain the expertise necessary to advance up the ladder. What most want instead are jobs where they can start out and re-enter again later in their lives, possibly on a part-time basis and possibly in a different city. Pay scales for these jobs, however, are relatively flat.

One other occupation has been mapped even though it employs only 344,559 women. Private household cleaners and

TABLE 4.2 LEADING OCCUPATIONS FOR WOMEN

OCCUPATION	NUMBER	% OF EMPLOYED FEMALE LABOR FORCE	% FEMALE	APPROXIMATE WEEKLY EARNINGS, 1981
Secretaries	3,823,248	9.18	98.8	$229
Elementary Teachers	1,722,000	4.14	75.4	$311
Bookkeepers	1,640,333	3.94	89.7	$222
Cashiers	1,428,066	3.43	83.2	$166
General Office Clerks	1,353,251	3.25	82.1	$199
Registered Nurses	1,214,868	2.92	95.9	$331
Waitresses	1,195,341	2.87	87.7	$144
Nursing Aides, Orderlies, and Attendants	1,136,455	2.73	87.7	$167
Textile Sewing Machine Operators	780,708	1.88	94.2	$156
Assemblers	725,729	1.74	49.7	$205

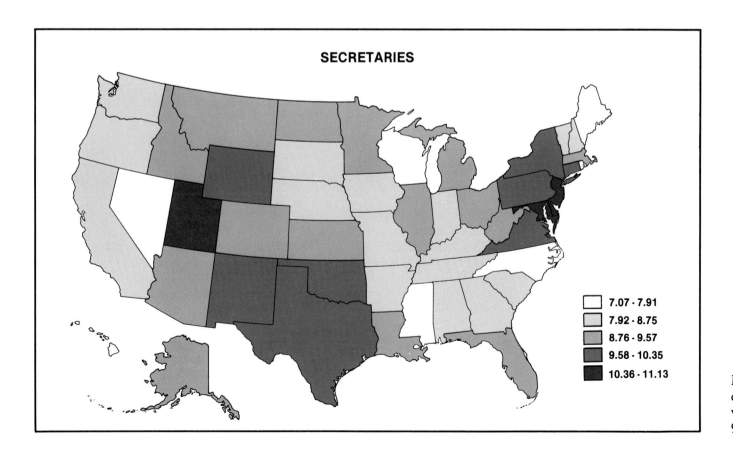

SECRETARIES

7.07 - 7.91
7.92 - 8.75
8.76 - 9.57
9.58 - 10.35
10.36 - 11.13

Map 4.6 Secretaries, as a percentage of all employed women, 1980. U.S. average is 9.18%.

servants were included because the distribution is so dramatic and the job so gender-specific (94.9% female).

Secretaries, represented as a percentage of all employed women, are centralized in two areas of the country (Map 4.6): the mid-Atlantic states, with Maryland at its core, and selected southwestern states. In addition to Maryland's value of 11.13%, values in Delaware, New Jersey, and Utah also are especially high. Since this is a map of residences of secretaries, not place of work, commuting patterns into Washington, D.C., Phildelphia, and New York City, metropolitan areas requiring large numbers of secretaries because of their economic activities, explain part of the concentration in surrounding states.

The lowest value on the map belongs to Hawaii where only 7.07% of its employed women are secretaries. Other particularly low states are Maine, Nebraska, North Carolina, and Rhode Island. Below-average areas include parts of New England, the South, Midwest, and West coast. Note that the total range of participation on this map is small, a difference of only 4 percentage points. Similar ranges are characteristic of all the six common occupations mapped; the small range here indicates the pervasiveness, and incidentally, importance, of secretaries in our society. How often we hear bosses proclaim that their business or whatever would fall apart if it were not for their secretary. They are the acknowledged glue.

It is unfair to group all secretaries into one category since they obviously vary greatly in their responsibility and training, but this label is the lowest division available through the census. Secretaries are the leading occupation for females. Its 3,823,248 members are twice the number in any other occupation. In addition, the occupation is 98.8% female, an increase over the 1970 figure of 97.8% female. This is the only occupation among the six with increased female participation during this time period.

Weekly wages for secretaries are relatively low ($229). In comparison, highly trained females who are computer systems-analysts earn $420 per week. The employment rate in 1980 for secretaries was high though, with only 3.21% of the female experienced civilian labor force who self-identified themselves as secretaries not employed (as opposed to 6.03% unemployment in the entire female labor force). More secretaries work full-time (78.5%) than the reference of 68.7% full-time employment for all female workers. The number of employed secretaries increased 39.7% between 1970 and 1980 and, therefore, we may conclude that it is still a growing occupation although it does fall behind the average increase of 43.9% for all employed females. Finally, the occupation is dominated by white women with 91.7% of all secretaries

falling in this racial category. Blacks represent 5.6% of secretaries, American Indians .4%, Asians 1.0%, and Hispanics 3.7%. For reference these same groups represent 84.5, 11.2, .5, 1.9, and 5.2% of all employed women.

If secretaries represent an assisting role, then teachers represent the nurturing role (Map 4.7). Elementary teaching as an occupation includes proportionally more of the female labor force in parts of the South and Southwest, in the Dakotas and Montana, and in Alaska than it does in other parts of the United States. Louisiana leads the country with 6.50% of its employed women engaged in this occupational pursuit. Alaska follows with 6.04%. Most of these areas represent traditional cultures that would encourage women to assume traditional roles.

The lowest value belongs to Nevada with only 2.83% of its women engaged in this category. Washington and Delaware follow at 3.29% and 3.30%. Low areas are evident along the West coast, in Colorado and Wyoming, Minnesota, parts of the Northeast, and Florida.

Elementary teachers represent 4.14% of all employed women, the second leading occupation for women. The occupation is only 75.4% female, the lowest percentage among any of the six occupations mapped. Between 1970 and 1980 the female dominance of elementary education declined 8.4 percentage points from a 1970 high of 83.8% female. The percentage of women as elementary teachers is high throughout the South with some of the highest values found in Alabama and Arkansas. Alaska, Oregon, and Washington have some of the lowest values. Some parents commend the increased participation of males in what has been a traditionally female domain because of the role-modeling effects. Current efforts to increase teacher salaries will undoubtedly have an effect upon the male–female balance. Elementary-teacher salaries at the current level are not sufficient to support a family without moonlighting and/or summer employment. The $311 average weekly earnings for women is viewed by many as supplemental income provided by the second wage-earner in the family.

As a group, female elementary teachers experienced only 1.57% unemployment in 1980 and 75.48% worked full-time. The occupation has grown since 1970 at a rate of 37.88%, slightly below the average increase in jobs for women. Finally, employment by race or ethnic origin is close to the reference for all employed women. White women are slightly overrepresented whereas Hispanic women are underrepresented. Of elementary teachers 86.1% are white, 11.6% black, .4% American Indian, 1.1% Asian, and 2.8% Hispanic.

The teaching profession offers one of the interesting ironies of life. At the elementary level we entrust our children

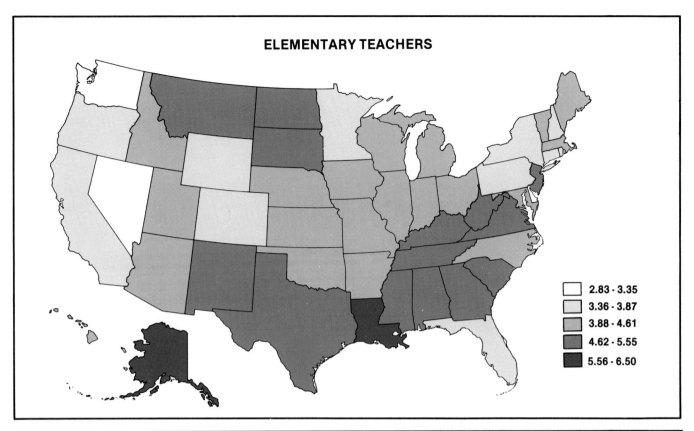

ELEMENTARY TEACHERS

☐	2.83 - 3.35
☐	3.36 - 3.87
☐	3.88 - 4.61
☐	4.62 - 5.55
■	5.56 - 6.50

Map 4.7 Elementary teachers, as a percentage of all employed women, 1980. U.S. average is 4.14%.

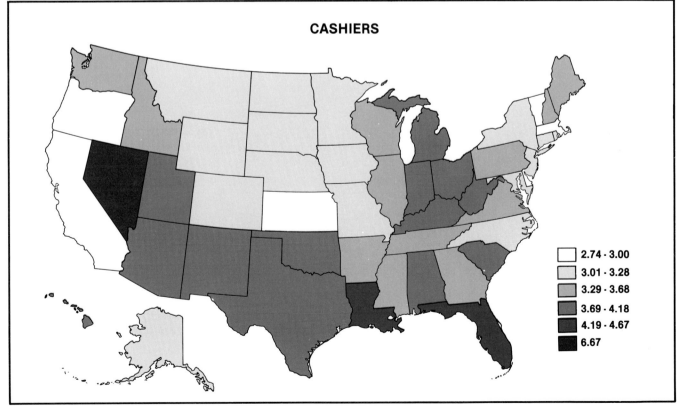

CASHIERS

☐	2.74 - 3.00
☐	3.01 - 3.28
☐	3.29 - 3.68
☐	3.69 - 4.18
■	4.19 - 4.67
■	6.67

Map 4.8 Cashiers, in sales, as a percentage of all employed women, 1980. U.S. average is 3.43%.

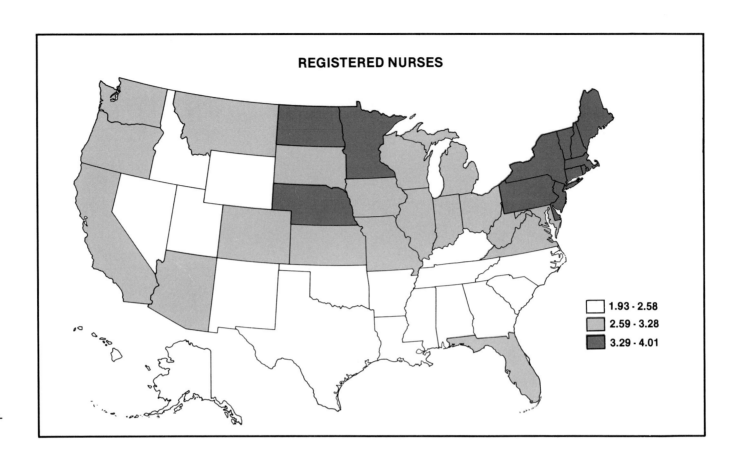

REGISTERED NURSES

Legend:
- 1.93 - 2.58
- 2.59 - 3.28
- 3.29 - 4.01

Map 4.9 Registered nurses, as a percentage of all employed women, 1980. U.S. average is 2.92%.

to women, but at the secondary level women represent only 56.4% of the 849,698 employed secondary teachers. Have women lost their nurturing advantage when it comes to teenagers? At the postsecondary level female participation falls even further to 36.3%. Why have the female ranks thinned in the classroom at this level? Salaries and tradition have kept elementary teaching largely a woman's job. Has the competition and career commitment at the other end kept college teaching a male profession? Male–female ratios, of course, change with field in postsecondary education. At this level female teachers of the health specialities, English, and foreign languages actually outnumber their male counterparts. Teaching ratios are highly male-dominated in physics and engineering with only 9.9 and 11.3% female participation.

Now to cashier, the mystery occupation with no professional associations, unions, or support groups (Map 4.8). Cashiers in sales represent the occupation of 1,428,066 women in the United States, the fourth leading occupation. Yet we are hardpressed to create a public image of a cashier in our mind's eye. The existence of a smock (a semi-uniform), for example, is dependent on store policy. Still cashiers exist everywhere and are needed in our consumer society.

A significantly higher proportion of women devote themselves to this occupation in Nevada than in any other state (6.67% of employed women). One might question whether this state is the most product-oriented of them all. Nevada forms the western anchor for high values of this variable across the Southwest and into selected parts of the South. Florida and Louisiana, in fact, represent the next highest values following Nevada. Similarly above-average values are found in a group of states representing the industrial Midwest.

The lowest participation in this occupational category belongs to the women in Vermont where only 2.74% are cashiers. Other low values are found in Delaware, Kansas, Massachusetts, and Oregon. Low areas are evident along the West coast, the northern Plains and Midwest, and in parts of the Northeast.

Cashiers represent 3.43% of all employed women and the occupation is assuredly female-dominated with 83.2% of the jobs belonging to women. This is a slight decline from a 1970 value of 84.0% female. The proportion of cashiers who are women varies somewhat with geographical location. California represents the greatest male infiltration with only 74.65% of cashiers there being female. New Jersey, New York,

Oregon, and Rhode Island also have relatively low female-participation rates.

Cashiers are best described by their pay and terms of employment. The average weekly earnings for cashiers in 1981 was only $166 per week, and this was for full-time jobs. Is it worth it? Even though there was as much as 8.8% unemployment in 1980, this occupation is probably the epitome of easy access and flexible employment. In fact, the number of female cashiers doubled from 1970 to 1980, far above the rate for other occupations. Employment by racial/ethnic group parallels the proportions for all employed women except that there are slightly more white women and slightly fewer black women than expected. Cashiers are 86.5% white, 9.2% black, .5% American Indian, 1.8% Asian, and 5.6% Hispanic.

With registered nurses we return to known territory. Most women at some point in their young lives wanted to be a nurse with its image of starched whiteness, competence, and caring. Nursing as a profession for women is prominent in the East and Midwest (Map 4.9). Massachusetts has proportionally more nurses among its employed women (4.01%) than any state. Pennsylvania and Delaware follow with percentages of 3.83 and 3.77 respectively. Do not jump to the conclusion that there is more need for nurses in these parts of the country (more hospitals and beds, more practicing physicians) or that more satisfactory working conditions attract nurses. Since the range in participation is only 2.08, the actually minor variations have been exaggerated by the mapping process. Registered nurse is one of our most ubiquitous occupations.

Registered nurses are relatively less important to the female employment picture in Arkansas where only 1.93% of employed women fall in this category. Louisiana, Mississippi, Oklahoma, and Texas also have low proportions of nurses in their female populations. These states form the core of a low-percentage region across the southern half of the country. The area extends northward into the intermontane states, as well.

Nurses represent the sixth occupation for women with 1,214,868 participants in 1980. Since 95.9% of registered nurses are women, it is among the leading female-dominated occupations. In 1970 nursing was 97.3% female. Indiana has the greatest percentage of women among its nurses (97.96%) with New Hampshire, New Jersey, and Vermont displaying similar tendencies. More men in New Mexico have entered the profession than elsewhere as evidenced by a reduction in female-dominance to 91.66%. Alaska, Arkansas, Louisiana, and Tennessee all have female participation rates in the 93% range.

Weekly earnings for female nurses averaged $331 per week in 1981, the top earnings among the group of 10 occupations in Table 4.2. With 1.4% unemployment and 70.0% full-time employment, it appears as if a critical demand for nurses exists. Between 1970 and 1980 the number of nurses increased 66.4%, far above the average increase. The obvious question to be posed is why even larger numbers of young women are not turning to this profession. Nurses outwardly represent a desirable occupation because of their post-high-school training and economic security. The "dirty work" aspects and subservient role in the medical pecking order may diminish their prestige somewhat. Low salaries and high stress are additional factors.

Racial/ethnic composition among nurses puts more emphasis upon white and Asian women than expected. Of female nurses, 88.2% are white, 7.4% black, .3% American Indian, 3.6% Asian, and 2.0% Hispanic. Among female nursing aides, orderlies, and attendants (all less prestigious jobs), the racial composition shifts. Here 69.3% are white, 26.5% black, .9% American Indian, 1.5% Asian, and 5.0% Hispanic.

Waitresses, known as one of the pink-collar occupations because of their uniform color, totaled 1,089,159 women in 1980 (Map 4.10). They provide necessary services, but as we shall see, are not treated well. This occupation, in fact, is among the most stressful jobs for women because the waitress lacks power and independence. If the waitress is in it for the tips, she has no alternative but to respond to customer demands with friendliness and efficiency. Rewards other than financial are minimal.

Areas of high employment extend across the north central and northwest states of this country plus Florida, Hawaii, and Nevada. Nevada has the highest proportion of its employed women as waitresses—6.09%. This, of course, goes hand in hand with the Nevada entertainment industry. Surprisingly North Dakota has the second highest proportion at 4.90%. Since this state has the highest proportion of females among waitresses (96.2%), North Dakota's position is partly explained.

States with low employment in the waitress occupation exist throughout the South, with the exception of Florida. Mississippi has the lowest value for this variable (1.64%) followed by Alabama and South Carolina. Parts of the metropolitan Northeast also have low values.

Although this is a female-dominated occupation with 87.7% of waitresses being female, men have made slight inroads since 1970 when waitresses were 90.6% female. As might be expected, the waiter has more cachet in certain situations. For example, New York has the lowest female dominance with only 74.9% of its waitresses being female. Louisi-

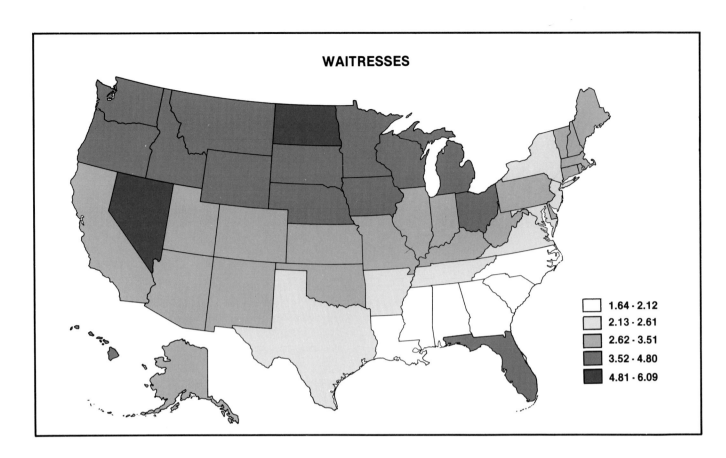

WAITRESSES

☐	1.64 - 2.12
☐	2.13 - 2.61
☐	2.62 - 3.51
☐	3.52 - 4.80
☐	4.81 - 6.09

Map 4.10 Waitresses, as a percentage of all employed women, 1980. U.S. average is 2.87%.

Map 4.11 Private household cleaners and servants, as a percentage of all employed women, 1980. U.S. average is .83%.

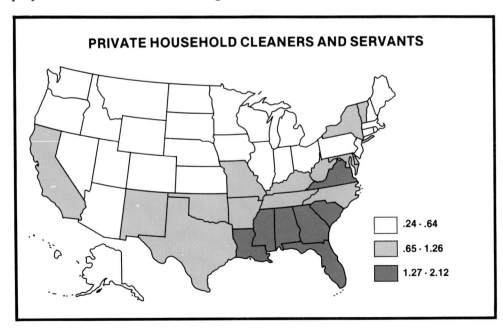

PRIVATE HOUSEHOLD CLEANERS AND SERVANTS

☐	.24 - .64
☐	.65 - 1.26
☐	1.27 - 2.12

ana and Nevada also have more mixing of the sexes in this occupation. Possibly a positive correlation exists between number of waiters and classiness of dining. One would expect more chic restaurants in all three of these states. In addition, the French background of Louisiana may make it easier to approve of the male waiter.

Waitresses' weekly earnings in 1981 totaled only $144, the lowest of any occupation on the top 10 list. Of course, the possibility exists that tips were not included in this reporting. Coupled with low wages, waitresses also experienced 9.8% unemployment in 1980, the highest rate among the six occupations mapped. In addition, only 38.3% of waitresses worked full-time. The terms of employment clearly are not ideal. The occupation has increased 21.1% in female numbers since 1970, less than the average for all female employment. Since Americans are spending more of their food dollar on dining out, lack of rapid growth in the occupation of waitress suggests that families are spending more and more of this food dollar in the type of fast-food restaurants that do not employ waitresses or waiters. Waitresses are overwhelmingly white (92.0%). Blacks account for 4.0% of the total, American Indians .5%, Asians 2.1%, and Hispanics 3.6%.

Private household cleaners and servants are represented in the final map in this set (Map 4.11). Chosen not because of their numbers (344,559 or .83% of employed women), this category of domestic help was included to document a strongly regional phenomenon that is perhaps vanishing. The jobs included in this category sound like a list from an *Upstairs/Downstairs* script, including kitchen maid, pantry maid, upstairs maid, and downstairs maid. It is suspected, however, that most of these women are daytime help performing a cleaning function especially since 94.2% of private household help live away from their place of work. In the Midwest these people are called cleaning women, but the terminology varies with locale. Launderers, ironers, cooks, housekeepers and in-home child-care people are not included as they fall in other occupational categories.

The Deep South dominates the pattern of private household cleaners and servants. Louisiana has the greatest participation in this category with 2.12% of employed women. Alabama, Georgia, and Mississippi follow. Florida, South Carolina, and Virginia are not far behind in areas surrounding the core. Are these all remnants of a class society?

The lowest value on the map belongs to Nevada, followed by Utah, Alaska, North Dakota, and Minnesota in that order. Values are particularly low across the northern half of the country where there is little tradition of servants.

As with the other occupations, this one too is highly female in composition (94.9%). Since 1970 female participation has declined somewhat from the then 96.0% level. Alabama has the highest predominance of females in this occupation with 97.73%; Kansas follows with 97.01%. Nevada has the most male integration with 81.58% of its private household cleaners and servants being female. Hawaii and Maine also have low percentages.

Weekly earnings for this group of women are $124 per week for full-time work, lower than that for waitresses. Unemployment in 1980 was 5.1%, but only 30.2% were employed full-time, truly a meager existence. The most dramatic fact, however, is that the number of women in this occupation in 1980 was less than half of what it was 10 years before.

As older women retire, younger women are not replacing them. The proliferation of small businesses that specialize in home cleaning on a contract basis is another factor supplanting some of the jobs. As women increase their full-time participation in the labor force, especially in the higher paying professions, the need for a clean house does not disappear. This is, in fact, when the use of such services increases. Future trends will be interesting to follow.

The other factor that radically differentiates this occupation from the others that are mapped is its racial/ethnic composition. Blacks dominate. Of all the women employed as private household-cleaners and servants, 39.6% are white, 54.7% black, .5% American Indian, 1.3% Asian and 9.6% Hispanic.

MALE-DOMINATED OCCUPATIONS

Occupations long dominated by men have not been discussed so far in this chapter. Women as doctors, lawyers, or company presidents are repeatedly singled out for media coverage to show that women are being integrated into employed society, but despite this attention, women in high-visibility jobs represent but a token segment of all working women. For example, according to the 1980 census, there were 57,310 female physicians in the United States. This represented 13.28% of all doctors, but only .14% of all employed females. The percentages become much smaller when such professions as architects (.02% of employed females) or judges (.01%) are considered.

Small numbers present problems to the mapmaker; they increase the chances of misrepresentation, especially when working with sample data such as the census. No female judges are indicated in Hawaii or New Hampshire by the census, yet according to another source there were six trial judges in Hawaii's state courts in 1980. Obviously some caution must be exercised in discussing the five female dentists in South Dakota or the three female firefighters in Wyoming. Instead of individual occupational analysis, some of these smaller numbers have been grouped together for mapping.

States here have been assigned a "grade" based on female integration into a set of male occupations. Data for 10 male-dominated occupations (architect, clergy, dentist, engineer, farmer, firefighter, judge, lawyer, physician, and police) have been tabulated to present a "report card" (Map 4.12). States were ranked for each of the 10 occupations according to the female participation rate in that occupation. Rhode Island, for example, had the lowest participation rate for females as architects (1.98%) and received a 1 ranking. Virginia, in contrast, had the highest value (12.88%) and, therefore, received a 50 ranking. Subsequently, rankings for all 10 occupations were tallied. A state could flunk one of the 10 tests and still receive a high grade for their acceptance of women into the set of occupations, just as a student can flunk one quiz and still ace a course. Vermont, for example, did very poorly on dentists (only 3.01% female, the third lowest ranking), but still managed to get an A based on its performance in the other occupations. Perhaps the responsibility for a grade should not be placed on a state (and thereby assume

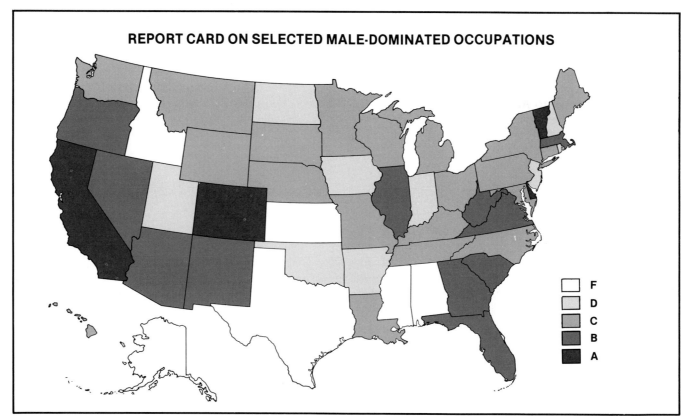

REPORT CARD ON SELECTED MALE-DOMINATED OCCUPATIONS

F
D
C
B
A

Map 4.12 Report card on selected male-dominated occupations, based on composite
ranking of female participation rate in 10 occupations,
1980.

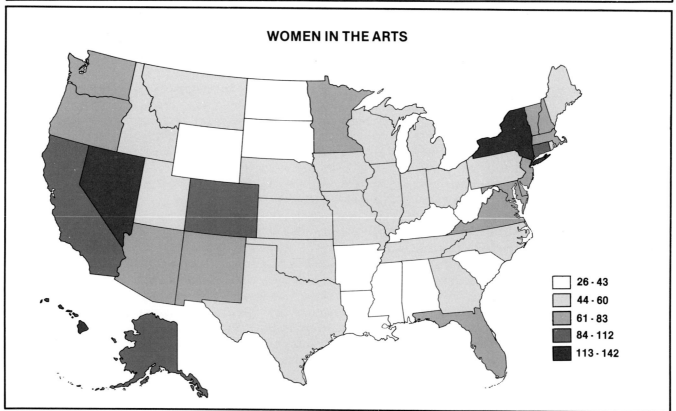

WOMEN IN THE ARTS

26 - 43
44 - 60
61 - 83
84 - 112
113 - 142

Map 4.13 Women in the
arts—women employed in the
arts as a rate per 100,000 resident population, 1980. U.S. average is 69.

that societal attitudes have some effect upon participation rates). Perhaps the responsibility lies with the women of the state and their degree of commitment to nontraditional occupations.

The high grades on the map belong to Alaska, Vermont, Delaware, Colorado, and California in that order. States with a grade of B join these five states to form regional concentrations in the West (with an obvious gap provided by Idaho and Utah), the far southeastern corner of the country, some mid-Atlantic states, some New England states, and Illinois.

Alabama, Kansas, Mississippi, Idaho, and Texas have failed the test. Activists, legislators, and professional associations as well as the women of these states owe it to themselves to take a closer look at why they have received such poor grades. When joined by the D students, poor grades characterize parts of the intermontane West, parts of the Midwest, the western half of the South, and parts of the Northeast.

Both Alabama and Texas have no rankings above 25 and thus have consistently performed in the bottom half of the class. Alabama did especially poorly on clergy, lawyers, and firefighters whereas Texas's primary bad mark belonged to the clergy. Kansas, Mississippi, and Idaho had at least one ranking above 25 (Kansas with police; Mississippi with engineer, judge, and firefighter; and Idaho with engineer, judge, and police), but the remainder of their marks were so low as to lead to an overall failing grade. Clergy was the worst category for all three states. Kansas can add judge and lawyer to its list of particularly bad representative percentages; Mississippi should add architect, dentist, farmer, and lawyer; and Idaho architect, farmer, and physician.

Of the five states that passed with an A only California had no individual grades in the bottom half of the class. In Alaska engineers rank below 25, whereas in Vermont dentists do, as stated before. In Delaware engineers are the culprit, and in Colorado farmers form the low-percentage links. Especially high rankings belong to both engineers and lawyers in California and Colorado. Colorado adds police to this list. Alaska had the most diversified list of very high marks with clergy, farmer, firefighter, judge, lawyer, physician, and police all topping the list. In Vermont women as clergy, firefighters, judges, and lawyers did especially well. In Delaware women as farmers and physicians received particularly high marks.

Women can probably look to the five A states for enlightened attitudes toward women in nontraditional occupations. Some of the B states can be looked to for understanding and acceptance as well. There are, however, three surprises on this list, based on all the other findings in this atlas—Georgia, South Carolina, and West Virginia. How did they make it? South Carolina actually had the highest ranking in the country for dentists, engineers, and firefighters. Other than police, which received a 44 ranking, the remaining occupations all received mediocre grades. For Georgia dentists and engineers had 49 and 48 rankings, but remaining occupations were average or lower. In West Virginia police and farmers had especially high grades whereas the remainder of the grades were not outstanding.

WOMEN IN THE ARTS

The spatial variation in one final category of employment for women tells us something further about the character of our states. This category is women in the arts. Women in each state who were employed primarily as authors; musicians and composers; actors and directors; painters, sculptors, craft-artists, and artist printmakers; and dancers, in the 1980 census were compared with the total population of that state. The result is a female-artist-rate per 100,000-resident population (Map 4.13). Other than indicating how prominent women in the arts are in each state, the map also gives an indication of how likely you are to know an artist personally, depending upon where you live.

Unfortunately this measure does not include all women active in the arts and, therefore, is not a true measure of female cultural activity. Amateur artists as well as those citizens who support the arts through donations, attendance at functions, and/or volunteer time all have a big impact upon the cultural status of a community. The map includes only those women who identified themselves as belonging to one of the previous five categories on an employed basis. Many of them are probably self-employed, but assuredly, many belong to professional companies of dancers or musicians. Quality, of course, cannot be assessed from the map data.

The map displays a strong East coast/West coast polarity. Colorado forms a high anomaly in what is otherwise a vast expanse of average or below-average representation. Nevada has the highest value, with 142 women in the arts per 100,000 population. Hawaii follows at a rate of 129; New York is next with 126. New York's inclusion was expected as it has long been acknowledged as the primary cultural center of this country and is certainly a magnet for women in the performing arts. But Hawaii and Nevada? Both of these states have exceptionally high numbers of dancers. Since the occupational classification does not differentiate between those women who may be associated with classical ballet or modern dance companies and those who are with folk-dancing groups (perhaps in Hawaii) or stage shows (assuredly in Nevada), the broadly defined dancer category inflates the values for both of these states. If one were to subtract all dancers from their state totals (a rather unfair procedure), Hawaii's rate would decrease to 96, placing it between Alaska and Colorado in the ranking. Similarly, Nevada's rate would decrease to 91, putting it slightly below Hawaii's new position. Both states would, therefore, remain well above average in women's participation in the arts. New York at the top would, in this case, be followed by California and then Alaska.

The lowest rank in the country belongs to Mississippi and West Virginia (both 26). Arkansas follows with a rate of 28 and Wyoming is next with 29. The northern Plains and portions of the South and mid-South join these four states in the exceptionally low category. Perhaps legislators and potential patrons there need to reaffirm the undeniable importance of the arts to quality of life.

Composite values such as women in the arts obscure many of the internal variations in each of the five categories. For example, New York has the highest rate for authors with 3,931 of such women residing there (rate of 22). Alaska, Nevada, and California follow with rates of 20, 18, and 18 respectively. The reader is again cautioned about rates; Alaska only has 79 female authors and a low female population provides the high rate. California, in turn, has 4,309 authors, but a female population higher than that of New York, creates in effect, a relatively lower rate. Authors include novelists, of course, but also jobs as diverse as poets, television writers, ghost-writers, librettists, and verse writers for greeting cards. Nevada has the highest rate for musicians and composers (36); Hawaii, Nebraska, New York, and Minnesota follow. Musicians and composers include such obvious positions as a violinist in a symphony orchestra, but choir directors, opera singers, and piano players of all sorts are part of the category,

too. Not surprisingly, New York has the highest rate for actors and directors (26) with California following. Unexpected jobs within this category include dramatic coaches, extras, narrators, and pageant directors. Hawaii has the highest rate for painters and other graphic artists in the category (54); New Mexico, Vermont, and Colorado follow with rates of 52, 50, and 48 respectively. Certainly these 4 states are among the most scenic of our 50; residence in any of them could provide inspiration for the creative spirit. Graphic artists, of course, may include commercial endeavors as diverse as cartoonists, ice sculptors, medical illustrators, or stained-glass artists. Dancers, discussed previously, includes chorus girls, square-dance callers, and strippers, to name a few.

Dancers are dominated by females (75.2% female) whereas musicians and composers are not (30.3%). Authors are 44.3% female, actors are 32.8%, and painters are 47.9%. Of the five occupational groups, actors and directors are more likely to be working full-time (69.0%) followed by painters (61.1%), dancers (51.4%), authors (49.5%), and finally musicians with only 21.3% full-time employment. The highest unemployment rate is found among actors and directors (19.7%), with dancers following at 11.8%. The remaining categories have unemployment ranging from 4 to 6%; probably a difficult criterion to assess in a largely free-lance business. The most dramatic increase since 1970 has occurred among women who are authors—a 147% increase in the number of employed female authors. The male increase, in contrast, was only 30.5%. Another large increase occurred among female painters (117% increase) with dancers and actors experiencing above average but more modest gains (67.8 and 64.4% increases). Female musicians and composers increased minimally by 17.2%.

CHAPTER FIVE

EDUCATION

INTRODUCTION

Women's persistence in the pursuit of education and their eventual attainment levels are reflections of many personal decisions made at different points in the life-cycle. The reasons behind dropping out of high school, the decision to go to college or not, and the drive to finish a professional degree can be complex. Continuation of education may be viewed strictly in economic terms—expectation of return on an investment. Education also has vocational utility: the higher the educational level, the more opportunity for career choice. In addition, many women pursue educational goals to improve their psychological well-being and quality of life. Although education decisions are made at the personal level, data that are aggregated for larger units, such as counties or states, reveal definite regional patterns in educational status. Regional variation in educational level reflects a variety of economic variables. The variation also suggests a societal influence in education decisions. There seems to be an acceptance of education for women in some parts of this country as well as a prejudice against it in other parts.

This chapter opens with a map of high-school graduates, a standard measure of educational level. Two measures of educational attainment from opposite ends of the spectrum follow—illiterate women and women with "brains." The percentages of college degrees to women at two academic levels are then presented as well as female participation in specific disciplines. Next, college majors favored among graduating senior women are graphically portrayed. Finally, two special aspects of women's higher education are presented—locations of women's colleges and of women's studies programs.

EDUCATIONAL ATTAINMENT

Levels of educational achievement among women in the United States are represented on the following three maps. Since education is often used as an indicator of status or well-being, regional disparities such as are apparent in these maps are especially important. Education levels, however, are one of the more easily modified parts of a population

profile. Compulsory public education, bilingual education, and efforts to retain the potential high-school dropout should assure more standardization in the future than is evident now.

High-school graduates is a standard descriptive measure of potential productivity and quality of life in a population. Such data are, for example, part of the decision process used to assess the labor force prior to locating new industrial plants. The percentage of women 25 and older in a state who are high-school graduates is the subject of Map 5.1. These women have passed their normal years for high-school attendance, and the map thus reflects a long-term pattern rather than a current completion rate. It includes women who were of high-school age before compulsory education, women whose family depended upon youthful earnings to supplement the family income, and women who grew up in areas of the country where high schools did not exist at all or did not exist for minorities. High-school graduation is a significant milepost in life. The receipt of a diploma has a direct impact upon other decisions. In the aggregate, high-school graduation data in an area are directly related to other population variables such as income, job options, and, possibly, even health.

The gradual rise in median years of school completed for both females and males is presented in Table 5.1. The data are for persons 25 and older. The peak in 1980 of 12.4 years for females indicates the changing emphasis upon longer school participation. The rise is, of course, accompanied by a rise in societal expectations regarding the amount of education needed to function as an adult.

State averages for female high-school graduates range from 52.5% for South Carolina to 82.2% for Alaska. South Carolina is joined at one end of the scale by Alabama, Arkansas, Georgia, Kentucky, Louisiana, Mississippi, North Carolina, Tennessee and West Virginia (at percentages ranging from 53.1 to 56.4). Florida is the exception among the southern states with an average of 66.2% high-school graduates, near the national average of 65.8%. Florida has attracted new industrial workers as well as affluent retirees in recent decades through aggressive marketing and its climatic amenities. Both of these groups have increased the average educational levels.

Alaska is joined by Utah, Wyoming, Colorado, and Wash-

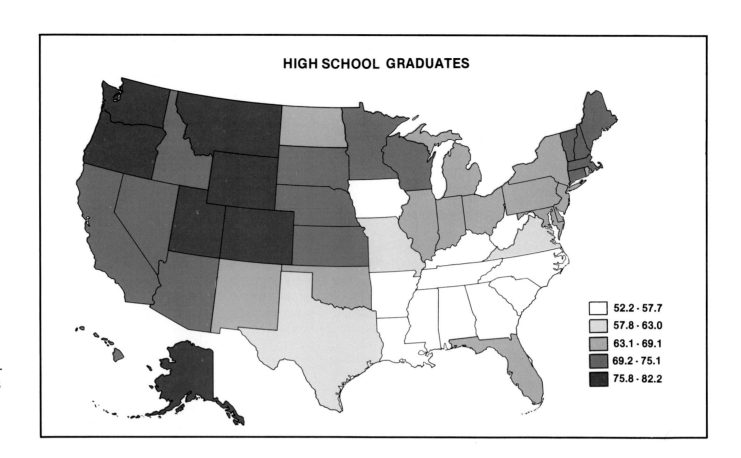

HIGH SCHOOL GRADUATES

52.2 - 57.7
57.8 - 63.0
63.1 - 69.1
69.2 - 75.1
75.8 - 82.2

Map 5.1 High-school graduates—percentages of females 25 years and older who are high-school graduates, 1980. U.S. average is 65.8%.

TABLE 5.1	YEARS OF SCHOOL COMPLETED	
YEAR	FEMALE	MALE
1940	8.7	8.6
1950	9.6	9.0
1960	10.9	10.3
1965	12.0	11.7
1970	12.1	12.2
1975	12.3	12.4
1980	12.4	12.6

TABLE 5.2 HIGH SCHOOL GRADUATES IN SMSAs

LOCATION	%	LOCATION	%
Anaheim–Santa Ana–Garden Grove, Calif.	78.9	Minneapolis–St. Paul, Minn.-Wis.	79.8
Atlanta, Ga.	66.2	Nassau-Suffolk, N.Y.	74.7
Baltimore, Md.	61.0	New Orleans, La.	61.9
Boston, Mass.	76.9	New York, N.Y.-N.J.	61.9
Buffalo, N.Y.	66.7	Newark, N.J.	68.5
Chicago, Ill.	66.2	Philadelphia, Pa.-N.J.	64.9
Cincinnati, Ohio-Ky.-Ind.	61.8	Phoenix, Ariz.	74.5
Cleveland, Ohio	67.8	Pittsburgh, Pa.	67.1
Columbus, Ohio	71.2	Portland, Oreg.-Wash.	78.4
Dallas–Fort Worth, Tex.	68.5	Riverside–San Bernardino–Ontario, Calif.	69.2
Denver-Boulder, Colo.	80.4	Sacramento, Calif.	76.5
Detroit, Mich.	66.8	St. Louis, Mo.-Ill.	61.9
Fort Lauderdale–Hollywood, Fla.	70.1	San Antonio, Tex.	60.0
Houston, Tex.	68.4	San Diego, Calif.	75.9
Indianapolis, Ind.	68.2	San Francisco–Oakland, Calif.	77.7
Kansas City, Mo.-Ks.	73.5	San Jose, Calif.	77.8
Los Angeles–Long Beach, Calif.	68.6	Seattle-Everett, Wash.	81.2
Miami, Fla.	62.7	Tampa–St. Petersburg, Fla.	65.4
Milwaukee, Wis.	70.9	Washington, D.C.-Md.-Va.	79.1

ington for top honors (at 79.1, 78.2, 77.9, and 77.3% respectively). It is ironic that those states in which it is probably most difficult to get to school because of distance, difficult terrain, and uncertain winter weather also produce high proportions of high-school graduates.

High school graduates data for SMSAs reveal a similar geographical pattern (Table 5.2). Seattle-Everett has the highest percentage of women reaching this educational level (81.2%); Denver follows with 80.4%. No major metropolitan areas have percentages as low as those in the lowest map category. The lowest belongs to San Antonio with 60.0%; Baltimore follows with 61.0%.

The same data viewed at the county level would reveal an irregular arc dividing areas with a below-average percentage of high-school completions for women from the rest of the country. The dividing line for educational achievement starts on the Atlantic coast of Eastern Shore Maryland and progresses westward cutting across West Virginia, the hill areas of southern Ohio, Indiana, and Illinois, the Ozarks of Missouri, and diagonally through Oklahoma, ending at El Paso, Tex. To the south and east of this line educational level is generally below average, with the exception of Florida. Rare patches of above-average exceptions occur, mainly associated with retirement areas, colleges, or state capitals. Georgia (excluding Atlanta, its environs, and the coastal areas) has an exceptional number of counties in the lowest category. The cotton-rich Delta area south of Memphis and coal-mining counties in eastern and south central Kentucky join Georgia. The Mexican border area of Texas provides another area of pronounced low educational achievement as do the bayous of Louisiana and the old tobacco region of southern Virginia.

In contrast, counties to the north and west of the dividing line have average or above-average levels of educational achievement. If the counties in the western half of the country that are home to large numbers of native American women or Hispanics were subtracted from the distribution, the result would be a uniformly above-average pattern. Small exceptions still exist, such as the portion of North Dakota dominated by relatively recent immigration. Northern and western coastal areas of Alaska, where delivery of school services is difficult, form another anomalous low. Exceptionally high value areas across the West are associated with college-oriented counties, high-income counties (such as Johnson County, Kan., and Marin County, Calif.), and year-round resort areas. The Colorado ski counties are joined by those counties containing Jackson Hole, Wyo., Sun Valley, Idaho, and the Lake Tahoe area.

The distinctive and almost uniformly high percentage pattern in the northwest quadrant of the country can probably best be explained by looking at the age of the female popula-

tion. In Wyoming, for example, the median age among women is 27.3. In Alaska it is 25.7. Since a higher proportion of women in Wyoming and Alaska grew up within the time of compulsory education than did the women in South Carolina, for example, (where the median age is 29.4), the high-school completion percentage would logically be greater in Alaska and Wyoming.

Counties with the lowest percentage of female high-school graduates are Taliaferro County, Georgia (24.0%) located in the east central part of the state between Augusta and Atlanta; Zavala and Starr counties, Texas (25.3 and 26.9%) near the Mexican border southwest of San Antonio; and Wolfe and Jackson counties of eastern Kentucky (27.0 and 27.1%). All of these counties are far below their state averages. The Georgia county has a large indigent, black population. Hispanics dominate the Texas counties. The Kentucky counties are part of a long-established poverty pocket in the old coal-mining areas.

Counties with the highest percentage of graduates are Summit, Pitkin, and Gunnison counties, Colorado (95.5, 95.1, and 91.3%) in ski country USA; Los Alamos county, N.M. (92.9%), site of a high-technology government research center; and the Juneau census area in Alaska (91.5%). Jobs associated with recreation facilities in Aspen and other towns in the Colorado mountain area attract an educated, mobile, and youthful portion of the population looking for glamour and not job security. The same people also have college degrees. Los Alamos County was created to isolate the secret nuclear-weapons research center there. Its jobs are almost exclusively for highly educated people. Juneau, a government center, magnifies the high status of Alaska in general.

Map 5.2 is a surrogate measure for illiteracy—percentage of women 25 years or older who have completed four or fewer years of elementary school. This measure approximates conventional illiteracy definitions based on schooling, but not those for functional illiteracy based on ability to perform adult reading tasks such as using a road map or completing a short income-tax form. The measure here also does not include the self-educated woman, of course, and, therefore, some error is inherent in the data.

Illiteracy by this measure is lowest in Iowa (1.0%) followed closely by Vermont, Nebraska, Minnesota, and Wyoming. The Northeast, Midwest, and West all rank generally low. Exceptions are states with large ethnic and black populations such as New Jersey, New York, and Rhode Island. Illiteracy among women is highest in Louisiana (7.1%) followed by Texas and South Carolina. The entire South, with the exception of Florida, Maryland, and Virginia, falls into the low end of the educational spectrum. It seems certain that illiteracy in the South represents past educational failures rather

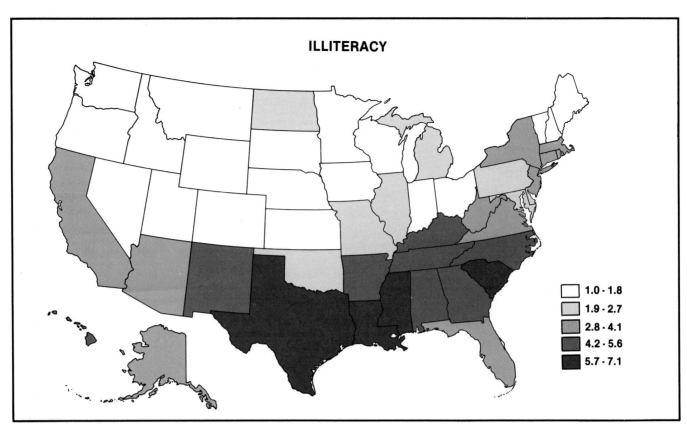

ILLITERACY

☐	1.0 - 1.8
☐	1.9 - 2.7
☐	2.8 - 4.1
☐	4.2 - 5.6
■	5.7 - 7.1

Map 5.2 Illiteracy—percentage of females 25 years and older who completed 4 or fewer years of elementary school, 1980. U.S. average is 3.3%.

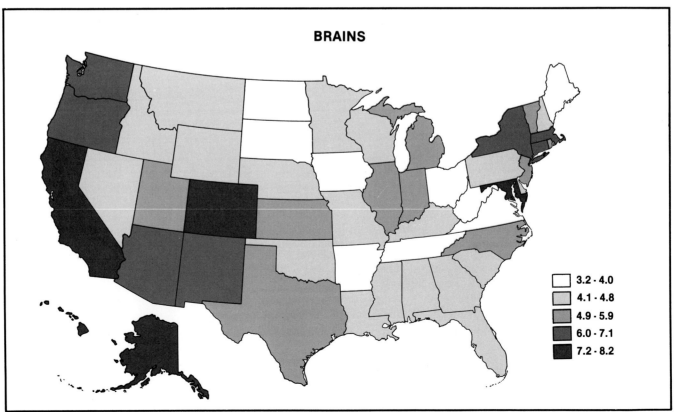

BRAINS

☐	3.2 - 4.0
☐	4.1 - 4.8
☐	4.9 - 5.9
☐	6.0 - 7.1
■	7.2 - 8.2

Map 5.3 Brains—percentage of females 25 years and older who completed five or more years of college, 1980. U.S. average is 5.3%.

Atlas of American Women

than current trends. In the future one would expect these percentages to be much lower. The numbers of women pursuing education degrees in these same states should guarantee regional improvement.

Map 5.3 shows where women locate after they have achieved a highly educated level. Where the "brains" are, or percentage of women 25 or older who have completed 5 or more years of college, is in many ways a residential preference map. The map reflects a composite locational decision made by a highly mobile segment of the population. As such, it may well be a surrogate for places with such desiderata as high salaries, availability of challenging jobs, environmental amenities such as climate or recreational opportunities, etc. Some women, of course, exhibit a strong attachment to place and remain where they were reared and educated.

Arkansas represents the low end of the "brain" scale at 3.2%. Other southern states are included in the low category with the exception of Maryland and Virginia, locations of the bedroom communities for people working in Washington, D.C. Midwestern states such as North and South Dakota, Iowa, and Ohio also appear at this low end. For many years these states have experienced a "brain drain." Young people are educated in their home state, at the expense of the local taxpayers, and then leave for jobs in more attractive locales. Some states in this same area have recently shown a reversal in this population movement. Young people are still leaving the state after they receive a college education, but are returning later in the life-cycle to establish permanent roots with their young families.

Brains are attracted to our noncontiguous, exotic states of Alaska (8.2%) and Hawaii (7.9%). Maryland and California are followed by Colorado, New York, Connecticut, and Washington in popularity. Somehow this is not a surprise. All states are associated with a large metropolitan area, a source of employment for women in the professions, and some even have well-known life-style images as well.

COLLEGE GRADUATES

Women graduates receiving bachelor of arts or bachelor of science degrees in 1979–80 represent 49.0% of the total bachelor's degrees conferred (Map 5.4). The data are for both publicly and privately controlled institutions of higher learn-

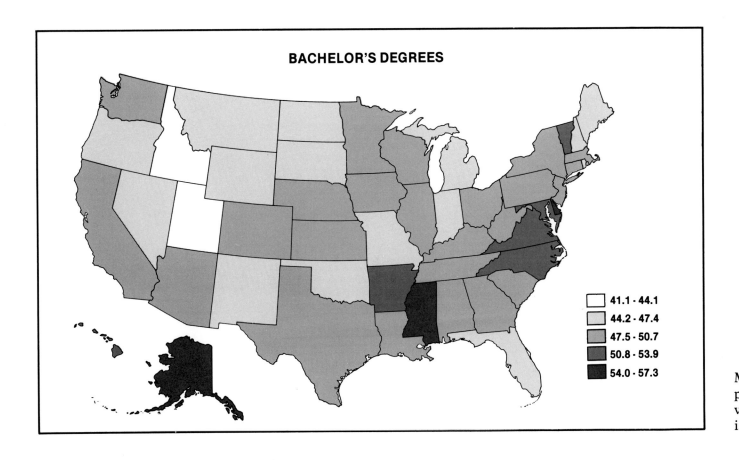

BACHELOR'S DEGREES

41.1 - 44.1
44.2 - 47.4
47.5 - 50.7
50.8 - 53.9
54.0 - 57.3

Map 5.4 Bachelor's degrees—percentage awarded to women, 1979–80. U.S. average is 49.0%.

ing and represent four- as well as five-year programs. The 455,303 graduates represent a steady increase in women graduates in the last 10 years.

States with higher-than-expected women graduation rates, based on the male/female ratio of the state population, include Alaska, Delaware, and Mississippi. Although data for these states reflect the growth in female enrollment in the 1970s, the data may also indicate low interest in college education among males. In Alaska, for example, alternate post-secondary employment opportunities for males may discourage them from pursuing a college degree. Males represent 53.0% of the population in Alaska, but only 42.7% of the degrees and 39.9% of the total enrollment in higher education. Mississippi and Delaware graduates portray similar profiles and accentuate a larger southern phenomenon. Traditionally college graduation as a stepping-stone to success is not held in the same high regard by southern males as it has been in other parts of the country. Conversely, educated females are acceptable among southern values.

Utah at 41.1% and Idaho at 43.9% represent the states with the lowest percentage of bachelor's degrees awarded to women. Both states are dominated by the Mormon culture that emphasizes woman's traditional role in the home. The fact that 15.0% of Utah's women graduates in 1976–77 had home economics as a major, a proportion higher than any other state, is some testimony to this influence. Utah and Idaho form the focus of a northwestern "sink" regarding female participation in higher education at all levels.

The states producing the most women graduates are New York with 42,639 and California with 40,168. These two states also have the two highest female populations in the United States. This fact, plus a long tradition of quality state educational institutions, explains the high numbers. Although the proportion of women enrolled in higher education is 51.4%, the number of men attending full-time still exceeds that of women. The female part-time re-entry student over 35 entering college for the first time or returning to finish an undergraduate degree accounts for the difference.

Students participating in postbaccalaureate degree programs migrate from their home states more frequently than undergraduates and, therefore, the regional patterns on Map 5.5 reflect student locational decisions rather than public attitudes toward educated women in their state. Students are attracted by specific departments or even professors, avail-

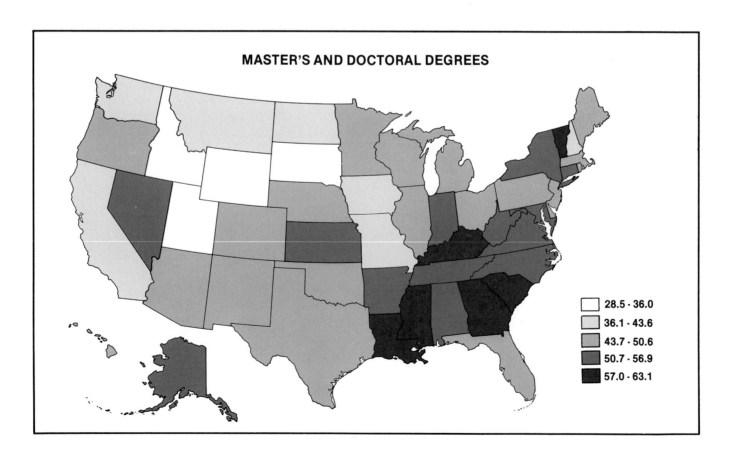

MASTER'S AND DOCTORAL DEGREES

28.5 - 36.0
36.1 - 43.6
43.7 - 50.6
50.7 - 56.9
57.0 - 63.1

Map 5.5 Master's and doctoral degrees—percentage awarded to women, 1979–80. U.S. average is 47.5%.

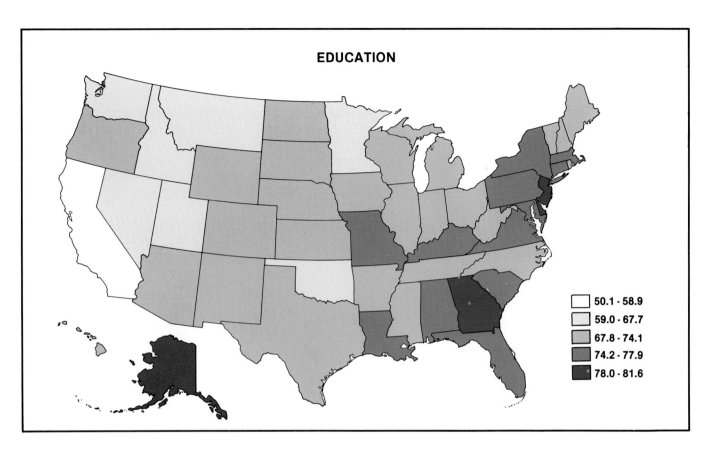

EDUCATION

☐	50.1 - 58.9
░	59.0 - 67.7
▒	67.8 - 74.1
▓	74.2 - 77.9
█	78.0 - 81.6

Map 5.6 Education—percentage of degrees in this major awarded to women, 1976–77. U.S. average is 72.2%.

ability of financial aid, and research facilities in their choice of graduate schools. Perhaps perceived attitudes toward women on campus form a small part of the decision-making process.

Something must be attractive about graduate programs in the southeastern states (with the exception of Florida) and selected states in the Northeast. Vermont has the highest percentage of graduate degrees (master's and doctoral combined) awarded to women—63.1%. On the other hand, what is it about South Dakota that discourages women doctoral students (lowest proportion at 8.1%)? Part of the mystery is revealed by looking at the majors of degree recipients (see the next section).

Women receiving master's degrees represented 49.4% of the total degrees awarded whereas their proportion of doctoral degrees contrasts dramatically at 29.5%. The 147,519 master's degrees to women in 1979–80 far exceed the 9,667 doctoral degrees awarded in that same year. The states granting the highest number of master's and doctoral degrees to women are New York and California for reasons cited earlier.

Although women have doubled their production of doctorates earned in the last decade, this area is obviously one where more inroads can be made to break the cycle of male domination of higher education. Low doctoral output perpetuates low proportions of women as college professors.

MAJORS

The percentage of undergraduate degrees to women in each of 21 disciplines in 1976–77 confirms those fields dominated by one sex or the other (Table 5.3). Stereotypically, almost all the degrees in home economics are to women and almost none of the degrees in engineering.

Although all of the majors exhibit some regional patterns when data by state are plotted, two disciplines in particular have been selected for this discussion. Education, a female-dominated major, attracts higher proportions of women than the national average among most of the eastern and southern states as well as Alaska (Map 5.6). This major is most prominent in Alaska where 81.6% of the degrees were awarded to women. The next leading state is Georgia with 80.0%. Relatively low proportions of women in education are evident in the far western states with California the lowest at 50.1%. Women in Georgia appear to be perpetuating a regionally traditional slot for women in society when they pursue educa-

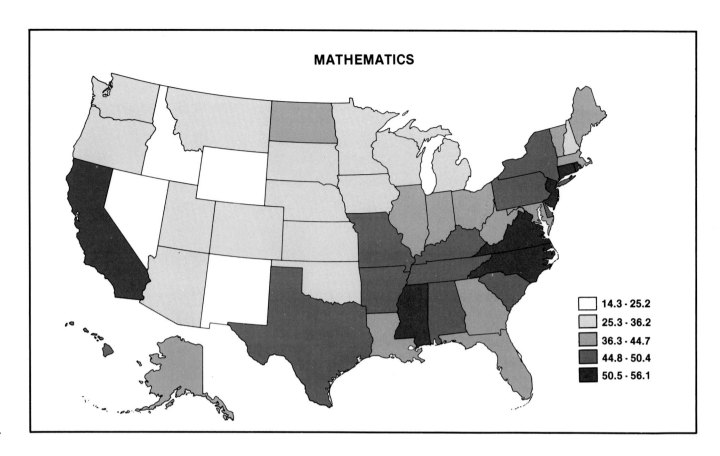

MATHEMATICS

☐	14.3 - 25.2
☐	25.3 - 36.2
☐	36.3 - 44.7
☐	44.8 - 50.4
☐	50.5 - 56.1

Map 5.7   Mathematics— percentage of degrees in this major awarded to women, 1976–77. U.S. average is 41.8%.

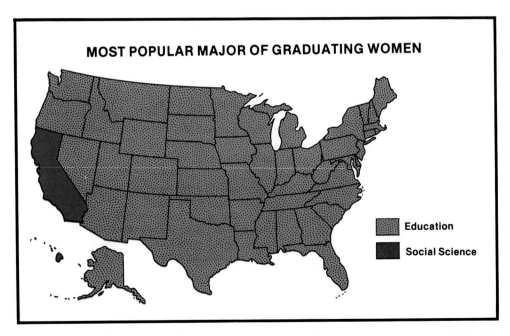

MOST POPULAR MAJOR OF GRADUATING WOMEN

☐	Education
☐	Social Science

Map 5.8   Most popular major of graduating women, 1976–77.

tion as a major. Women in California, in contrast, appear to have found alternative occupations. Based on population, California should have four times as many women education graduates as Georgia, but in 1976–77 California graduated 2,124 women and Georgia 2,167 women in education. The movement of women out of education into other disciplines is causing a deficit of elementary and secondary teachers in the country. Map 5.6 indicates that there is a regional imbalance in this deficit.

Mathematics, one of the male-dominated disciplines, appeals to women in several East coast states plus Mississippi and California (Map 5.7). The highest proportion of female math students is in Rhode Island with 56.1%. The lowest proportion of 14.3% is in Nevada, just one of the many northern and western states in a mathematics wasteland as far as women are concerned.

Much has been written about "math anxiety" among women. Sex differences in attitudes toward mathematics are formed as early as third grade. Early socialization, therefore, may lead to lack of motivation at higher levels and low performance on tests. Is there something in the curriculum orientation of the elementary and secondary schools in California, Connecticut, Mississippi, New Jersey, North Carolina, Rhode

Atlas of American Women

Island, and Virginia that encourages women to pursue a non-traditional major in college? Alternately, are children in Idaho, Nevada, New Mexico, and Wyoming still telling each other that math is a boy's subject because males have aptitude for spatial tasks?

Education is the most popular major among women nationwide except in California and Hawaii (Map 5.8). Based on number of baccalaureate degrees awarded in 1976–77, women selected education a total of 103,590 times, twice as much as the next most popular degree in the social sciences (see Table 5.3). The intensity of this major ranged from 5.8% of the women graduates in California to 41.9% in Arkansas (the U.S. average was 24.5%). When the second most popular major in each state is examined, a more complex regional picture emerges (Map 5.9). The social sciences (including anthropology, archaeology, economics, history, geography, political science, sociology, criminology, international relations, ethnic culture studies, urban studies, and demography) dominate New England and the East coast states as far south as South Carolina with outliers in the socially aware states of Colorado, Oregon, and Alaska. The health professions (including nursing, occupational therapy, physical therapy, public health, medical-record librarianship, speech pathology and audiology, hospital and health-care administration, along with other subspecialities) is a northern phenomenon with pockets in the South. Business and management (including accounting, business statistics, banking and finance, investments and securities, hotel and restaurant management, marketing and purchasing, real estate, insurance, personnel management, and labor and industrial relations) is a popular degree in the South and Hawaii. Business and management and the social sciences are male-dominated disciplines, but because of the large numbers of degree recipients with these majors, these fields are still popular among women on an absolute scale.

Leading fields among women at the master's level are education, followed by public affairs and services (primarily social work), health professions, business and management, letters (English, literature, classics, linguistics, and philosophy), and library science. At the doctoral level women are specializing in education, followed by psychology, letters, social sciences, biological sciences (biology, botany, zoology, bacteriology, pathology, physiology, microbiology, biochemistry, biophysics, ecology, and others), foreign languages, and physical sciences (physics, chemistry, astronomy, atmospheric sciences and meteorology, geology, and oceanography). Stereotyping finally begins to dissolve at this level.

If we were to wave a magic wand and cancel all education majors and remove them from the head counts, the statistical effect on women's participation in higher education is dra-

TABLE 5.3 MAJORS OF GRADUATING SENIORS 1976–1977

MAJOR	% TO WOMEN	NUMBER OF DEGREES AWARDED TO WOMEN
Home Economics	95.9	16,688
Health Professions	79.2	45,381
Foreign Languages	75.9	10,564
Education	72.2	103,590
Fine Arts	61.6	25,579
Psychology	56.7	26,816
Letters	56.5	26,589
Area Studies	56.5	1,656
Interdisciplinary Studies	47.4	15,843
Public Affairs and Services	44.7	16,240
Communications	44.3	10,278
Mathematics	41.8	5,893
Social Sciences	39.5	46,110
Biological Sciences	35.8	19,380
Theology	25.4	1,500
Computer and Information	24.0	1,531
Business and Management	23.4	35,547
Agriculture and Natural Resources	22.3	4,777
Architecture and Environmental Design	21.1	1,932
Physical Sciences	20.3	4,500
Engineering	4.6	2,217

Map 5.9 Second most popular major of graduating women, 1976–77.

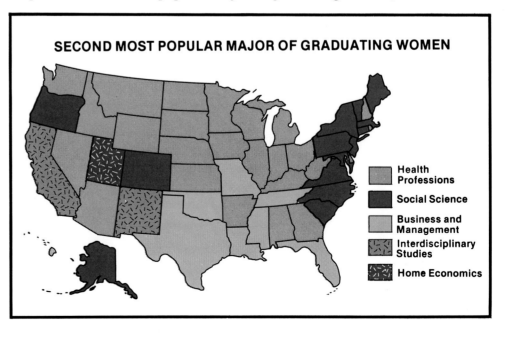

SECOND MOST POPULAR MAJOR OF GRADUATING WOMEN

Health Professions

Social Science

Business and Management

Interdisciplinary Studies

Home Economics

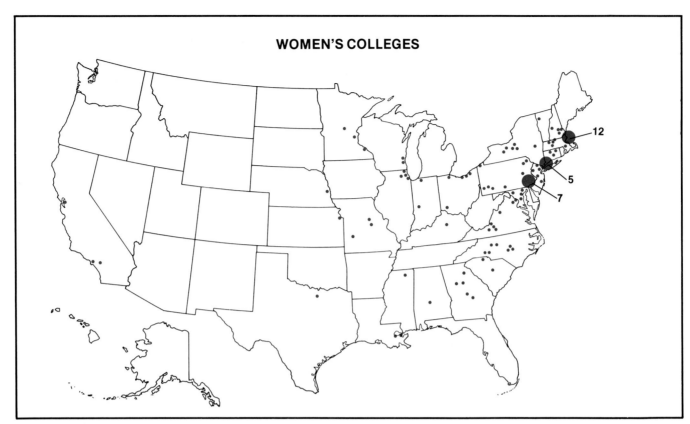

WOMEN'S COLLEGES

Map 5.10   Women's colleges, 1983.

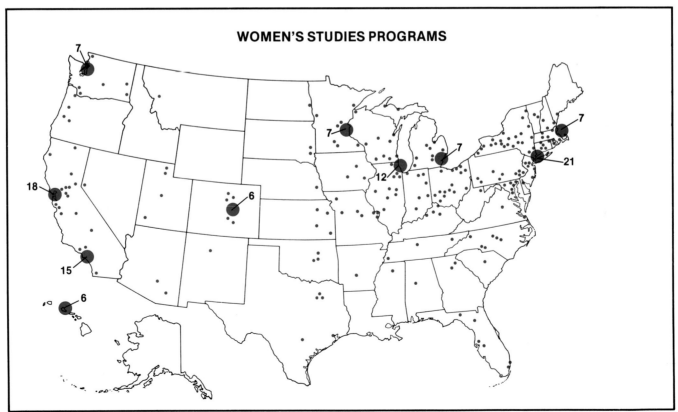

WOMEN'S STUDIES PROGRAMS

Map 5.11   Women's studies programs, 1981.

matic, especially at the graduate-school level. Removing education majors would reduce women's share of baccalaureate degrees from 46.3 to 41.5%, master's degrees from 47.3 to 34.9%, and doctoral degrees from 24.4 to 21.2% (calculations using 1976–77 data). Total numbers of degrees to women in each of these categories would become 319,886, 66,003, and 5,321 respectively. Education degrees are the major factor in the distribution pattern of graduate degrees shown on Map 5.5. For example, 70.9% of all master's degrees to women in Kentucky are in education, 75.0% in Mississippi, 76.3% in South Carolina, 67.4% in Louisiana, and 69.5% in Georgia. The national average is 55.8%.

WOMEN'S COLLEGES

The 111 active women's colleges are concentrated in the northeastern quarter of the United States with the urban areas of Boston, New York, and Philadelphia as major centers (Map 5.10). The remaining colleges are scattered unevenly throughout the eastern states. There are only 12 women's colleges west of the Mississippi, including 3 in California.

Fifty-nine of the colleges are church-related: 43 with Catholic affiliations and 16 with various Protestant ties. Catholic schools are distributed throughout the northeastern quadrant and account for all of the schools in Indiana, Kansas, Minnesota, Nebraska, and Vermont and high proportions in Illinois, New Hampshire, Ohio, and Pennsylvania. Remarkably, there are no Catholic women's colleges in New York state although there are some schools with historical connections to Catholicism. There are no Catholic schools in the South with the exception of St. Mary's Dominican College in New Orleans, and Sacred Heart College in Belmont, N.C. The Catholic school pattern is highly correlated with the distribution pattern of that church generally. All of the Protestant schools are located in the South with the exception of Wilson College and Cedar Crest College in Pennsylvania.

The highest concentration of independent women's schools is in Massachusetts, including the well-known Mount Holyoke, Radcliffe, Smith, and Wellesley Colleges, members of the Seven Sisters schools. The only college in this prestigious group to have gone coeducational is Vassar. Two of the women's schools are state-controlled, public institutions (Douglass College of Rutgers State University in New Brunswick, N.J., and Texas Woman's University in Denton, Tex.).

The oldest women's college is Salem College of Winston-Salem, N.C., founded as a day school for girls in 1772 by the Moravian church. Fifty-seven of the colleges were established in the nineteenth century and they vary widely in affiliation and geographical location. The nine schools founded following World War II are Catholic-supported with one exception.

WOMEN'S STUDIES

In 1981 there were 330 universities, colleges, and community colleges with women's studies programs offering minors, certificates, and degrees (Map 5.11). San Diego State appears to have been the first to establish an official program, and Cornell, San Francisco State University, University of Massachusetts, and University of Washington were other early innovators. All five date from approximately 1970, with some development as early as 1967. The growth rate for women's study programs has been spectacular. Many of the programs have passed from courses on women to programs to departments with line budgets, administrators, and a full curriculum. In other words, women's studies has arrived on many campuses.

Women's studies programs, however, have not arrived equally everywhere in America. Large clusters of schools appear in metropolitan areas with Boston, Chicago, Los Angeles, New York, and San Francisco dominating the map. These urban areas support numerous institutions of higher learning and responded early to a demand for women-oriented studies. California and New York support such programs at a rate higher than expected based on the number of institutions of higher learning in each state. Michigan, Minnesota, Colorado, and Ohio follow. In contrast, no women's studies exist in Alaska, Idaho, Louisiana, and Wyoming and there are only token programs in Alabama, Arkansas, Delaware, Maine, Mississippi, Montana, Nebraska, Nevada, New Mexico, North Dakota, South Carolina, and West Virginia.

Research has shown that large schools are more likely to adopt women's studies than smaller schools because they are already structurally well differentiated and can easily accept new programs. Public schools respond to demands for curricular innovation more readily than private schools. Sectarian schools are most conservative. Women's colleges, for obvious reasons, also lack special women's studies programs.

Women's studies programs may be short-lived phenomena, as material about women is gradually "mainstreamed" into courses in established disciplines. A healthy component of the women's studies picture, however, is the recent establishment of research centers devoted to the study of women (28 by 1982). Most are campus-based, but independent of the university political structure. They support individual scholars as well as interdisciplinary research projects, providing not only information about women to be used in women's studies courses, but information germane to public-policy decisions. They have a chance to become as established as the urban and population institutes of the past decade. These centers have good credentials, impressive lists of research grants, and well-focused missions.

CHAPTER SIX
SPORTS

INTRODUCTION

This chapter examines the participation of girls and women in organized sports. Helped by Title IX regulations, participation at all levels has expanded rapidly since 1972, putting more and more of the country's female athletes in the public eye. Women have eagerly embraced athletics, accepting the healthy body/healthy mind dictum and enjoying the fun.

Organized athletic competition for girls usually begins at the junior or senior high-school level. In most sports, it is a question of then or never, for female athletes operate under the same pyramid system as males: lots of teams at the skill-learning level and then fewer and fewer player positions as athletes mature and progress up the ladder. Very little room exists at the top whether that level is defined as being an Olympian or a professional athlete.

The maps herein start with participation rates in athletics among high-school girls. The most popular and second most popular interscholastic sports by state are presented. Following are maps examining the regional intensity of six selected sports at the high-school level. Basketball, track and field (outdoor), and volleyball were chosen for their nationwide appeal; softball (fast pitch), soccer, and field hockey were included for their strong regional associations. These same sports are then mapped at the intercollegiate level to examine persistence in regional patterns. A map of the home states of the 1984 Olympic team members is included to cap the discussion of regional impact on sports-activity distribution. Since only a few of the sports offered at the high-school level can be considered lifelong sports, alternatives are sought later in life. Bowling, a competitive sport with regional appeal, is the subject of the final map.

Something interesting has happened among the women in this country in the last decade. Young women, almost in mass, have decided to take care of and use their bodies. How many female joggers do you see now that never were there before? This emphasis starts early in life, thanks to the work of physical-education instructors, recreation departments, and parent volunteers. Appropriate data on recreational or leisure-time sports are not available, however, or this chapter would be full of such maps because recreational sports affect a greater percentage of women than do organized sports.

HIGH-SCHOOL SPORTS

Girls' participation in organized high-school sports has undergone significant recent growth. In 1971 only 294,015 girls were involved, but by the 1983–84 school year the number of participants had climbed to 1,747,346. In contrast, boys' participation during the same period actually decreased by 363,318 boys to its 1983–84 level of 3,303,599 participants. Most of the growth can be attributed to the equal opportunities provided by Title IX of the Education Amendments of 1972. Some of the growth, however, should be assigned to the women's movement itself, increased interest in physical activity, and parental pressure on school boards to provide athletic activities for their daughters as well as their sons.

Girls have found that it is fun to compete as an athlete, and team sports also offer socialization, which heightens the experience. Sports have grown rapidly as an extracurricular activity for girls, competing with music, drama, student government, and other school-sponsored activities. Sports have become especially important in rural areas with small high schools where the alternatives are not abundant. Finally, although this is hardly in the mind of a high-school freshman as she tries out for the basketball team, participating in sports at an early age probably promotes values such as discipline and leadership and may lead to a longtime interest in physical activity that will assure a healthier life and more varied leisure time.

Data used in this section of maps are from the National Federation of State High School Associations for 1983–84. Members of this association represent approximately 89% of public and private high schools. The tabulations include only athletes in high schools (no junior highs or middle schools). In addition, the data do not include intramural participation, an important alternative for girls not able to participate at the varsity level. Participation in a sport, the measure used in the following maps, must be explained further. Often, high-school athletes double or even triple in several sports because there are usually three distinct sports seasons at the high-school level. For example, some girls who play basketball in the winter may also participate in track and field in the spring. The participation rate, therefore, should be viewed as composed of participation units, not number of girl athletes.

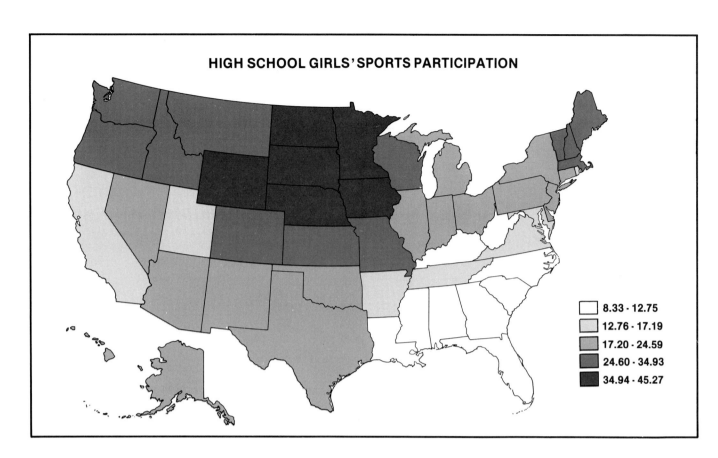

8.33 - 12.75
12.76 - 17.19
17.20 - 24.59
24.60 - 34.93
34.94 - 45.27

Map 6.1 High-school girls' sports participation—percentage of girls who were 10 to 14 years of age in 1980 participating in sports in 1983–84. U.S. average is 19.42%.

Participation in high-school sports (Map 6.1) is perhaps the best measure of the acceptability of organized sports for girls within our society. Map data were compiled by dividing the number of girls high-school sports participants in 1983–84 for each state by the number of girls in each state who were 10 to 14 years of age in the 1980 census (and by 1983 of high-school age). On the average, 19.42% of girls supposedly eligible to participate actually did, with possible duplications mentioned earlier.

The map displays some striking regional patterns. A dominant core of high participation exists in the northern Plains. South Dakota has the highest rate at 42.27%. Nebraska follows at 38.97%. Around the core there are above-average states to the west, south, and east. Participation at a similar level exists in northern New England. All of these states are among our most rural, supporting the lack-of-alternatives tenet expressed earlier.

In contrast, low rates of sports participation characterize the South, Utah, and California. The lowest value belongs to Alabama with 8.33% participation. Mississippi has 8.70%. The southern states and Utah represent traditional cultures, as expressed by other variables in other parts of this atlas. Perhaps "nice girls don't sweat" really is a motto of these

areas. Perhaps they are just slower to change and accept the girl as athlete. Ironically, California, home of physical fitness gurus and many 1984 female Olympians, is also in the below-average category with 14.89% participation.

The NFSHSA gives data for 32 girls' sports. A few of these, such as baseball in Alabama, California, Georgia, and South Carolina; football in California and Mississippi; or ice hockey in Massachusetts, represent girls playing on boys' teams. Other sports such as judo, decathalon, or pentathalon have limited involvement. The top 20 sports in terms of number of participants are listed in Table 6.1 along with the number of schools with each sport and the number of states having programs in that sport. The big two are basketball and track and field (outdoor) with high numbers of participants, number of schools involved, and nationwide availability. Volleyball, tennis, and cross-country have similar universality, but smaller numbers of total participants. In contrast to other popular sports, softball (fast pitch), soccer, and field hockey have regional status only. Team size explains part of the variation in participation. Basketball, track, and volleyball all average 23 to 25 players per program implying, of course, varsity/ junior varsity teams in some instances. Tennis teams average 13.9 players per team, cross-country teams 10.7 players, and golf only 7.4.

A map of the most popular girls' sport (based on number of participants) reveals some interesting regional concentrations (Map 6.2). Basketball dominates the map although the pattern is irregular. Twenty-five states claim it as the top girls' high-school sport. Track and field follows with eight first-place positions and volleyball is next with seven, both sports similarly dispersed. Softball, in either slow- or fast-pitch format, presents the most agglomerated pattern with intensity in the Northeast and outliers in California, Florida, and North Carolina. Field hockey dominates only in Delaware.

Analysis of the second most popular girls sport (Map 6.3) emphasizes the large extent of track-and-field competition with 23 positions. Basketball comes in second with 16 and volleyball third with 8. The territorial extent of softball is expanded somewhat and field hockey disappears.

Putting the patterns from the two maps together in one's mind emphasizes the predominance of girls' basketball in American culture. California and Utah in the West; Illinois, Nebraska, and Wisconsin in the middle; and Florida, New Jersey, New York, and Connecticut in the East constitute the only "untouched" states. In all nine states, however, basketball is the third most popular sport. With this groundswell of grassroots support for girls' basketball across the nation, it seems only a matter of time until professional basketball for women is a financial success.

TABLE 6.1 PARTICIPANTS IN GIRLS' HIGH SCHOOL SPORTS			
SPORT	NUMBER OF PARTICIPANTS	NUMBER OF SCHOOLS	STATES HAVING PROGRAM
Basketball	390,678	16,366	50
Track and Field (Outdoor)	351,274	13,992	50
Volleyball	269,498	11,603	48
Softball (Fast Pitch)	194,270	7,831	31
Tennis	114,177	8,221	49
Cross Country	87,316	8,176	50
Swimming and Diving	78,491	3,781	42
Soccer	69,374	2,562	33
Field Hockey	49,188	1,509	18
Gymnastics	38,684	2,278	40
Softball (Slow Pitch)	32,100	1,672	10
Golf	24,851	3,344	42
Track and Field (Indoor)	17,591	862	13
Badminton	7,361	382	5
Lacrosse	6,986	162	8
Bowling	6,449	540	10
Skiing (Downhill)	4,629	350	11
Skiing (Cross Country)	1,664	148	4
Riflery	611	102	6
Fencing	495	37	3

Map 6.2 Most popular girls' high-school sport, based on number of participants, 1983–84.

Map 6.3 Second most popular girls' high-school sport, based on number of participants, 1983–84.

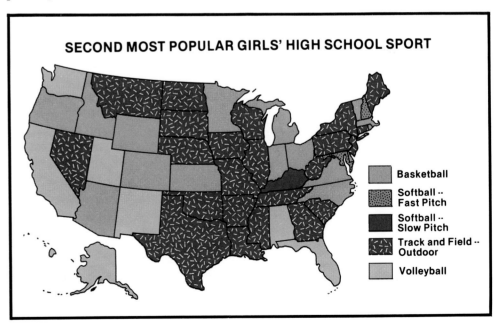

MOST POPULAR GIRLS' HIGH SCHOOL SPORT

Basketball
Softball -- Fast Pitch
Softball -- Slow Pitch
Track and Field -- Outdoor
Volleyball
Field Hockey

SECOND MOST POPULAR GIRLS' HIGH SCHOOL SPORT

Basketball
Softball -- Fast Pitch
Softball -- Slow Pitch
Track and Field -- Outdoor
Volleyball

Girls in New York have the greatest number of sports options with 19 different sports offered. Idaho represents the other end of the scale with only 6 sports (basketball, cross-country, golf, tennis, track and field, and volleyball). The offering of some sports is, of course, influenced by climate; only California, Colorado, Maine, Massachusetts, and Michigan offer downhill skiing as a sport. Selection is also dictated by school finances; cross-country is relatively inexpensive whereas gymnastics is at the other extreme. In addition, sports programs are determined in part by the available athlete pool. Sports such as golf, gymnastics, and tennis are expensive for parents because private lessons, special coaches, and membership in a club are sometimes viewed as necessary ingredients in starting early. High school is generally too late to begin any of these. Therefore, none of these sports fare well in poverty areas where the girls and their parents cannot afford the extras.

The intensity of a sport across states may be examined by expressing the number of participants in basketball, for example, as a percentage of total girls' sports participants in a state. Using this measure, maps are provided for basketball, track and field, and volleyball, the three biggest sports. In addition, activity in field hockey, softball, and soccer is mapped in order to examine their regional concentration.

Girls' high-school basketball dominates the pool of athletic participants in two sections of the United States (Map 6.4). One core area exists in the northern Plains states of Montana and North Dakota and another exists in Arkansas, Mississippi, and Oklahoma. These latter states form a concentrated focus of above-average basketball participation across the South (excluding the Atlantic Coast states of Florida, North Carolina, and Virginia). Basketball, although present throughout the country, is largely a western Middle West and Southern phenomenon in terms of intensity. Arkansas has the highest value with 48.92% of its athletic participants involved in basketball. North Dakota follows with 46.90%.

In contrast, basketball has few followers in California and the Southwest. Equally low interest is expressed in the northeastern quarter of the country and in Florida. The lowest participation rates belong to New York (13.37%) and New Jersey (13.96%).

Historical roots explain part of basketball's popularity for girls. As a competitive sport, basketball has been played by girls since shortly after it was invented by James Naismith in 1891. With modifications the game was introduced at Smith College by Senda Berenson. Convenience is also an explainer. Basketball was an easy sport to implement for girls after Title IX. Since basketball programs for boys exist in more schools than any other sport, the gyms were already there. In many cases all the athletic director had to do was draft

Map 6.4   Basketball, as a percentage of high-school girls' sports participants, 1983–84. U.S. average is 22.36%.

Map 6.5   Track and field—outdoor, as a percentage of high-school girls' sports participants, 1983–84. U.S. average is 20.10%.

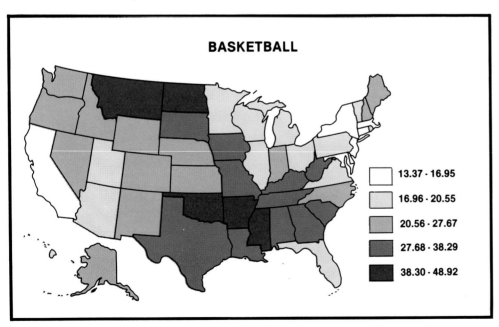

BASKETBALL

	13.37 - 16.95
	16.96 - 20.55
	20.56 - 27.67
	27.68 - 38.29
	38.30 - 48.92

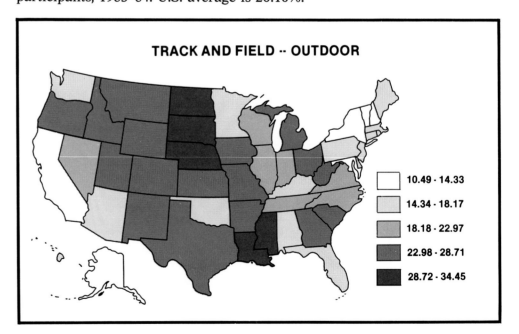

TRACK AND FIELD -- OUTDOOR

	10.49 - 14.33
	14.34 - 18.17
	18.18 - 22.97
	22.98 - 28.71
	28.72 - 34.45

an extra coach and become a wizard at scheduling gym practice times during any overlap in the girls' and boys' seasons.

Track and field (outdoor), the No. 2 sport for high-school girls, displays a patchwork pattern of concentration across the middle of the United States (Map 6.5). Areas of intensity exist in the contiguous north central states of Nebraska and North and South Dakota as well as the southern states of Louisiana and Mississippi. South Dakota has the highest participation rate at 34.45%. Louisiana follows with 29.91%. The remainder of the above-average states are dispersed from Oregon to South Carolina with notable gaps existing for Oklahoma and parts of the Midwest and South.

Athletes in both Mississippi and North Dakota concentrate their efforts in just basketball and track and field; participation in all other sports is at an average level or below. In fact, the two big sports occupy 73.15% of the participants in Mississippi and 76.42% in North Dakota. In contrast, basketball and track/field account for only 29.55% of the participants in California, 27.98% in Maryland, and 26.88% in New York.

Track and field has particularly low acceptance in Alaska (as do all the outdoor springtime sports), California, and parts of the Northeast. Vermont has the lowest participation rate at 10.49%. Alaska is next with 12.47%.

The same thinking that led to hesitation among Olympic committee members in allowing females to compete in endurance races exists at the high-school level in regards to track-and-field competition. This sport, in a public-opinion poll, was ranked last among six sports as suitable for female participation. Some of the myths about the female body and athletic competition are relevant here. Strenuous activity will damage the reproductive system, a blow to the breast will cause cancer, menstruation saps strength and makes females emotionally unfit for competition, females are weaker, and female aerobic capacity is less. The first two myths have no basis in fact. With regards to the third point, there is some disadvantage just before a menstrual period as fluid retention makes the body heavier and psychologically slower. As far as being the weaker sex, females have less arm strength than men, but their leg strength is potentially the same. The capacity for oxygen uptake (aerobic capacity) is the same for both sexes until puberty when girls' aerobic growth slows down. Training, however, can alter this situation. Top female runners have an aerobic capacity just 4.3% less than that of male runners. Restricting girls from participating in track-and-field events, grueling as some of the events may be, appears to have no basis in fact. To change public opinion is, of course, something else.

Volleyball belongs to the middle of the Midwest in Kansas and Nebraska (Map 6.6). Participation rates in these two states

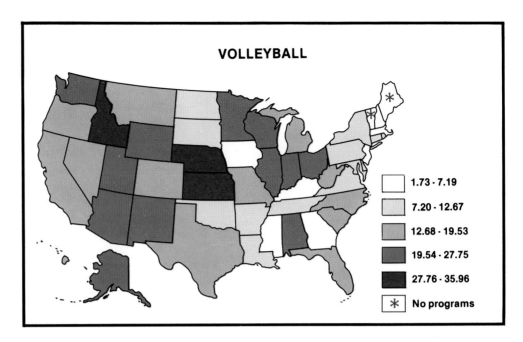

VOLLEYBALL

☐	1.73 - 7.19
☐	7.20 - 12.67
☐	12.68 - 19.53
☐	19.54 - 27.75
☐	27.76 - 35.96
✳	No programs

Map 6.6   Volleyball, as a percentage of high-school girls' sports participants, 1983–84. U.S. average is 15.42%.

are 30.50% and 35.96% respectively. Idaho takes third place with 28.78%. Given the popularity of beach and collegiate volleyball in California and Hawaii, this map may surprise all fans of the sport except for the girls in these three states who are actively involved in this highly competitive game. In many towns there, it is *the* prestige sport in high school, with intense competition for team slots. Other above-average areas include scattered states in the West plus Alaska, states in the Great Lakes area, and Alabama.

Volleyball is a minor sport in some of the Great Plains states, parts of the South, and throughout the Northeast. The lowest participation rate belongs to Georgia with 1.73%. New Hampshire follows with 2.13%. The entrenched fall sport of field hockey in the Northeast precludes acceptance of volleyball as an alternative. Maine and Vermont do not even have programs. Volleyball is largely, but not exclusively, a female sport at the high-school level. Boys' volleyball programs exist in 10 states, led by California, but even in California girls in the sport outnumber boys 7.4 to 1. The evolution of this strong female association with volleyball in the high schools can be explained by the three-sports school year. The traditional triad for boys is football, basketball, and outdoor track and field. Girls could adopt the latter two sports in the seasonal sequence and use the facilities already in existence for boys, but they need a replacement for football. Volleyball became that replacement in most places.

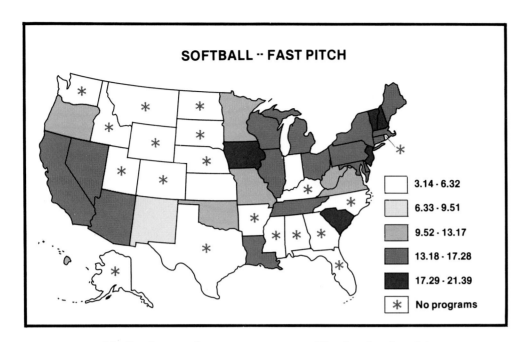

SOFTBALL ·· FAST PITCH

3.14 - 6.32
6.33 - 9.51
9.52 - 13.17
13.18 - 17.28
17.29 - 21.39
* No programs

Map 6.7   Softball—fast pitch, as a percentage of high-school girls' sports participants, 1983–84. U.S. average is 11.12%.

Map 6.8   Soccer, as a percentage of high-school girls' sports participants, 1983–84. U.S. average is 3.97%.

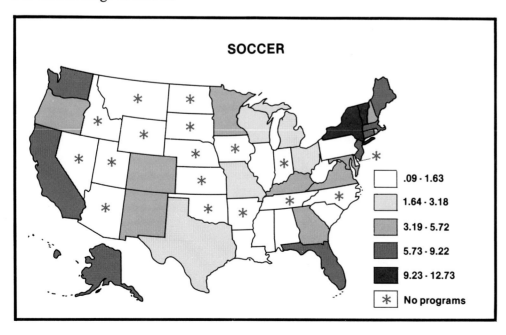

SOCCER

.09 - 1.63
1.64 - 3.18
3.19 - 5.72
5.73 - 9.22
9.23 - 12.73
* No programs

Softball, one of the regional sports, comes in two forms—fast and slow pitch. Fast-pitch programs at the high-school level exist in 31 states and slow pitch in 10. Only in Oklahoma do both programs coexist. Because fast pitch dominates the softball scene by a ratio of six fast-pitch players for each slow-pitch player and because fast-pitch is the form retained in college programs, it is the focus of this discussion (Map 6.7).

Fast-pitch softball is centered in the Northeast, parts of the Midwest, isolated states in the South, and in the southwestern corner of the country. The most-intense areas are scattered throughout the eastern half of the country. New Hampshire has the greatest participation with 21.39% of its girls' sports participants engaged in the sport. Vermont is next with 20.56%, followed by New Jersey with 20.24%. Nineteen states in the Rocky Mountains, Great Plains, and South, plus Alaska, do not have programs. Among those that do, token participation is present in Kansas (3.14%) and Indiana (4.60%).

If slow-pitch softball were incorporated into the map, the result would be an ascendency of softball in the eastern half of the country (but not Indiana). A less-intense area extends up and down the West coast. North Carolina dominates slow-pitch softball with a 25.07% participation rate. Florida and Rhode Island also have high rates (18.77 and 17.87% respectively).

Just as with volleyball, softball in either of its two forms is largely a girls' sport at the high-school level. Massachusetts has a few fast-pitch softball programs for boys and Alabama, Georgia, and Mississippi have insignificant numbers of male players involved in slow-pitch softball. The 416 total participants in boys' softball do not compare, however, with the 398,608 participants in boys' baseball. Saying boys' baseball is redundant since the sport belongs to males. In 1983–84, 23 high-school girls were playing on boys' baseball teams, hardly enough to form a league. All this number business is ironic because as boys mature into men with slower reflexes they turn from baseball to softball for recreational sport. Of course, recreational softball is popular among women as well.

Soccer as a girls' high-school sport displays even more regional concentration than softball (Map 6.8). The West coast, the Northeast, and Florida are the primary foci for this sport. New York has the highest participation rate with 12.73% and Vermont follows with 11.93%.

Seventeen states from Nevada to Delaware do not even have programs for girls. States with minimal participation include West Virginia (.09%) and Mississippi (.45%). Actually the seven girls in West Virginia are playing on boys' soccer teams. Low participation areas are scattered throughout the Midwest and South.

Soccer will be an interesting sport to follow in the upcom-

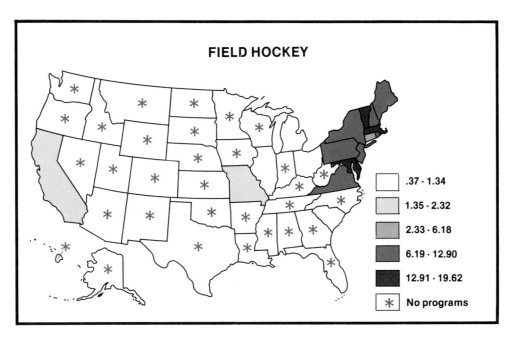

FIELD HOCKEY

□	.37 - 1.34
▨	1.35 - 2.32
▨	2.33 - 6.18
▨	6.19 - 12.90
■	12.91 - 19.62
✳	No programs

Map 6.9   Field hockey, as a percentage of high-school girls' sports participants, 1983–84. U.S. average is 2.82%.

ing years. An extensive youth soccer movement is taking place in this country and girls are prominent members of these teams. The wildfire growth can partly be attributed to the universal nature of the game. Parent volunteer participation ensures youth soccer's continued growth and soon, as the youngsters mature, parents will exert pressure upon school athletic administrations to include soccer as a varsity-level sport. Parents of boys see it as a safer alternative to football. Parents of girls see it as another opportunity for their daughters to participate in a team sport. The possibility of boys and girls on the same team, a rarity in the world of sports, does exist. The 61 schools in Kentucky that offer soccer, for example, do so on a coed basis. A girl with endurance can compete effectively at this age level because it is a noncontact sport. As of 1983–84, 4,882 high schools offered soccer to boys, almost twice as many as those offering the same sport to girls. Male participants outnumbered female by 2.5 to 1. As with the girls, the highest participation rates for boys are found on the East coast.

The final sport in this set, field hockey, has the most restricted regional concentration (Map 6.9). Although it is intensely important to the Northeast as far south as Virginia, only minor outliers exist in the remainder of the country. Vermont has the highest participation rate, with 19.62% of its girls' high-school sports participants engaged in field hockey. This puts field hockey there slightly below basketball and fast-pitch softball. Delaware has an equally high participation rate of 19.54%, and field hockey is the most popular girls' sport in the state.

Field hockey has a unique distribution in that a state either has it and it is popular, or the sport is nearly nonexistent. Participation in South Carolina, Michigan, and Illinois, for example, is only .37, .47, and .50%. The sport is not even offered in 32 states. Only California and Missouri form minor outliers to the Northeast home. Maybe crisp air, tartan skirts, fall foliage, and a lush bluegrass field are necessary preconditions to making this sport a success and they can only be found in combination in one region of this country. Early ties to New England date from 1887 when field hockey became a women's sport. Field hockey is not a high-school sport for boys nor a college sport for men. It is only at the Olympic games level that field-hockey competition exists for American males.

COLLEGIATE SPORTS

Title IX, enacted in 1972, has caused rapid change in collegiate sports for women as well. Sec. 106.41 states that "no person, on the basis of sex, may be excluded from partici-

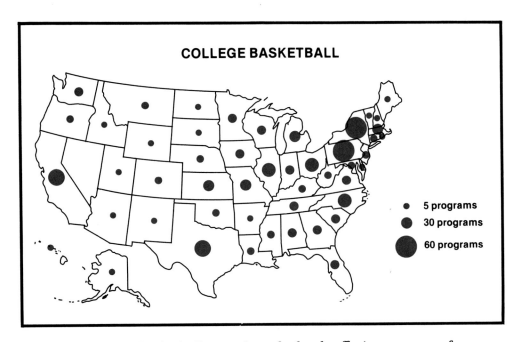

COLLEGE BASKETBALL

5 programs
30 programs
60 programs

Map 6.10 College basketball—number of schools offering programs for women, 1981. U.S. has 959 programs.

Map 6.11 College track and field—number of schools offering programs for women, 1981. U.S. has 497 programs.

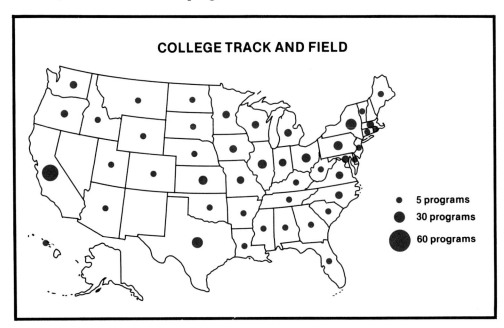

COLLEGE TRACK AND FIELD

5 programs
30 programs
60 programs

pation in, be denied benefits of, or be discriminated against in any interscholastic, club, or intramural athletics." Many interpretations, modifications, and court rulings have followed, but the legislation has provoked dramatic changes at the college level. More female athletes are competing, female varsity sports have been increased to match the number of offerings for males, larger portions of athletic budgets are going to women's programs, and more scholarship opportunities exist. Now the economically disadvantaged, but athletically gifted, female athlete has a chance to complete a college education.

Women's Sports magazine publishes an annual scholarship guide to colleges and universities (including selected community colleges). The first guide in 1976 contained only 348 schools, whereas the 1985 guide had almost 800 listings. Athletic scholarships for women are offered in 24 different sports. Some offerings have a regional flavor, such as lacrosse, which is a scholarship sport at the University of Maryland. At Boston College field hockey, lacrosse, and soccer are among their 9 scholarship sports. Most large schools offer scholarships in 7 to 9 sports, although in many cases the entire team is not on scholarship.

Data for the six maps that follow come from the *Women's Sports* guide and *The Directory of Athletic Scholarships.* Although this latter book is intended to assist the high-school athlete in identifying schools for possible scholarships in a chosen sport, it can be used to determine the number of schools in each state that have athletic programs in a sport. Using total number of schools presents a map-interpretation problem; let the reader beware. Less densely populated Rocky Mountain states never have a chance of appearing in the highest categories because the total number of schools in these states is small. Delaware and Rhode Island have a similar problem. Since the same proportional symbol is used for all six maps, comparisons among sports can be made.

Much of the geographical variation found in high-school sports is lost at the university level as athletic-program offerings are homogenized to conform with budget restrictions and Title IX regulations. Only enough players are needed to support a varsity (and possibly junior varsity) team, and because varsity sports are limited to premium athletes in order to be competitive, recruiting for these potential stars often is conducted nationwide. Rosters of teams, therefore, rarely contain only local talent. Schools that have no business having a softball team, for example, based on the regional pool of talent, will support a team composed mainly of imported players because of regulations, alumni loyalty, and desire for national reputation.

College basketball programs exist in all 50 states (Map 6.10). New York, a state with minimal basketball participation at the high-school level, claims the greatest number of programs (58) and forms the core of a northeastern concentration with an extension through the coastal southern states. Pennsylvania has 57 programs. Small numbers of schools have basketball programs in the Rocky Mountain and northern Plains states. The high for this region is Colorado with representation in 15 schools. Basketball, with a total of 959 programs, is the most popular college sport for women. In 42 states it either represents the most popular sport (as measured by number of schools offering basketball programs) or is tied with another sport for first-place honors. All this tends to confirm basketball's reputation as the No. 1 sport of American women.

Track and field, a sport that claimed the No. 2 spot in high school, falls to fourth place at the college level with only 497 programs (Map 6.11). Here California comes into its own with a dominating 50 programs. New York and Texas are the closest competitors with 29 and 28 programs respectively. The long training seasons in California and Texas undoubtedly do much to attract the track hopeful. Small numbers of schools participate in this sport in that continental V from Idaho to Arizona to North Dakota. Southern schools also have low participation. Although track-and-field college programs for women can be found in all 50 states, track is not the most popular sport in any state.

Volleyball emerges as the No. 2 sport at the college level with 816 programs (Map 6.12). California has the greatest number of programs with 65 and is followed distantly by Illinois, New York, and Pennsylvania with 47, 49, and 51 programs respectively. Small numbers of schools in the Mountain states and parts of the South have teams. The greatest concentration of this sport appears in the northeastern quarter in roughly the same states that displayed college basketball popularity. Volleyball is, in fact, the most popular sport (or tied for that position) in 13 states.

Softball, a sport that does not even exist in 19 states at the high-school level, is present in all but 2 states at the college level (Map 6.13). Alaska and Montana do not have programs, two areas where spring practice must get mired in the mud. Pennsylvania has the greatest number of participating schools (49), but California follows closely with 47. Softball's strong connections with the northeastern quadrant are maintained at the intercollegiate level. Softball ties for first-place popularity honors in 6 states. With 604 programs, it becomes the third-ranking college sport out of the six mapped.

Soccer is a minor sport for women at the college level with a total of only 59 programs in 24 states (Map 6.14). New York has the greatest number of teams with nine but Massachusetts is right behind with eight, confirming the far northeastern relationship. A strong correspondence exists be-

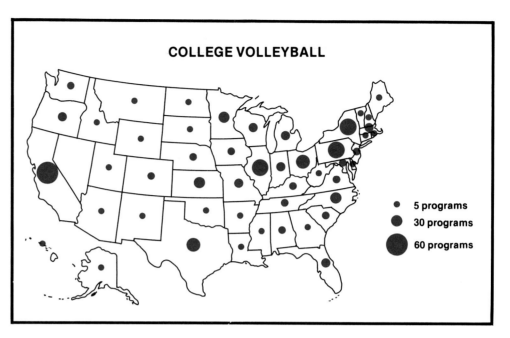

Map 6.12   College volleyball—number of schools offering programs for women, 1981. U.S. has 816 programs.

Map 6.13   College softball—number of schools offering programs for women, 1981. U.S. has 604 programs.

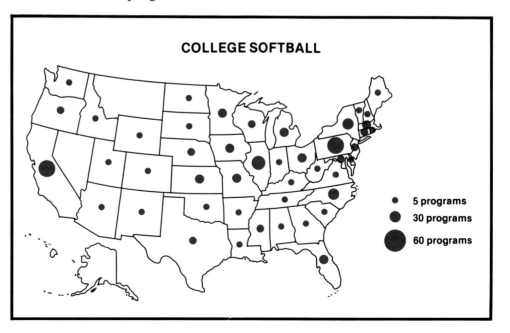

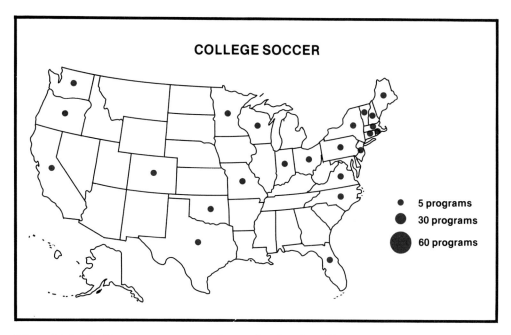

COLLEGE SOCCER

5 programs

30 programs

60 programs

Map 6.14 College soccer—number of schools offering programs for women, 1981. U.S. has 59 programs.

Map 6.15 College field hockey—number of schools offering programs for women, 1981. U.S. has 248 programs.

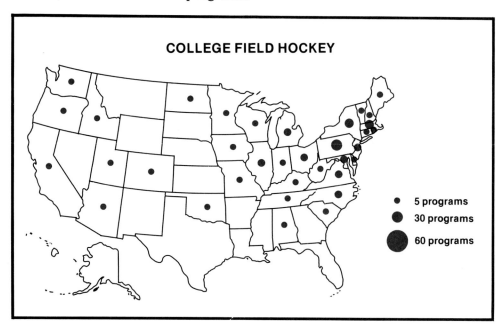

COLLEGE FIELD HOCKEY

5 programs

30 programs

60 programs

tween those states that had soccer for girls at the interscholastic level and those that offer it for women as a varsity sport at the intercollegiate level. The most prominent gaps remain in the intermontane West, Plains, and parts of the South.

In contrast, field hockey, a minor and intensely regionalized sport for high-school girls, assumes a more dominant position in college athletic departments (Map 6.15). Field-hockey players in Pennsylvania outnumber those in any other state (35 programs). Massachusetts and New York are the nearest competitors with 22 and 21 teams. With 248 programs throughout the nation, field hockey actually ties for popularity honors in New Hampshire and Vermont. What becomes most interesting, however, is how the sport has extended beyond what is normally the last western outpost of field hockey in St. Louis (with the exception of California). Scattered schools in the West and the South offer field hockey as a varsity sport for college women, bringing the total up to 35 states with programs.

OLYMPIANS

Olympic team members represent the premier amateur athletes at a given time in our country. Admittedly some of the best could be eliminated in qualifying rounds for one reason or another, but, in general, the team represents the pick of the crop. What is their regional pedigree? Map 6.16 tabulates the 1984 winter and summer female Olympic-team members, their sport, and their home state.

The map portrays 7 events for women in winter competition and 17 in the summer. Tennis was played only as a demonstration sport in Los Angeles, but it is included as well. Tennis has Olympic ties, however; it was a medal sport for women from 1900 to 1924 until the question of players' amateur status was raised. Both tennis and table tennis are scheduled to be included in the Seoul games in 1988. Rhythmic gymnastics, cycling, and synchronized swimming were added to the 1984 program of women's events. In addition, three separate shooting events for women were inaugurated in Los Angeles; until then women could be on the team with men. In equestrian events (show jumping, dressage, and three-day event) women and men compete with each other. Theoretically, yachting is in the same category, but women have not qualified in recent years. Current female membership on the International Olympic Committee may result in increased female participation if more events are added.

California is the home of far more female Olympic athletes than any other state. Two winter-team members and 53 summer-team members come from this state. Seventeen of the 43 track-and-field participants form the most impres-

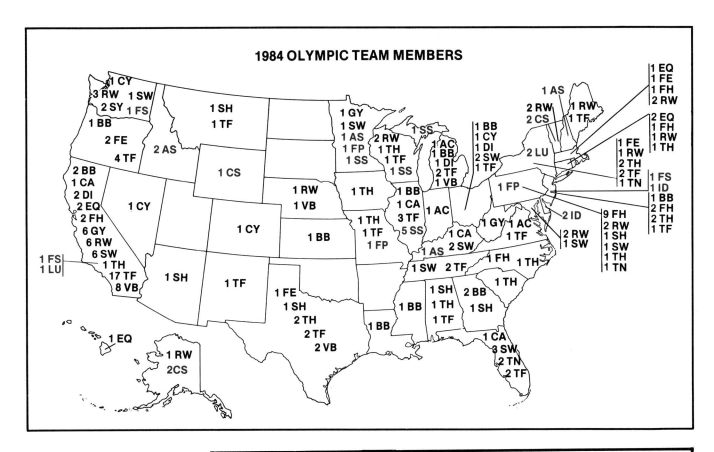

1984 OLYMPIC TEAM MEMBERS

Summer Olympics

AC Archery	TH Team Handball
BB Basketball	TN Tennis
CA Canoeing	TF Track and Field
CY Cycling	VB Volleyball
DI Diving	
EQ Equestrian	
FE Fencing	
FH Field Hockey	
GY Gymnastics	
RW Rowing	
SH Shooting	
SW Swimming	
SY Synchronized Swimming	

Winter Olympics

AS Alpine Skiing
CS Cross-country Skiing
FP Figure Skating -- Pairs
FS Figure Skating -- Singles
ID Ice Dancing
LU Luge
SS Speed Skating

Map 6.16   1984 Olympic-team members—home states.

sive participation total for California, but 6 of 8 female gymnasts and 8 of 12 volleyball players also show the state's athletic strengths. But California, in contrast to past Olympic teams, provided only 6 of the 18 female swimmers for the 1984 summer games and 2 of the 4 divers. No new "swimming state" has emerged, however, with team members dispersed among eight other states. Year-round training weather and prevalence of clubs to encourage competitiveness may be the secret of California's overall success.

Pennsylvania claims second-place honors with 16 1984 female Olympians coming from this state. Nine of 16 field-hockey players are from Pennsylvania, perpetuating at this level the same regional concentration for the sport seen in high schools and colleges. Illinois claims third place in the Olympic race (5 speed skaters make this state unique) and is followed by New York; then there is a tie among Florida, New Jersey, Texas, and Washington. New York has no specialties except for the luge, but Florida claims 2 of the tennis players. The alpine skier from Lexington, Ky., is perhaps the biggest geographical surprise.

Six states did not have any Olympic-team members in 1984. Although the distribution is related to population (the greater the population pool, the greater the probability of an elite athlete), nevertheless, the large relative gap in the middle of the country should cause some speculation. Many of these states are the same ones that have high participation rates among girls in high-school sports. Being an Olympic athlete requires talent and dedication combined with good coaching and training facilities. The location of the latter two factors may be partly responsible for the geographical distribution shown here.

LIFELONG SPORTS

Not all sports are lifelong sports. The aging body makes recreational basketball, soccer, or softball an impossibility if not an outright, high-risk-taking venture after a certain age. With regret we all make this decision to quit sooner or later. In addition to the problems of being a step slower to first base, the problems of organizing teams that are composed of busy, midlife women become overwhelming. The

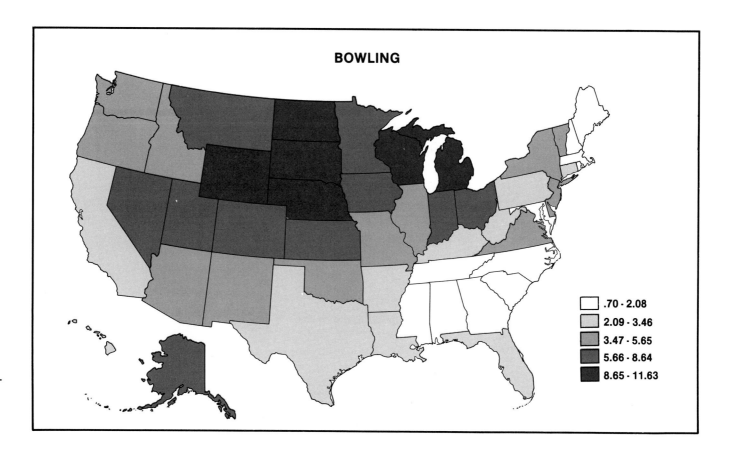

BOWLING

.70 - 2.08
2.09 - 3.46
3.47 - 5.65
5.66 - 8.64
8.65 - 11.63

Map 6.17 Bowling—percentage of women 15 years and older who are Women's International Bowling Congress members, 1983–84. U.S. average is 4.16%.

options for the competitive natures, therefore, are reduced with age. As a result, some women become exclusively spectators instead of participants.

Running, either competitively or jogging through the neighborhood, is a relatively recent entrant to the extended-sports category. Many older women, of course, take their exercise in the much less-demanding, derivative form of walking. Exercising, especially the currently popular aerobic exercises, takes care of the physical activity needs of many women, but this is a competitive sport only in the sense that maybe you can outlast your neighbor in a routine. Tennis and golf continue to enjoy popularity as the pace of competition is adaptable to age. Handicapping and doubles help. Many older women swim and bicycle, but rarely competitively.

Bowling is one option that is competitive but not overly strenuous. Data from the 1983–84 annual report of the Women's International Bowling Congress indicate that sanctioned membership in this organization as of July 31, 1984 totaled 3,804,882 women and 157,607 leagues. Of all the women in the United States who were 15 years or older in 1980, 4.16% belong to this group, a substantial participation for any adult sport.

As with other athletic phenomenon, bowling has regional popularity (Map 6.17). The most intense participation exists in a north central core of states. Other above-average rates extend from Nevada to Ohio with Illinois and Missouri providing a slight gap in a continuous pattern. Wisconsin has the highest participation with 11.63% of its adult women be-longing to WIBC. North Dakota follows with 10.96%. Although all states have some members (as do several foreign countries), the proportions become minor in Maine, for example, where only .70% of the women participate. Massachusetts, Mississippi, and New Hampshire represent other particularly low rates. Low participation rates extend across the southern tier of states from Hawaii to Florida and then up the East coast. Regions of particularly low-value states exist in the South and parts of New England.

At a first glance through the membership data, bowling appears to be both a metropolitan and a small-town sport in the Midwest. Since small towns do not provide the critical population mass to support a bowling alley, however, calling this sport a "county-seat sport" comes closer to the truth. In Midwestern snowbound areas it is a winter athletic/social diversion. The capital city for women's bowling is Detroit; it boasts first place in individual membership, number of leagues, and largest local tournament. Milwaukee ranks third behind Chicago even though Milwaukee's suburb of Greendale is the headquarters of the WIBC.

Bowling exists as a high-school sport for girls in 10 states with 6,449 total participants. Highest participation rates are found in Illinois, New Jersey, and New York. As a college sport for women, 43 programs are offered in 19 states with New York providing the most. It is unlikely, therefore, from these small numbers that women learn bowling through their school experiences; more likely the lore and skill of the sport are passed from friend to friend.

CHAPTER SEVEN

RELATIONSHIPS

INTRODUCTION

Increasing diversity among family units is transforming American society. Traditional marriage characterized by a lifelong, legal, sexually exclusive marriage between one man and one woman, with children, is no longer the normative condition. Other life-styles are proliferating in our pluralistic society. The evidence is insurmountable: Marriage is not permanent, more women are living alone, family size is decreasing, marriages are being postponed, premarital sex is increasing, remarriage is brisk, and the number of one-parent households is increasing. The maps in this chapter were selected to display the geographical distribution of some of these social phenomena. Data limitations preclude the portrayal of other important subjects, including married couples who do not live together (commuter marriages and two-location families), unmarried cohabitation, or lesbians.

The maps start with five census classifications of marital status for women: single, married, separated, widowed, and divorced. These are followed by crude marriage and divorce rates. Families are examined next with the two dominant roles for women singled out for consideration—married-couple families and single-parent (mother) families. Finally, the number of single-mother families below the poverty level and the feminization of poverty are examined.

MARRIAGE STATUS

Marital status is classified by the census into five categories: single (never married), married, separated, widowed, and divorced. All women 15 and over are included. In 1980 of the 91,414,347 women in this age category, 23.0% (21,037,493) were single, 54.8% (50,138,720) were married, 2.6% (2,404,936) were married but separated, 12.3% (11,231,965) were widowed, and 7.2% (6,601,233) were divorced. Although the divorce rate is climbing in this country and divorce seems to touch more lives than ever before, it is important to note the small percentage of women at a given time who are actually divorced. Obviously remarriage is rampant. The preferred relationship with members of the opposite sex remains marriage. Among men percentages for these same categories are 29.9, 60.3, 1.9, 2.5, and 5.4.

Being single is more prevalent in selected states in the Northeast, three upper Midwest states, and Hawaii than it is in the remainder of the United States (Map 7.1). Massachusetts and New York dominate this variable with 29.2 and 28.0% respectively of their relevant female populations in the never-married category. Some of this concentration may be attributed to migration to large metropolitan areas by young people in search of jobs and social activities. Students also fall in this category. Another possible interpretation is that being single in these states does not carry the stigma that it does in more conservative places. Society in the 12 high-ranking states may actually condone independent women and recognize that women can successfully go it alone. Perhaps these states even represent the vanguard of a demographic transition. The relative lack of single women in Arkansas, Idaho, Oklahoma, and Wyoming may be related to overall conservatism in local society. Perhaps being married is the common denominator for social activities in these states and "belonging" means not being single.

Marriage is the preferred relationship in Alaska, Idaho, Utah, and Wyoming (Map 7.2). Harsh physical environments may be a force in bringing couples together there, and, certainly, the emphasis on family life by the Mormons is even a greater factor in three of these states. Western and Plains states generally rank high on this measure. Low percentages of married women are seen in New York, Massachusetts, and Rhode Island with percentages of 48.9, 49.7, and 50.9. These states are at the center of a northeast metropolitan depression joined by Illinois and California, other states with large urban populations.

If you can reverse the order of the classification scheme in your mind, you will be looking at a map of those states where women are responsible for themselves (and perhaps their children) because they are single, separated, divorced, or widowed. There are a lot of women taking care of themselves in California, New York, Pennsylvania, and Illinois (4.4, 3.8, 2.3, and 2.2 million respectively, to be exact).

Separated women, those who no longer live with their husbands either through agreement or desertion, are concentrated in East-coast locations and California (Map 7.3). Maryland leads with 4.4% of its female population in this category. It is followed closely by North Carolina, New York, South Carolina, and New Jersey, in that order. Separation as an

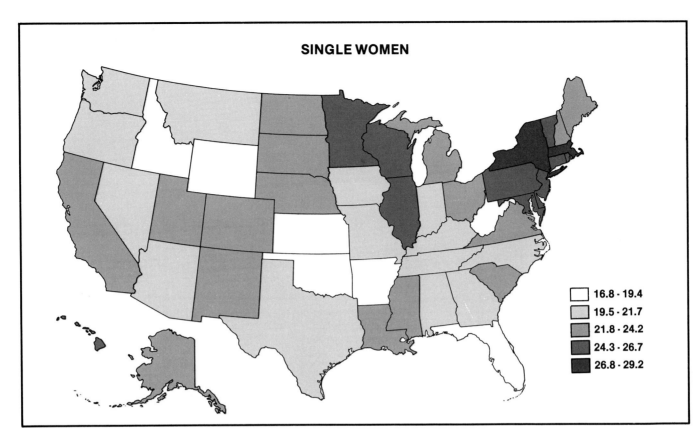

SINGLE WOMEN

	16.8 - 19.4
	19.5 - 21.7
	21.8 - 24.2
	24.3 - 26.7
	26.8 - 29.2

Map 7.1 Single women, as a percentage of all women 15 years and older, 1980. U.S. average is 23.0%.

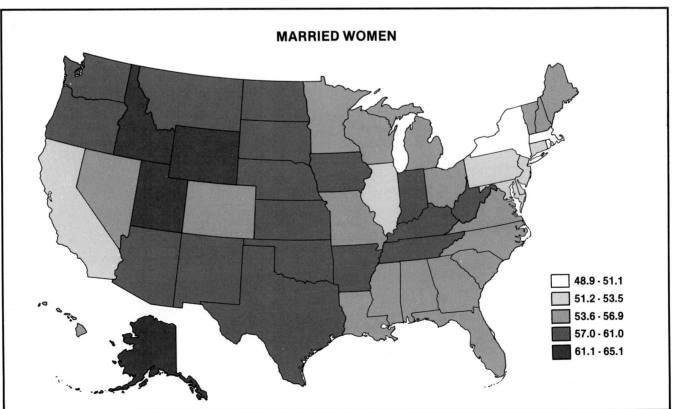

MARRIED WOMEN

	48.9 - 51.1
	51.2 - 53.5
	53.6 - 56.9
	57.0 - 61.0
	61.1 - 65.1

Map 7.2 Married women, as a percentage of all women 15 years and older, 1980. U.S. average is 54.8%.

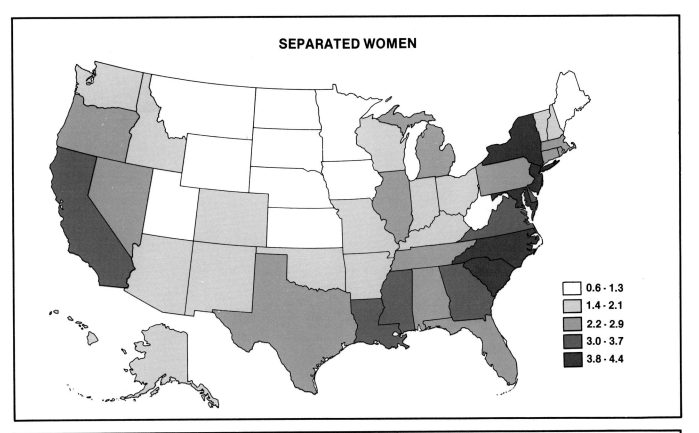

SEPARATED WOMEN

☐	0.6 - 1.3
▨	1.4 - 2.1
▨	2.2 - 2.9
▨	3.0 - 3.7
▉	3.8 - 4.4

Map 7.3 Separated women, as a percentage of all women 15 years and older, 1980. U.S. average is 2.6%.

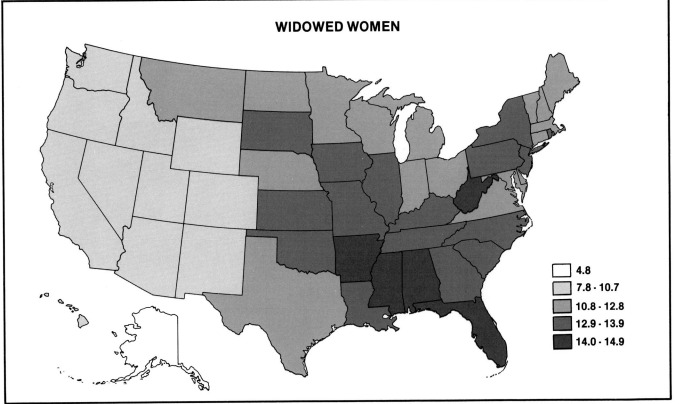

WIDOWED WOMEN

☐	4.8
▨	7.8 - 10.7
▨	10.8 - 12.8
▨	12.9 - 13.9
▉	14.0 - 14.9

Map 7.4 Widowed women, as a percentage of all women 15 years and older, 1980. U.S. average is 12.3%.

Relationships

alternative to an unhappy marriage is unheard of in the interior of the country. North Dakota and South Dakota at .6 and .8% form the lows. Marriage or dissolving marriage straight to divorce is the norm for this part of the country.

It is unclear whether these data represent trial separation, a period of counseling and perhaps reconciliation, or a semi-married state adhered to because of welfare laws or response to religious practices. In any case, it is the least common of the marital-status variables and represents a small portion of the female population.

Widows are relatively rare in the western half of the country (Map 7.4). The more youthful age of people in the western states would tend to depress this figure. Alaska has an exceptionally low percentage of women in this category—4.8%. Hawaii and Utah follow at 8.0 and 8.1%. The younger and somewhat transient population of Alaska may account for the lack of widows there. Although there are exceptionally high percentages of widows in Alabama, Arkansas, Florida, and Mississippi, all Sun-belt retirement areas, there are no similar highs in Texas and Arizona, other retirement areas. The highest percentage for this variable is in West Virginia at 14.9%, a state characterized by minimal out-migration. A

similar "nonmoving" tradition is present on the Plains and in the Northeast and may help account for the presence of widows in these secondary regions. Support systems in the form of family, friends, and social institutions encourage a widow's locational persistence even in a climate that may be somewhat difficult for an older woman.

Speculation on why widows do not remarry in Alabama, Arkansas, Florida, Mississippi, and West Virginia is interesting. Is the tea-and-bridge society with older women companions preferable to a new life with a possibly crochety old man? If one is financially set, this seems a reasonable choice given the relative unavailability of eligible males.

Do all divorced women live in California as the television sit-coms would have us believe? Not really, but California does have the second highest percentage of divorced women among its female population (9.9%). Nevada is highest with 12.8% (Map 7.5). Since California has a large female population, divorced women there total 620,693, compared with the 39,830 in Nevada. Colorado, Oregon, and Washington round out the western concentration of divorcees with an outlier in Florida. North and South Dakota at 4.3 and 4.5%, in contrast, have proportionally very few divorced women. They

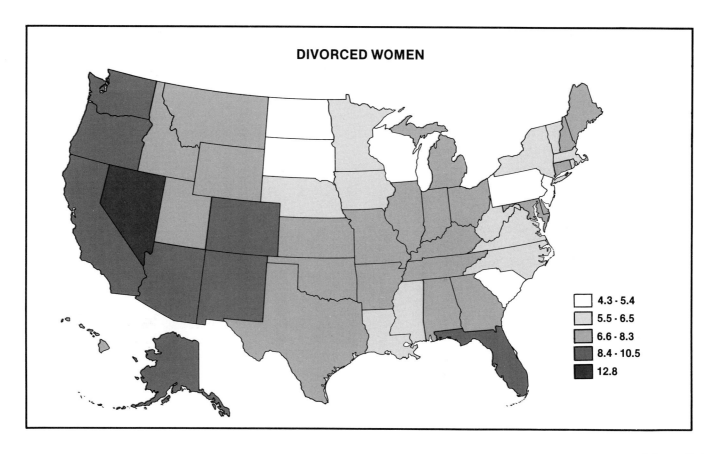

DIVORCED WOMEN

4.3 - 5.4
5.5 - 6.5
6.6 - 8.3
8.4 - 10.5
12.8

Map 7.5 Divorced women, as a percentage of all women 15 years and older, 1980. U.S. average is 7.2%.

are joined by South Carolina and Pennsylvania. The upper Midwest and East coast can be singled out as pockets of divorcelessness.

Divorced women are known to have high migration rates, especially when they are unencumbered with children. Starting over is the basis for many of these moves. The patterns on Map 7.5, therefore, are a combination of high divorce rates (compare this map with Map 7.7) and attractive resettlement areas. Social attitudes of potential friends, neighbors, and employers are a primary pulling factor.

When the five variables of marital attachment are considered in combination they create a complex picture of relationships in a state. The most "normal" state in the union, for example, is Michigan—it ranks right at the national average for all five measures, and, therefore, reflects the American image of marital relationships. Maine, New Hampshire, and Ohio are other typical states. They have lower-than-average separation rates, but rank near the average for the other variables. On the other hand, the most deviant states are New York, West Virginia, and Wyoming, each in its own way.

New York has an exceptionally high single and separation rate, combined with an exceptionally low married rate. It is the ultimate singles scene. Undoubtedly, the New York metropolitan area attracts single women both for job and social opportunities and some of the numbers reported here may be a result of in-migration. New York, however, is also at the center of nine states high in single women, a variable seemingly intrinsic to that part of the country. The extreme separation rate in New York may be attributed to large, urban, ethnic populations and the associated problems of desertion by husbands and welfare-assistance policies.

West Virginia, in contrast, has exceptionally low single and separation rates, but an exceptionally high widow rate. The married rate is above average and the divorce rate is below average. Marriage appears to be the preferred standard in West Virginia although the high number of widows indicates lack of remarriage.

Wyoming similarly has exceptionally low single and separation rates, but an exceptionally high married rate. Widows are below the national average whereas divorced women are right at the average. Again marriage is placed at a premium in Wyoming, possibly because of the scarcity of women.

MARRIAGE AND DIVORCE RATES

Wheareas Maps 7.1 through 7.5 portray a cumulative marriage status index, Maps 7.6 and 7.7 portray marriage and divorce activity during one year. The crude marriage rate for 1979 (or number of marriages performed per 1,000 population residing in area) varied from a low of 7.3 in Delaware to 17.3 in South Carolina. Actually Nevada was the high at 135.2, but because of its particular laws in regards to marriage and divorce and the resulting temporary migration of couples to Nevada, Nevada should really be considered in a class by itself. Marriage rates are low throughout the northeastern quarter of the United States and in California and Oregon. In contrast, rates are high in selected areas of the South, Oklahoma–Texas–New Mexico, Wyoming–Idaho–South Dakota, Alaska, and Hawaii.

Values for the crude divorce rate (number of decrees granted per 1,000 population) ranged from 3.0 in Massachusetts to 9.0 in Arkansas (plus 15.4 in Nevada). Catholic states (Louisiana plus selected northeastern states) have lower-than-average divorce rates. States where Baptists and fundamentalist religions are prevalent have higher divorce rates.

The divorce rate exhibits a similar pattern to that of marriage rate at first glance, but there are some notable changes. South Carolina has an exceptionally low ratio of divorces to marriages (.256) with South Dakota the next lowest (.300). This means, of course, that there are many more marriages going on than divorces in these states. In contrast, Alaska, Arkansas, California, Delaware, Indiana, and Oregon have high ratios (ranging from .796 for Oregon to .690 for California).

By putting the marriage and divorce rate together, individual states are seen to have certain characteristics. For example, Massachusetts, New Jersey, New York, Pennsylvania, Rhode Island, and Wisconsin are not active. Both the divorce rate and the marriage rate are low. Those few that get married appear to stay that way. Louisiana, Minnesota, and North Dakota, on the other hand, have a bit more activity. They represent traditional marriage with low divorce rates and average marriage rates. South Carolina is similar to these three states, but at a more frenzied pace. People in South Carolina strongly believe in marriage, but have a bit more trouble selecting a lifelong mate the first time around.

Tendencies toward decadence and restlessness are evident in other states. Connecticut, Delaware, and North Carolina, for example, have an average divorce rate and a low marriage rate. The trait is intensified in Alaska, Arizona, Arkansas, Indiana, New Mexico, and Wyoming where the divorce rate is high and the marriage rate is average. The epitome of this category, however, is Oklahoma and Nevada where both the divorce and marriage rates are high. These three sets of states reflect increasing social activity in the sometimes hectic pursuit of a partner. While divorce may once have been taboo in these same states, it obviously no longer is. Marital problems created by early marriage and

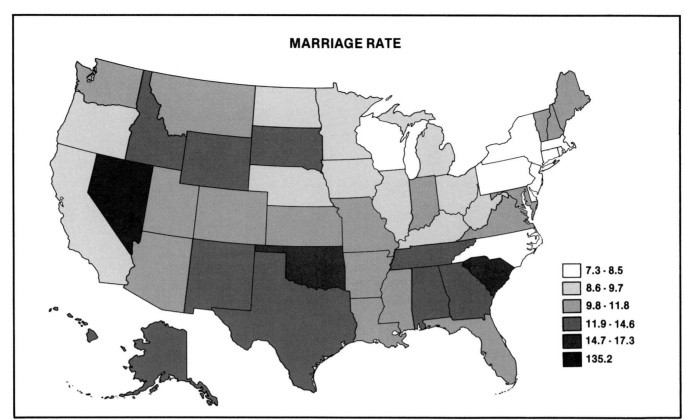

MARRIAGE RATE

☐	7.3 - 8.5
☐	8.6 - 9.7
☐	9.8 - 11.8
☐	11.9 - 14.6
☐	14.7 - 17.3
☐	135.2

Map 7.6 Marriage rate—marriages per 1,000 residents, 1979. U.S. average is 10.4.

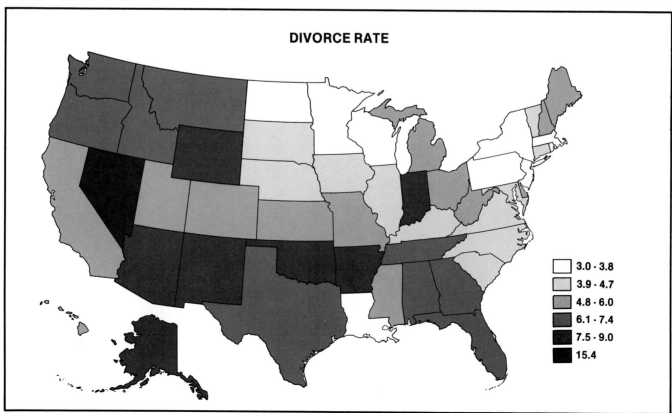

DIVORCE RATE

☐	3.0 - 3.8
☐	3.9 - 4.7
☐	4.8 - 6.0
☐	6.1 - 7.4
☐	7.5 - 9.0
☐	15.4

Map 7.7 Divorce rate—divorces per 1,000 residents, 1979. U.S. average is 5.3.

unreasoned choice of partner are being resolved in the divorce courts.

This marital instability is what the New Right thinks is wrong with American society—a decrease in the sanctity of the nuclear marriage. It is ironic that leaders in the movement come from states where the most work needs to be done to restore faith in marriage. Maybe they echo parochial problems rather than nationwide ones.

If you want to open a bridal-shop business, avoid Delaware or New Jersey, but you could do well in Oklahoma or South Carolina. If you are a marriage counselor, do not hang up your sign in Massachusetts, North Dakota, or New Jersey, but try Arkansas or Alaska.

FAMILIES

A family is two or more people related by birth, marriage, or adoption who reside together, by census definition. In 1980 there were 58,975,810 families in the United States with an average size of 3.27 persons. Approximately 85% of the American population, therefore, participated in a family relationship. How important to the total family picture is the married-couple family with children under 18 or the single-parent (female) family, two categories where women play significant roles?

Married couples with their own children under 18 represent 41.5% of family relationships (Map 7.8). This category includes blended families with children from previous marriages. Highs in Utah and Wyoming (54.2 and 49.5%) can be attributed to the family ideals associated with the Mormon religion, a significant influence in these states. The youthful adult population in these states plus Alaska also explains the concentration.

Women's magazines often portray the young, healthy family with children in clean clothes all posed with their dog and station wagon before a new house, supposedly depicting all that is right with American society. This "Better Homes and Gardens" image fits the central part of the country as well as Alaska and Hawaii, and upper New England.

Although the nuclear family is the dominant preference in all these states, they are not necessarily the target market for family-oriented products. If advertisers go with numbers alone, California (2.4 million families in this category), New York (1.7 million), Texas (1.6 million), Pennsylvania (1.3 million), Ohio (1.2 million), or Illinois (1.2 million) would be the more profitable site for an advertising blitz than Utah (.2 million), Alaska (.05 million), or Wyoming (.06 million).

Florida, in contrast, has very few married-couple families with children (33.2%). Although Florida has an average proportion of married couples compared with the rest of the country, many of these couples are older, possibly with children who have left home. New Jersey, New York, and Rhode Island, representing other lows ranging from 38.1 to 39.7%, just do not have very many married women (see Map 7.2). Nevada, another low state at 39.6%, has an average number of married couples, a youthful population, but not very many children, possibly due to voluntary childlessness.

A map of single mothers (7.9) displays an almost perfect inverse relationship to the previous map of married-couple families. Where married-couple families with children were, single mothers are not, and vice versa. Single-parent (female) families with related children under 18 account for 9.5% of all families. These groups are concentrated in the South (excluding Florida) plus New York. Mississippi leads the nation with 12.6% of its families in this category, followed by New York with 12.0%, and Georgia and Louisiana with 11.7%. California, at an above-average percentage of 10.5, has the most women in this category (600,000). These patterns are consistent with general profiles developed for these women. Single mothers maintaining a family are likely to be young, divorced or never married, and black or Hispanic. Single mothers are largely an urban occurrence with 43% of female householders residing in cities greater than a million population. Eighty percent of black single mothers are in metropolitan areas, as are 90% of Hispanic single mothers.

For individual metropolitan areas, New York has the highest percentage of single mothers with 14.21 (Table 7.1). New Orleans follows with 12.68%; Chicago, Detroit, and Newark are next. At the other end of the scale are Nassau-Suffolk and Pittsburgh.

Being a PTA president in states with large percentages of single mothers can provoke headaches. Single parents decrease the pool of potential volunteers by half and these people are already overextended by other demands on their time, including full-time jobs.

The percentage of single mothers is low throughout the Plains and Mountain states, just as was the percentage of separated women. North Dakota has the lowest percentage at 5.1% followed by Wyoming at 5.6% and Iowa and Nebraska at 6.2%. Although the divorce rate is particularly high in some of these same states (for example Idaho, Montana, and Wyoming), remarriage and blended families may change temporarily single mothers into remarried mothers at a faster rate than elsewhere in the nation.

The family relationships encompassed by Maps 7.8 and 7.9 represent 51.0% of all families. Other unmapped possibilities include: married-couple families without children or with children over 18 (40.9% of all families), single parents (male), unmarried couples with children, female householder without children (such as daughter living with mother), or female

TABLE 7.1 SINGLE PARENT (FEMALE) FAMILIES IN SMSAs

LOCATION	%		
Anaheim–Santa Ana–Garden Grove, Calif.	7.78	Minneapolis–St. Paul, Minn.-Wis.	7.93
Atlanta, Ga.	10.78	Nassau-Suffolk, N.Y.	6.02
Baltimore, Md.	10.92	New Orleans, La.	12.68
Boston, Mass.	9.12	New York, N.Y.-N.J.	14.21
Buffalo, N.Y.	8.23	Newark, N.J.	11.52
Chicago, Ill.	11.51	Philadelphia, Pa.-N.J.	9.53
Cincinnati, Ohio-Ky.-Ind.	8.84	Phoenix, Ariz.	7.28
Cleveland, Ohio	9.30	Pittsburgh, Pa.	6.04
Columbus, Ohio	10.16	Portland, Oreg.-Wash.	8.87
Dallas–Fort Worth, Tex.	8.47	Riverside–San Bernardino–Ontario, Calif.	8.61
Denver-Boulder, Colo.	8.97	Sacramento, Calif.	10.50
Detroit, Mich.	11.25	St. Louis, Mo.-Ill.	8.92
Fort Lauderdale–Hollywood, Fla.	6.39	San Antonio, Tex.	9.84
Houston, Tex.	8.64	San Diego, Calif.	10.33
Indianapolis, Ind.	9.52	San Francisco–Oakland, Calif.	9.64
Kansas City, Mo.-Ks.	9.18	San Jose, Calif.	8.99
Los Angeles–Long Beach, Calif.	10.79	Seattle-Everett, Wash.	8.75
Miami, Fla.	8.87	Tampa–St. Petersburg, Fla.	7.56
Milwaukee, Wis.	9.97	Washington, D.C.-Md.-Va.	10.80

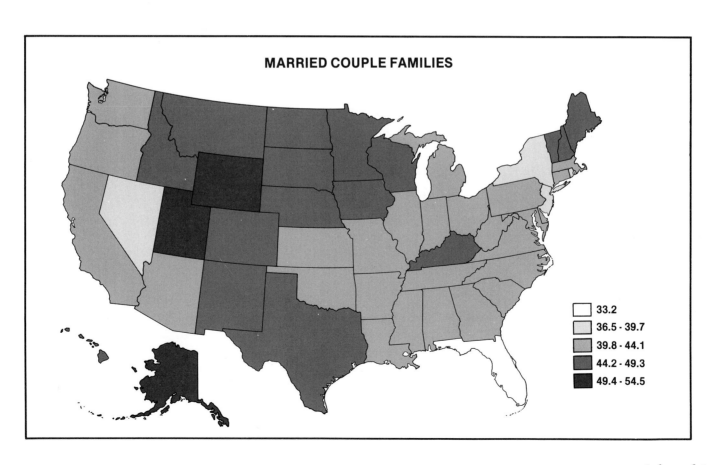

MARRIED COUPLE FAMILIES

☐	33.2
☐	36.5 - 39.7
☐	39.8 - 44.1
☐	44.2 - 49.3
☐	49.4 - 54.5

Map 7.8   Married-couple families, with own children under 18, as a percentage of all families. U.S. average is 41.5%.

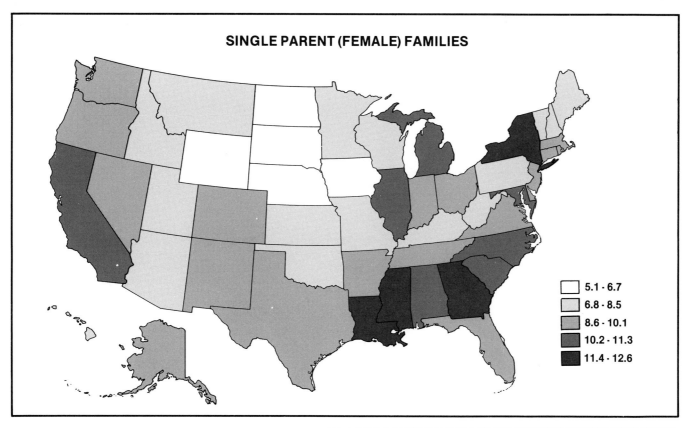

SINGLE PARENT (FEMALE) FAMILIES

	5.1 - 6.7
	6.8 - 8.5
	8.6 - 10.1
	10.2 - 11.3
	11.4 - 12.6

Map 7.9 Single-parent (female) families, with related children under 18, as a percentage of all families. U.S. average is 9.5%.

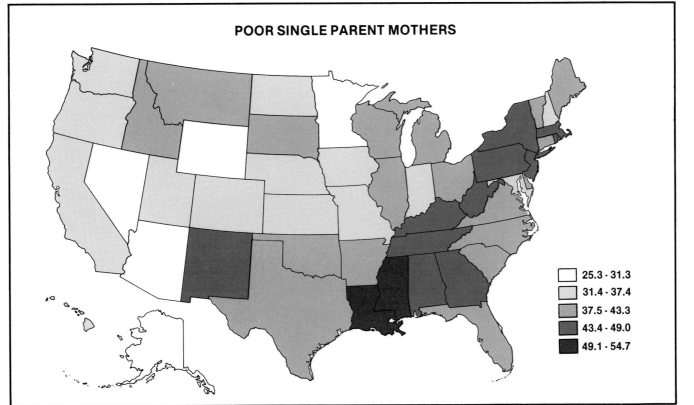

POOR SINGLE PARENT MOTHERS

	25.3 - 31.3
	31.4 - 37.4
	37.5 - 43.3
	43.4 - 49.0
	49.1 - 54.7

Map 7.10 Poor single-parent mothers—percentage of households headed by women with children under 18 who are below poverty level, 1980. U.S. average is 40.5%.

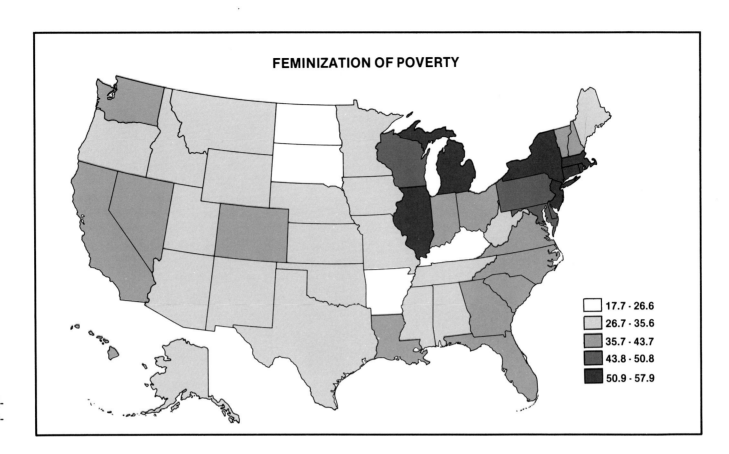

FEMINIZATION OF POVERTY

17.7 - 26.6
26.7 - 35.6
35.7 - 43.7
43.8 - 50.8
50.9 - 57.9

Map 7.11   Feminization of poverty—percentage of families below poverty level with female householder (no husband present) and related children under 18, 1980. U.S. average is 40.2%.

householder with children 19 or over. The census does not provide breakdowns for the latter four categories, which together total only 8.1% of all family relationships.

POVERTY

To what extent are single-parent mothers with children under 18 a burden upon society? Two different but closely related measures examine this question from the perspective of the single-parent mother and that of welfare institutions. Poor single-parent mothers, or the percentage of households headed by women with related children under 18 that are below the poverty level, are portrayed on Map 7.10. Poverty level is based solely on money income and does not include such noncash items as food stamps, medicaid, or public housing. In 1980 for families with a female householder, the poverty level for two people was $5,415, for three people it was $6,366, and for four people it was $8,382. On the average 40.5% of single parents (female) fall in this poverty category with significant variation across the country.

The lowest percentage on Map 7.10 is 25.3% in Nevada. Relatively few poor single mothers are located in the West and central Plains where it is assumed women are either working to support their families at a higher level or some combination of welfare/alimony/child support brings the family income above the poverty level in the majority of cases. At the other extreme, poor single mothers are the dominant situation in Louisiana (52.5%) and Mississippi (54.7%). Here low education level and low labor-force participation rates increase the probability of poverty among single-parent mothers.

The arbitrary poverty level figure may overdramatize the plight of some southern women who either because of a low cost of living (heating bills are low) or self-sufficiency (home gardens help) can maintain a similar, albeit low, standard of living to women living on slightly more money but in a more-expensive urban environment elsewhere in the country. Nevertheless, 44,598 women in Mississippi and 66,600 in Louisiana fall into the poverty category. The future of their children and the need to break the poverty cycle should be the enduring concern of public officials in these states and at the federal level.

The feminization of poverty is a convenient catchword, but is it a reality? Map 7.11 confirms the condition in selected areas of the United States. Of all families below the poverty level, 40.2% are headed by women with children under 18. North and South Dakota at 17.7 and 23.5% represent the low end of this spectrum. In these states families below the poverty level are more likely to be married-couple families. However, in eastern metropolitan states plus Michigan and Illinois, poverty-stricken families are likely to be headed by a female single parent with children under 18. These states have an awesome responsibility with regards to public assistance. Welfare to single-parent mothers absorbs a disproportionate share of tax dollars and caseload for social workers. The single-parent mother is important in these states, from the view of the welfare institution.

It is ironic that in Mississippi and Louisiana, where being a single mother is an almost certain path to poverty, single mothers represent an average to low proportion of the family poverty picture. Other family classifications such as married-couple families or married couples with no children under 18 (including couples over 65) are at normal proportions of the poverty picture, too. The difference is that many families of all types are below the poverty level in these two states (19.5% of all families in Mississippi and 15.3% in Louisiana, compared with a U.S. average of 9.6%). Single-parent mothers, therefore, are lost in the general misery.

CHAPTER EIGHT

PREGNANCY

INTRODUCTION

Having babies is in the unique domain of women. When and if to have children has increasingly become a matter of choice with improved contraceptives, increased use of legalized abortion, and rapidly increasing career opportunities outside the home. Historically early marriage and immediate childbearing was the dominant pattern. Higher education for women was rare and few women worked outside the home. Now that women have educational and work futures, reproductive choice is a fundamental concern. Although it is a personal choice, societal attitudes affect the aggregate data and produce regional variation. Some parts of the country have been slower to change than others.

This chapter opens with a map of the fertility rate for women 15 years or older. The total pool is somewhat diluted since one-third of these women have never had children. Even among women who have been or are married, 16.8% are not mothers through choice or infertility. A map of the birthrate follows to provide a current comparison to the cumulative fertility rate. Next regional variations in out-of-wedlock births are considered. The possibility of bastardy-prone societies where women pass on values and practices to their children is explored. Bastardy appears to have racial associations, with 9.3% of all births to white women being to unmarried women in 1980 whereas 23.6% of Hispanic births and 56.4% of black births were to unmarried women.

Teen-age pregnancy is the subject of the next two maps on fertility and unmarried mothers. Teen-age mothers present a significant problem to some parts of this country just because they soon become a burden on the welfare system. Early pregnancies lead to truncated education, inadequate vocational training, economic dependency and poverty, and social isolation. Who would wish this on anyone?

Contraceptive use is difficult to document, but the next map we see deals with use rate of family-planning services, a limited facet of the entire picture. Maps on abortion rates and an abortion-to-live births ratio complete the chapter. The last three maps, of course, are connected with the volatile moral issues of this decade. From the maps, the reader will soon appreciate that averting or terminating pregnancies has a regional component.

FERTILITY AND BIRTHRATES

The fertility rate, or children ever born per 1,000 women age 15 or older, is a crude measure of fecundity for the American population at a given time (Map 8.1). The denominator or standardizing measure is more generous than actual fact. It encompasses, for example, young teens, most of whom have not yet thought about having children. It also includes women who never intended to have children, further diluting the pool of childbearing women. Nevertheless, total fertility rate is an indicator of number of births per woman, albeit an underestimated one. More accurate data are not available at the state level.

Utah leads the nation with a fertility rate of 2,299 or 2.3 children per woman. The youthful population in this state, combined with the strong family emphasis of the Mormon religion, explains the high value. Idaho, Mississippi, North Dakota, and South Dakota also have high fertility rates and help form a southern concentration and a northern Plains and Rockies concentration of this variable.

Massachusetts has the lowest fertility rate in the country at 1,680 children per 1,000 women, followed closely by New York, Connecticut, and New Jersey. A northeastern low in this variable is clearly visible just as there was a high in the same area for proportion of women who are single. Women in California, Colorado, and Nevada belong to a different lifestyle, one which is in direct conflict with large families.

Family size, although a largely personal decision, still has some cultural preconditions such as ethnicity and race that encourage repeated births. When fertility rates for five groups (white; black; Hispanic; American Indian, Eskimo, and Aleut; and Asian and Pacific islander) within the same state are compared, several generalizations can be derived. The fertility rate among white women is never the highest in a state, when data for such comparison are available. (In eight states there is an insignificant nonwhite population and thus no comparisons are possible.) The highest fertility rate for white women in the 42 surveyed states is 2,150 in South Dakota, followed by 2,129 in West Virginia. The highest fertility rate among black women is 2,761 in Mississippi followed by Arkansas at 2,736. Black women have the highest fertility

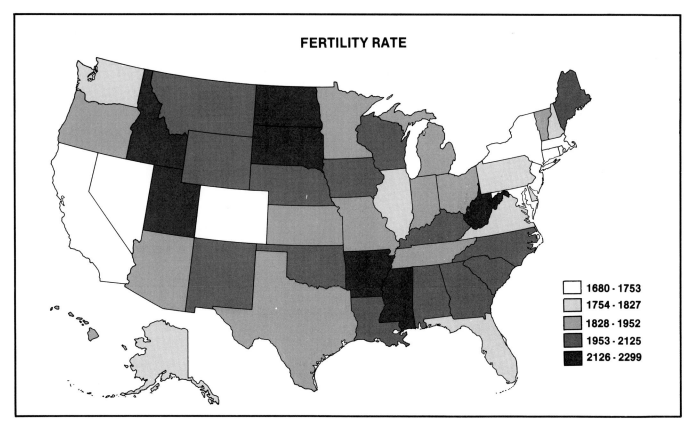

FERTILITY RATE

☐	1680 - 1753
☐	1754 - 1827
▨	1828 - 1952
▨	1953 - 2125
■	2126 - 2299

Map 8.1   Fertility rate—children ever born per 1,000 women 15 years or older, 1980. U.S. average is 1,865.

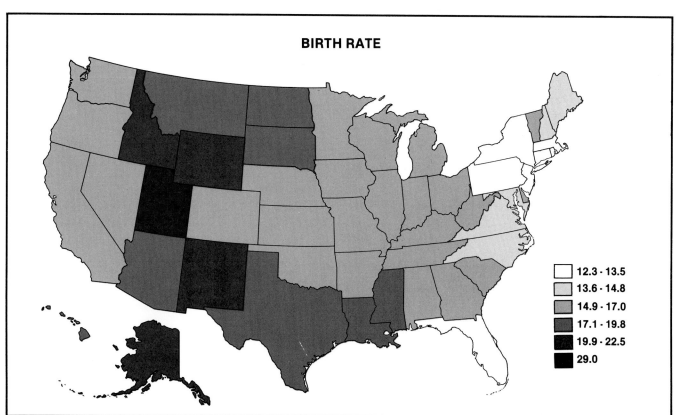

BIRTH RATE

☐	12.3 - 13.5
☐	13.6 - 14.8
▨	14.9 - 17.0
▨	17.1 - 19.8
■	19.9 - 22.5
■	29.0

Map 8.2   Birthrate—births per 1,000 residents, 1979. U.S. average is 15.6.

rates among the five ethnic/racial groups in 17 states. Hispanics have their highest fertility rates in Texas (2,521) and in New Mexico (2,518). They exceed other groups in a total of 13 states. The highest fertility rate among all groups is that of American Indians in South Dakota (2,878). Other exceptionally high rates may be found among native American groups in Alaska, Arizona, and Montana. The highest fertility rate among Asian and Pacific islanders is in Hawaii, where it reaches 2,094. This is the only state where women of this ethnic group have a higher rate than the remainder of the population.

Predispositions to high fecundity among ethnic groups in American society are complex to explain, but the prevalence of the extended family and poverty are two important factors. Extended families and their strong social dependence encourage large families—there is always someone available to share the child-care responsibilities and expenses. High birthrates in the past may have been for economic reasons in rural areas; more hands to help with the harvesting. Presumably some aspects of this philosophy extend to modern times, even when extra people are not needed in mechanized agriculture. The relatively recent pioneer status of the Dakotas, for example, plus the large proportion of immigrant groups from peasant Europe, where large families were common, may explain, in part, the high birthrates there. Poverty and associated variables such as low educational level, poor use of family planning strategies, and low participation in the labor force all combine to encourage large families. To the rural, black southern woman, having another child is often no big deal, certainly not a stigma, in or out of wedlock. Religious beliefs and concomitant bans on birth control are, of course, other factors to encourage high fertility rates.

As might be expected for a highly developed country, the U.S. fertility rate is below the world average. Even lower rates occur throughout Europe with an especially low 1.5 children per woman average in West Germany, Luxembourg, Sweden, and Switzerland. Developing countries, of course, have much higher rates. In Oman and Saudi Arabia the figure reaches 6.9 children per woman. In Africa, Kenyan women bear 7.9 children, on the average.

Whereas Map 8.1 depicts the cumulative effects of childbearing over many years, Map 8.2 is the current birthrate for a given year (1979). Crude birthrate is calculated from the number of births in a state per 1,000 residents.

The birthrate is much higher in Mormon Utah (29.0) than in the next highest state of Alaska (22.5). A set of intermontane western states dominate; three of these (Idaho, Utah, and Wyoming) also have large Mormon populations. Two states with large and conservative Catholic populations, Louisiana and New Mexico, also exhibit high birthrates; their religions encourage large families.

States with low birthrates, in large part, parallel those with low fertility rates on the previous map. Massachusetts is the lowest with a rate of 12.3, followed closely by Rhode Island and Connecticut. States in the lowest category are in the Northeast with the exception of Florida. All are states with comparatively older populations.

Comparison of Maps 8.1 and 8.2 indicates a close relationship between the two variables, confirming a persistence in childbirth pattern. There are, however, several states where the two patterns do not correspond. In North Carolina and West Virginia the long-term fertility rate is proportionally much higher than the current birthrate. This occurs to a lesser extent in Alabama, Arkansas, Maine, and Wisconsin. Possibly in previous generations, a time when the older women in the population were rearing children, a large family was an economic necessity. Older children supplemented the family income through their own earnings as well as provided required labor for labor-intensive farming such as tobacco, cotton, fruits, and vegetables. Large families also ensured financial support in old age, an important factor especially among proud groups where "going on welfare" was anathema.

In Alaska, California, and Colorado, the current birthrate is comparatively much higher than the fertility rate. Hawaii, Nevada, Texas, and Wyoming also maintain this trend, but to a lower degree. All of these states have proportionally large youthful populations, a major factor in determining childbirth activity. Although women are currently active in producing children in these states, eventual family size may be quite small. If this happens, the fertility rate at some point in the future would remain low, as it is now.

Bastardy is something we rarely talk about. It, too, has geographical variation and hence implications for public policy. By doing some minor calculations, the date provided by the census on children born and children born to ever-married women can be used to derive the number of children ever born to never-married women. Standardizing the data by the number of women in the never-married category provides a rate. Admittedly this measure contains some error. For example, those women who were married at the time of the census, but had given birth to a child out of wedlock at a previous time would have all their births counted as legitimate in this case. In addition, this may be one of those census questions that is difficult to answer truthfully, even if anonymity is promised. The measure used in Map 8.3 is thus only an estimate.

The highest rate of out-of-wedlock births per 1,000 women 15 years or older occurs in Mississippi (424). This means there are .4 out-of-wedlock births per woman in Mississippi. The next highest value occurs in Louisiana (366), followed by Alabama, South Carolina, and Georgia. What we

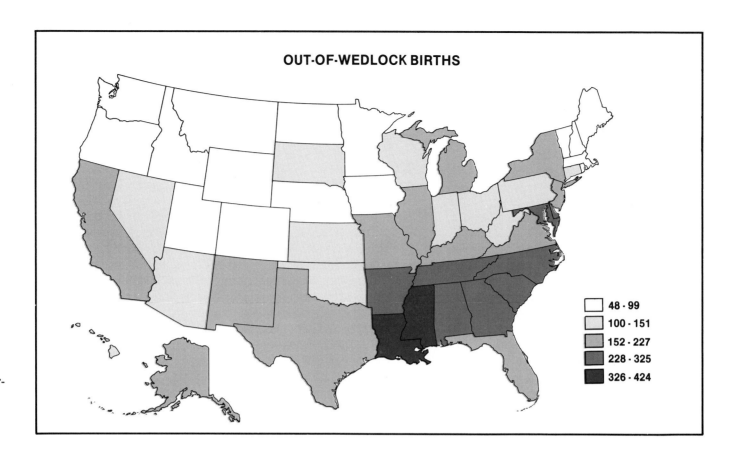

OUT-OF-WEDLOCK BIRTHS

☐	48 - 99
☐	100 - 151
☐	152 - 227
☐	228 - 325
■	326 - 424

Map 8.3 Out-of-wedlock births—births per 1,000 never-married women age 15 or older, 1980. U.S. average is 178.

are looking at, therefore, is a largely southern phenomenon. The only nonsouthern states to enter this end of the listing at all, and these at a considerably lower rate, are those with large urban populations—New York and Illinois.

The lowest rate in the nation is in New Hampshire (48). This state is followed by Idaho, Wyoming, Utah, Vermont, Iowa, and North Dakota. Women in these states are not necessarily chaste, they just do not become pregnant through their sexual experiences, or if they do, they use abortion as a way to end the pregnancy. Low rates for bastardy may be found throughout parts of the Northeast and the northern states of the West.

Rates are dramatically different at the two ends of the bastardy scale. The rate for Mississippi is almost 10 times that for New Hampshire. In terms of numbers, Mississippi had 90,731 out-of-wedlock children born to its women whereas New Hampshire had only 4,197 as of 1980. The relevant female population of Mississippi is, however, only two and one-half times that of New Hampshire. Since many of these women are a burden upon the public financial resources of society because they are unemployed and, in many cases, unemployable, this appears to be a private world that deserves some public scrutiny.

How common are bastard children? The national average, calculated by the above method, is 2.2% of all children born to women enumerated in the 1980 census. The percentage is as low as .4% in Idaho. Other low states include Iowa, New Hampshire, North Dakota, Utah, and Wyoming. The variable, however, does reach 4.1% in Mississippi where approximately 1 in 25 children were born out of wedlock. Other high states include Delaware, Georgia, Louisiana, Maryland, New York, and South Carolina.

Procreation of children outside of marriage used to be an index of the moral state of a community. Now social scientists prefer to consider it deviant behavior, one that upsets models of community interaction. In recent years research has focused upon illegitimacy among teen-agers, in large part because they present a distinct social welfare problem.

TEEN-AGE PREGNANCY

Teen-age pregnancy is a traditional and ongoing problem in the United States. It prompts a lot of rhetoric through its ties to sex education, teen-age morals, and abortion, but the problem remains large. In 1980, 983,551 births in the United

States had been recorded to young women who were then 15 to 19 years old. Of these, 447,711 children were born out of wedlock. Actually the adolescent birthrate is declining, but only because abortion and contraceptive use have increased.

Why is teen-age pregnancy a problem? It interrupts education and, therefore, aspirations for the future, including potential earning power and occupational choice for the couple. If the child is born out of wedlock, additional financial and life-goal problems are encountered for the mother and the child. In addition, pregnancy-associated medical problems are greater for teen-age mothers and their offspring.

The maps that follow portray teen-age fertility rate and teen-age out-of-wedlock births as a percentage of all births to teen-agers. Fertility rates for married and unmarried teen-agers as well as racial differences are discussed.

The fertility rate among teen-agers (Map 8.4) is low in comparison with the rate for all women (94 births per 1,000 women age 15 to 19 as opposed to 1,865 births per 1,000 women 15 years and older). This is to be expected because not as large a proportion of young women are actually at risk of becoming pregnant (not sexually active) as in the larger group of all adult women. Moreover, pregnancy is more often not a direct goal of sexual activity among teen-agers.

The fertility rate among teen-agers is exceptionally high in those same southern states encountered before. Mississippi is the highest state with 173 births per 1,000 women 15 to 19 years old. Louisiana, Arkansas, Georgia, and Alabama follow with rates from 141 to 149. The fertility rate is exceptionally low among teen-agers in Connecticut, Massachusetts, Minnesota, New Hampshire, Rhode Island, and Vermont with values ranging from 44 to 56.

Although this may appear to be mixing apples and oranges, comparison of relative rankings of the teen-age fertility rate with the crude birthrate for all women (Map 8.2) affords a more accurate analysis of current trends than a comparison of adult and teenage fertility rates would. The teen-age fertility rate, after all, encompasses activity over only a few years and, therefore, approaches being a birthrate in itself.

Hawaii, Idaho, Nebraska, and North Dakota have much lower teen-age fertility rates than expected based on the current pregnancy performance of the population-at-large in these states. Colorado, Minnesota, Montana, and Utah follow this trend to a lesser extent. In other words, residents of these

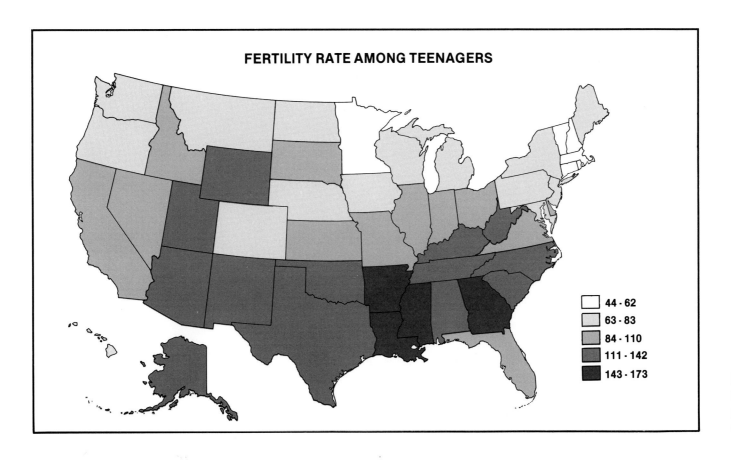

FERTILITY RATE AMONG TEENAGERS

44 - 62
63 - 83
84 - 110
111 - 142
143 - 173

Map 8.4   Fertility rate among teen-agers—children ever born per 1,000 women 15 to 19 years of age, 1980. U.S. average is 94.

states probably do not consider teen-age births a problem for, if their perceptions reflect reality, teen-agers are not as active as the adult population. On the other hand, residents of Arkansas, Florida, North Carolina, and Tennessee should have more concern. So should residents in Alabama, Georgia, Kentucky, and West Virginia. In these states teen-agers have much higher fertility rates than expected based on birthrates among all women. Although the teen-age fertility rate is very high in Mississippi, local residents may not perceive it that way, because the crude birthrate is high there, too.

In general, Maps 8.2 and 8.4 exhibit few regional similarities except in selected parts of the Northeast and Southwest. Thus a lack of correlation in behavioral patterns between the two populations is indicated. Another set of societal forces must be operating for teen-agers alone in some parts of the country. Propensity toward early marriage may be a possible explanation. So might out-of-wedlock births and social composition of the population.

In general, states that have exceptionally low teen-age fertility rates have low percentages of teen-agers married, and those with high fertility rates have a high married percentage. Within this generalization, however, three distinct societal groups emerge. There appears to be a set of states where teen-age marriage is common and so is teen-age pregnancy within marriage: Idaho, Kentucky, Oklahoma, Utah, West Virginia, and Wyoming. In another set of six southern states, births to teen-agers are high and a large proportion of these can be attributed to out-of-wedlock births: Alabama, Arkansas, Georgia, Louisiana, Mississippi, and South Carolina. Finally, there is a set of states where teen-agers do not get married and they do not have children out of wedlock: Massachusetts, New Hampshire, Rhode Island, and Vermont. All of the other states fall in the cracks between these broad categories. If one were to select average states in regards to teen-age behavior (no extremes in percentages or rates in comparison with the rest of the country), they would be California, Colorado, Hawaii, Maine, Missouri, and Nebraska.

Some racial comparisons give further perspective to the issue. In California, the state with the highest number of out-of-wedlock births among teen-agers, 35.8% of these 41,141 births are to teen-age women of Hispanic origin. These women, however, constitute only 23.0% of the female teen-age population of the state. Similarly, births to teen-age blacks in California are more numerous than expected, based on

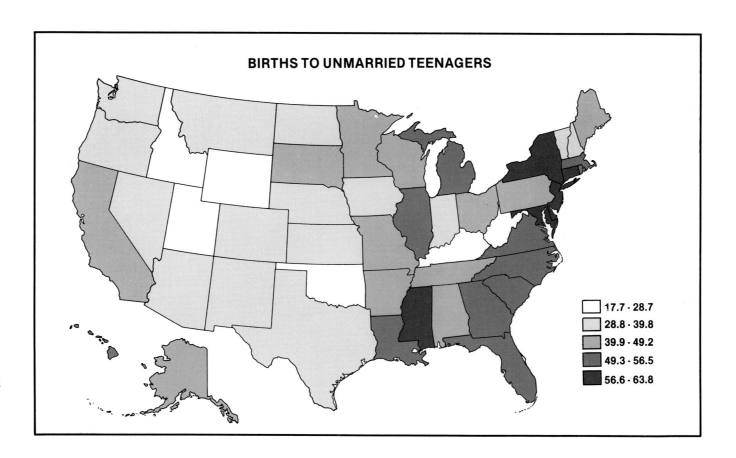

BIRTHS TO UNMARRIED TEENAGERS

17.7 - 28.7
28.8 - 39.8
39.9 - 49.2
49.3 - 56.5
56.6 - 63.8

Map 8.5 Births to unmarried teen-agers, as a percentage of all births to teen-agers, 1980. U.S. average is 45.5%.

their 9.4% share of the population. Black teen-agers have 30.5% of total illegitimate births to teens.

Similar patterns are evident in other states. New York has high percentages of births to blacks (55.5% of illegitimate teen-age births, but 16.8% share of relevant population) and teen-age women of Hispanic origin (21.9% of illegitimate teen-age births, but 11.1% share of relevant population). In Illinois 69.9% of its 28,335 illegitimate births to teen-agers are to blacks although the latter constitute 18.0% of the population. In Texas, of 27,005 out-of-wedlock births to teen-agers, 58.2% are to black teen-agers who constitute 14.2% of the population. The black dominance continues in Florida and Ohio, other states with high numbers of illegitimate births. In Mississippi blacks are responsible for 92.9% of the teen-age illegitimate births.

The most striking data in all these teen-age pregnancy variables, and perhaps the set that will be retained in the reader's mind, are out-of-wedlock births to teen-agers as a percentage of all births to teen-agers (Map 8.5). The highest percentage is in New Jersey with 63.8%. Maryland, Delaware, New York, and Mississippi follow. In fact a dramatic and unsettling total of 14 states have more births to never-married teen-agers than to married teen-agers. The only balancing factor is that the fertility rate among teen-agers in New Jersey and New York is especially low to begin with. Still we are talking about 13,350 illegitimate children in New Jersey and 31,116 in New York born to women who were 15 to 19 years old in 1980. The out-of-wedlock phenomenon dominates in certain parts of the eastern United States. Lows for this variable, in contrast, are 17.7% in Wyoming and 19.4% in Idaho. Other western states such as Montana, Oklahoma, and Utah follow, along with Kentucky and West Virginia.

Eight out of 10 Americans favor sex education for teen-agers, but only 3 states (Kentucky, Maryland, and New Jersey) actually require it. Seven more states encourage sex education in the schools (Delaware, Iowa, Illinois, Kansas, Minnesota, Pennsylvania, and Utah). All other states either do not have a policy dealing expressly with sex education or leave the decision to local jurisdictions. Six states encourage the teaching of birth control (Connecticut, Illinois, Maryland, Michigan, Minnesota, and North Dakota), whereas 3 states actually discourage such instruction (Kansas, Ohio, and Utah). Abortion discussions are encouraged only in Illinois and explicitly discouraged in Connecticut, Louisiana, and Michigan. In 11 states parental consent is necessary for a child's attendance at sex-education classes (Arizona, California, Connecticut, Idaho, Louisiana, Maryland, Michigan, Nebraska, Nevada, New Jersey, and Washington).

Perhaps a bit more emphasis upon sex education in those very states where the fertility rate among teen-agers is high

and/or out-of-wedlock births dominate would turn the tide and solve part of the problem. That bloc of southern states, especially Mississippi and South Carolina, is the prime target.

FAMILY-PLANNING SERVICES

Use of contraception is a difficult variable to analyze because it is such a personal decision, one that need not be reported to any data-collection agency. Map 8.6, therefore, represents only a small aspect of a larger issue—those women who have visited a family-planning clinic. Of all women in the 15–44-year-old group, only 8.7% used these facilities. Data are from surveys conducted by the Alan Guttmacher Institute for 1981. The services included those provided by health departments (40% of all family planning clients), Planned Parenthood affiliates (27%), and hospitals, neighborhood health centers, and community action groups (33%). These largely federally funded programs served a total of 4.6 million women in 1981. Most of the women served had low incomes (80% of all patients served) and were white (69%). Some were teen-agers (33%), and most had never borne a child (60%). Of the women at risk in the low- income group, it is estimated that 39% visited clinics and 19% visited private physicians for contraceptive advice. Of the remainder who did not use clinics or private physicians, some women used prescription contraceptives obtained in an earlier year, some used nonprescription methods purchased in a drugstore, some used alternate methods of birth control such as the rhythm method, and some used no birth control at all.

The rate of use of family-planning services is somewhat distorted because it is calculated from patients served as a percentage of all women in the 15–44 age range. Some of these women are not sexually active, are infertile, are surgically sterilized, are intentionally pregnant, or are trying to become pregnant. It would have been better to standardize the number of women served in clinics by only those women at risk of having an unintended pregnancy, but such data are not available by state.

The map values range from a rate of 3.8% in Utah to 16.7% in Vermont. The upper Midwestern states represent a distinct nonuse area with Illinois and Michigan at the core. Florida, Hawaii, and New Jersey are other states where clinic services are used by small proportions of women of childbearing ages. In contrast, high-use areas are scattered and no particular spatial concentration is evident.

Assuming that low-income women are the target group of these services, comparing use rate with the percentage of families below the poverty level in all states provides an addi-

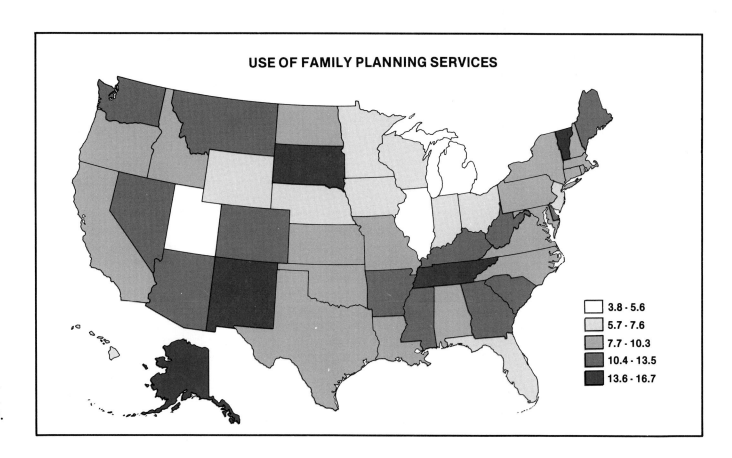

USE OF FAMILY PLANNING SERVICES

Legend:
- 3.8 - 5.6
- 5.7 - 7.6
- 7.7 - 10.3
- 10.4 - 13.5
- 13.6 - 16.7

Map 8.6 Use of family-planning services—women served as a percentage of all women 15 to 44 years of age, 1981. U.S. average is 8.7%.

tional perspective. States that do not use these facilities as much as expected based on poverty level include Alabama, Louisiana, and Mississippi, although all three states have higher-than-average number of services per 100,000 women (10.1, 13.2, and 33.3 respectively). Better public-relations work needs to be done in these states if the clinics are to accomplish their goals. In contrast, women living in Alaska, Arizona, Nevada, and Vermont use family-planning services more than expected based on poverty alone. These states, however, have an above-average rate of services available.

ABORTION

Legalized abortion has been a reality in this country since laws were enacted between 1973 and 1975. Although this well-known method of interrupting an unintended pregnancy finally has been brought out of the backrooms, abortion services are still not uniformly available across the country. Its usage appears to define, in part, the moral character of a region.

Women getting abortions are concentrated in the 20-to-24 age range (35.4% of total abortions) with women aged 15 to 19 the next most common users (28.6%). These women are overwhelmingly white (70.4%) and unmarried (79.4%). Most have had no prior births (57.9%) and no prior induced abortions (67.0%). The majority of abortions occur with less than 9 weeks of gestation (51.5%) and an additional 26.8% fall within the 9-to-10-week range. Three percent of women aged 15 to 44 obtained legal abortions in 1980.

Legalized abortion counts vary widely depending upon who is doing the survey and the variation in state laws related to reporting. The data used here are those collected by the Alan Guttmacher Institute and are based on direct surveys of the providers of abortions. The numbers are greater than those published by the Centers for Disease Control, a group that uses summary information provided by state health departments.

The resident abortion rate, or the total number of abortions obtained by state residents per 1,000 resident women aged 15 to 44, is displayed in Map 8.7. In large part this is a phenomenon belonging to the populous coastal areas. Parts of the Northeast (with the exception of Connecticut and Rhode Island), Florida, and parts of the West coast all have high rates. New York and California have the highest rate at 43.6 abortions per 1,000 women. Large parts of the upper Midwest, Plains states, border South, and intermontane West have relatively few abortions. Utah has the lowest rate (12.0), followed closely by North Dakota, South Dakota, and West Virginia. The highs in the pattern are not strictly urban-related as, for example, Illinois and Texas have only average rates. States thought to be socially advanced tend to correspond with those areas on the map in the two highest categories. Abortion is avoided in states that are highly Catholic, such as Louisiana or Rhode Island, and in fundamentalist religious areas of the South.

Other factors affecting spatial variation of abortion services include lack of medicaid funding in all but 14 states. In 1977 the Hyde Amendment limited federal funding of abortions and since medicaid is a state–federal venture, states alone must provide the bulk of abortion funds for medicaid-qualifying patients. States providing "medically necessary abortions" to indigent women include Alaska, California, Colorado, Connecticut, Hawaii, Maryland, Massachusetts, Michigan, New Jersey, New York, North Carolina, Oregon, Pennsylvania, and Washington. In most states, therefore, poor women must fund abortions on their own. Some teen-agers may be restricted in obtaining abortions by the parental consent and notification required in seven states (Louisiana, Maryland, Massachusetts, Minnesota, Montana, North Dakota, and Utah). Availability of abortion services, however, is probably more important than legislative constraints in determining geographical variation of abortion.

Availability of abortion services corresponds closely with the actual occurrence of abortions. When travel to another county or state becomes part of the abortion procedure, some women choose to carry an unwanted child to term rather than deal with the hassle. Cost, lack of know-how about finding a nonlocal facility, fear of postabortion problems that require diagnosis and treatment, and the jeopardizing of privacy when a woman must be away from work or home for a relatively long time—all may restrict abortion use. It appears expedient, therefore, that a reasonably dense network of abortion facilities exist if women are to have freedom of reproductive choice. This is especially important to teen-agers and low-income women. As of 1980, 78% of the counties had no abortion services, with 28% of women of reproductive age living in these counties. Large gaps in abortion facilities

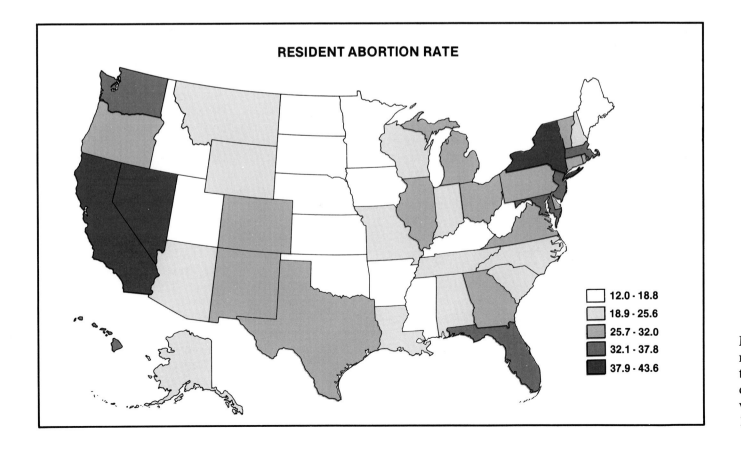

RESIDENT ABORTION RATE

12.0 - 18.8
18.9 - 25.6
25.7 - 32.0
32.1 - 37.8
37.9 - 43.6

Map 8.7 Resident abortion rate—total number of abortions obtained by state residents per 1,000 resident women 15 to 44 years of age, 1980. U.S. average is 29.1.

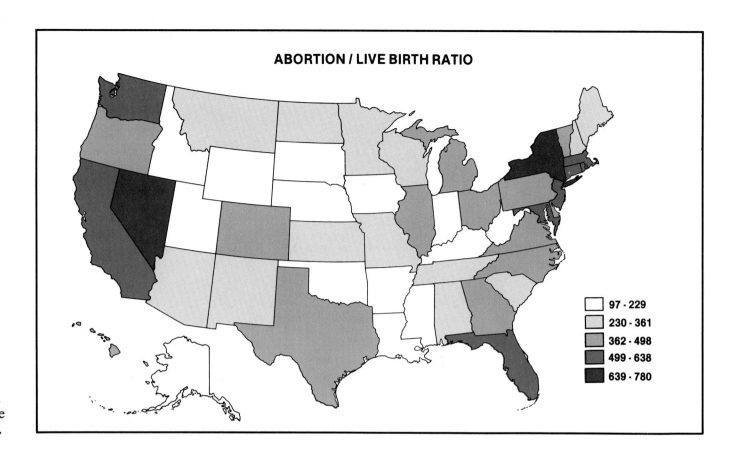

ABORTION / LIVE BIRTH RATIO

97 - 229
230 - 361
362 - 498
499 - 638
639 - 780

Map 8.8   Abortion/live birth ratio—abortions per 1,000 live births, 1980. U.S. ratio is 428.

occur in the middle of the country. Nonmetropolitan areas, in particular, are poorly served.

The percentage of residents obtaining abortions out of state is a standard measure of adequacy of facilities. More than half of the abortion-seekers of South Dakota, West Virginia, and Wyoming elect to go out of state to obtain an abortion. More than one-quarter of such women in Idaho, Indiana, Kentucky, Maryland, Mississippi, and Missouri must leave the state. In 1980, 92.6% of all abortions in the United States were obtained in-state as opposed to only 56.2% in 1972, so obviously some progress is being made about availability of facilities.

The abortion ratio or number of abortions per 1,000 live births (Map 8.8) comes close to addressing the moral issue of abortion. Putting such information in ratio form makes a dramatic statement about abortion, but readers are warned about the confounding nature of ratios. In the present case both Rhode Island and Connecticut have low birthrates and average abortion rates. Together these numbers yield a higher-than-average abortion ratio and overemphasize the situation. With this caveat, the pattern on this map appears similar to that on Map 8.7. New York and Nevada lead the nation with rates of 780 and 697 abortions per 1,000 live

births respectively. Massachusetts and California follow. The District of Columbia (not shown on the map) actually has more abortions than live births.

Rather than pointing a finger at these states and alleging decadence, asking why abortion is used so frequently in some places and not others is more appropriate. After all, even women sexually active for purposes of pleasure would logically avoid pregnancy. Pregnancy just is not compatible with liberated sexual mores. What is it, therefore, in the attitudes of the women who live in these states that leads to such a high incidence of abortion? Maybe abortion in these areas is an accepted means of birth control, albeit an expensive and medically risky one. Maybe the women are poor users of contraceptives through ignorance, religious prejudice, or not wanting to appear prepared for sexual encounters. Maybe these women are shifting for perceived health reasons from oral contraceptives and IUDs to less effective methods of contraception. Any of these undocumented attitudes could produce a high abortion ratio.

In turn, areas with low abortion ratios but high out-of-wedlock percentages provide equal consternation. Mississippi is a prime example. One obvious answer is that abortion facilities may not be available for reasons of distance or cost. Another may be that societal attitudes make abortion an unviable alternative to an unwanted pregnancy. Carrying an unplanned child to term is more acceptable.

Compared with other industrialized countries, the United States has a high concentration of abortion among its young and unmarried, but a much lower abortion rate for those women over 35 because of the wide utilization of contraceptive sterilization in America. U.S. abortion rates are higher than those in Western Europe, but lower than in Eastern Europe where limited contraceptives are available. Canada has a lower legal abortion rate than the United States because of restrictive laws and poor availability of service.

CHAPTER NINE

HEALTH

INTRODUCTION

Women live longer lives than men, have comparatively lower death rates, and constitute small proportions of those dying in a given year. These three facts are the basis for the introductory maps in this chapter. While establishing that women, on the average, live long lives, the maps also suggest that one of the public-policy issues for the future needs to be old, old women, those 85 years and older. As their numbers increase, thanks to life-prolonging methods of modern medicine, so do their requirements for assistance and understanding.

Geographical variation in the cause of death is the focus of the next set of maps. The geography of death provides clues to the epidemiologist who studies the complex causes of disease. Maps of major cardiovascular disease, cancer, and accidents, the three leading causes of death for women, introduce the topic. In addition, refined categories of the same diseases are mapped (diseases of heart, cerebrovascular diseases, arteriosclerosis, breast cancer, and cancer of the reproductive organs) in order to pinpoint spatial variation in morbidity. Next, deaths from cirrhosis of the liver, a surrogate for alcoholism, is presented. The section closes with a map of reported cases of gonorrhea, a sexually transmitted disease. Deaths from this disease are rare, but infection has reached epidemic proportions in some parts of our society.

Finally, the quality of women's health while they are alive is addressed in a set of maps. Because of lack of data by state for everyday health concerns, this part of the atlas is brief. Percentage of the female population that is disabled is the subject of one map. Fragmented behavioral-risk data (overweight, cigarette smoking, and lack of seat-belt use) are also presented as one way of predicting future health trends.

LONGEVITY

This section starts with one of the more positive aspects of death—women are living longer than they ever have before. A woman born in the United States in 1982 is expected to live 78.2 years, 7.4 years longer than her male counterpart. Life expectancy for both sexes has increased dramatically since 1900 when the life expectancy for women was 48.3 years, but the gap in favor of women has widened. Various explanations have been advanced for the male/female discrepancy in longevity including life-style (the inherent risks of male behavior involving alcohol and fast driving), hazardous working conditions for traditional male occupations, a possible biological protection against heart disease for women, increased use of health care among women (more apt to visit a physician), and the beneficial side-effects of being pregnant (better health habits established during this experience delay death later in life).

As women increase their participation in the labor force, many people have predicted that their incidence of stress-related diseases and deaths (especially cardiovascular mortality) will increase as well. So far, though, there is little evidence that work outside the home is contributing to increased female mortality. On the contrary, participation may encourage a longer life because of psychological well-being.

Switching from theoretical longevity projections to real lifetimes enables us to look at regional patterns of death. Three measures are mapped: average lifetime for women, death rate for women in 1978, and female deaths as a percentage of all deaths in 1978.

Spatial comparisons of the average lifetime for women can be derived from Map 9.1. The map is based on well-known data collected by the National Center for Health Statistics directly from death certificates. It represents the average lifetime of all women dying in the 1969–71 period. Death is counted by place of residence, not place of death. Note that even for women dying during this period, the average lifetime was 74.64 years.

Women live the longest in the Plains states and in the West with the notable exceptions of Alaska and Nevada. Another small pocket of longevity occurs in five New England states. In contrast, the average lifetime is shorter in the South and selected portions of the industrial-metropolitan northeast quadrant. The shortest lifetime is in South Carolina (72.29 years), closely followed by Mississippi and Louisiana. Your chances of living a longer life, if you are a woman, are increased substantially by living in North Dakota where the average lifetime is 77.01 years. Minnesota and Hawaii are good second choices. Whether these regional differences can

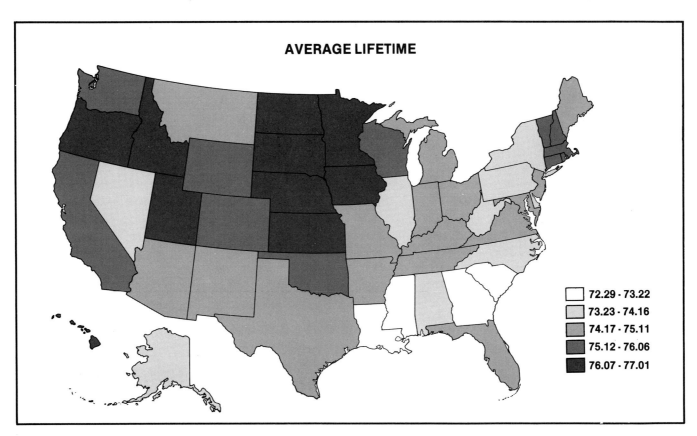

AVERAGE LIFETIME

☐	72.29 - 73.22
☐	73.23 - 74.16
☐	74.17 - 75.11
☐	75.12 - 76.06
☐	76.07 - 77.01

Map 9.1 Average lifetime, of women dying from 1969 to 1971. U.S. average is 74.64 years.

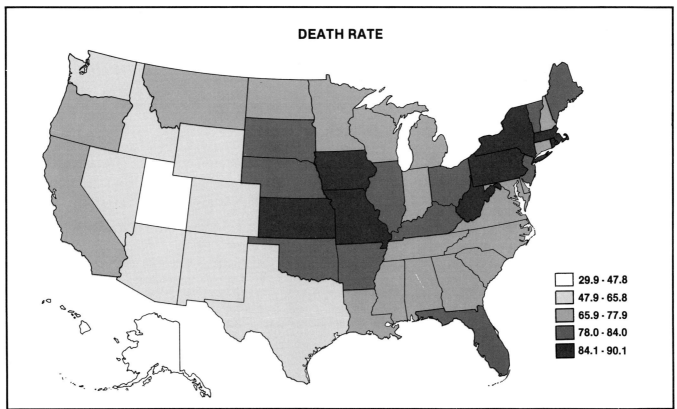

DEATH RATE

☐	29.9 - 47.8
☐	47.9 - 65.8
☐	65.9 - 77.9
☐	78.0 - 84.0
☐	84.1 - 90.1

Map 9.2 Death rate—deaths per 10,000 resident women, 1978. U.S. average is 74.9.

be related to life-style, environmental hazards, and/or the history of health-care systems remains unresolved. As with most problems in medical epidemiology, the ecology is complex and defies simple explanation.

Research shows that among Americans, those of Oriental heritage live the longest whereas whites, blacks, and Hispanics follow with shorter lives in that order. Such an influence explains part of the pattern of shorter lifetimes in the southern half of the country where both blacks and Hispanics constitute larger portions of the female population than they do in other sections. Another indicator of longevity is marital status, especially among older women. Being married promotes good health habits, compliance with medical regimens, and reduces the depression and anxiety associated with a major illness such as cancer. All such forms of psychosocial support tend to add extra years to an older person's life. Reference to the map of married women will confirm some regional similarities in the two variables, although the association is not absolute. Since these maps represent two different populations of women, caution should be exercised in any comparison.

The crude death rate per 10,000 resident women is portrayed for 1978 in Map 9.2. No estimate is available for the number of women living in each state at midyear 1978, so the 1980 census figure has been used as a standardizing measure instead. The average death rate is 74.9 per 10,000 women. Interpreted another way this means that .7% of the females in this country died in 1978 for a total of 872,498 deaths. For the same time period, the death rate for men was 95.8 (1,055,290 deaths).

The death rate is particularly high in the middle of the Midwest and in part of the Northeast. The state with the highest death rate is Pennsylvania at 90.1 followed by Missouri at 89.0. In general a continuous belt of high rates extends from the Plains (South Dakota through Oklahoma) eastward to Maine. Florida is an outlier. Connecticut, Indiana, and New Hampshire, however, form oases of "averageness."

Low areas of death rates extend throughout the West with an irregular shape from Washington to Texas to Arizona enclosing a consolidated area of low rates. Alaska, at 29.9 deaths per 10,000 women, and Hawaii, at 38.6, represent the lowest values.

A reasonable question posed by this map is the relationship of the overall death rate of women to the age structure of females in a state. Since the death rate increases progressively with each age group (the death rate among young girls from birth to 4 years of age is an exception to this generalization), one could logically expect that areas of the country with a high median age (indicating more older women and/or lack of young women) would also have high death rates.

The expected relationship of death rate with median age of the female population is maintained in most states. Alaska and Utah are good examples of low median age and low death rate, whereas New York and Pennsylvania are good examples of high death rates and high median age. Some notable exceptions occur. Mississippi and South Dakota have more deaths than expected based on the age of the population. Louisiana and Nebraska exhibit the same relationship, but to a lesser extent. Possibly socioeconomic conditions in the two southern states cause premature deaths. Possibly racial or ethnic factors contribute to the discrepancy in the other two states. In contrast, Nevada has fewer deaths than expected based on the median age of its female population. Connecticut, Maryland, North Carolina and Virginia exhibit similar trends. Florida has the same relationship, but to an even lesser extent. Here the unexpected becomes even more puzzling because Florida's women have the highest median age in the country (36.7 years), as would be expected in a retirement mecca.

Putting the information from the two maps together and synthesizing past average lifetimes with current death rates, it appears that Hawaii, Idaho, and Utah would be good places in which to be born, reared, and reside if you are interested in a long life. New York, Pennsylvania, and West Virginia are poor choices for a woman.

The third map in this series emphasizes that women do not die as frequently as men even though there are more women in the total population. Nowhere on Map 9.3 does the percentage of 1978 deaths attributed to women exceed that of men. The U.S. average, in fact, is 45.3%. Women approach death parity in the Northeast with Massachusetts the leader at 47.8% (53.4% of this state's population is women). An intermittent band for above-average values extends from Kansas to New Hampshire. On the other hand, the intermontane West plus Alaska and Hawaii are the places where female deaths constitute a low percentage of all deaths. Alaska has the lowest value at 33.4% whereas women there are 47.0% of the population.

A close relationship exists between female deaths as a percentage of all deaths and women as a percentage of the population. For example, Alaska has exceptionally low percentages of both variables. Conversely, Massachusetts, New York, and Rhode Island have exceptionally high values for percentage of deaths and percentage of the population. The interesting states to examine are those that deviate from the expected in the proposed relationship. Kansas has a much higher proportion of female deaths than expected; so do California, Colorado, New Hampshire, and Vermont. In all of these state the median age among females is average and, thus, overloading of the population in the higher age categories does not explain the unexpected distribution. At the oppo-

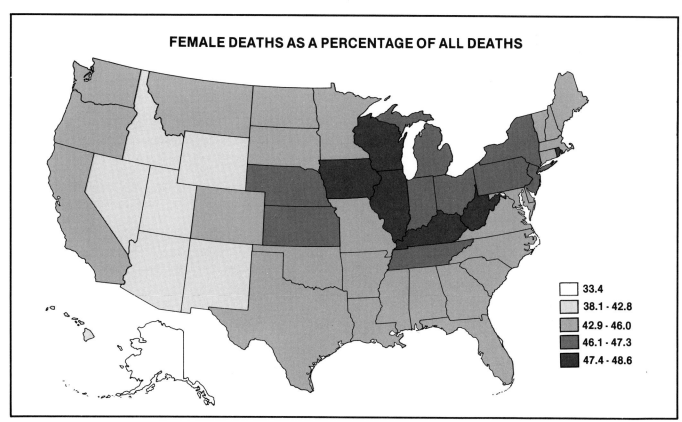

FEMALE DEATHS AS A PERCENTAGE OF ALL DEATHS

☐	33.4
☐	38.1 - 42.8
▨	42.9 - 46.0
▨	46.1 - 47.3
■	47.4 - 48.6

Map 9.3   Female deaths as a percentage of all deaths, 1978. U.S. average is 45.3%.

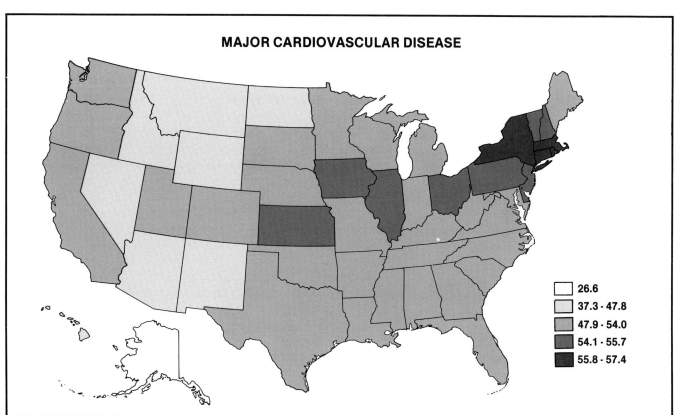

MAJOR CARDIOVASCULAR DISEASE

☐	26.6
☐	37.3 - 47.8
▨	47.9 - 54.0
▨	54.1 - 55.7
■	55.8 - 57.4

Map 9.4   Major cardiovascular disease, as a percentage of all causes of death, 1978. U.S. average is 53.2%.

site extreme, Alabama, Florida, and Mississippi have a lower proportion of female deaths than expected. So do Arkansas and Tennessee.

These three maps should raise the reader's awareness of elderly women in our society. Women's lifetimes are being extended, their death rates are declining, and in all parts of the country women do not die at as high a rate as do men. Even among older women, death rates have declined substantially. For example, in 1940 the crude death rate per 1,000 females was 33.9 for women 65 to 69. By 1980, this rate had improved to 17.2. For women 85 and over the 1940 figure was 227.6, but by 1980 it had declined to 147.5. Rates for men improved over the same time period, but the lower death rate always belongs to women. From 1940 through 1960 the ratio of male deaths to female deaths for people over 85 approached unity (lowest ratio was 1.06 in 1952, 1954, and 1955). Since 1960 the gap has expanded, however, so that in 1980 the mortality-sex ratio was 1.27 for even this most elderly group. In 1980 women constituted 69% of this 85-and-over group, totaling 1.6 million women. It has been estimated that 1 out of 14 people in the United States by the year 2000 will be a woman 65 or older. It is time we take this group of people, their contributions, and the problems they pose very seriously.

Much of the rethinking involving aged women will involve health care. Many physical and emotional problems are readily attributed to postmenopausal syndrome or to senility and thus these two topics have been the focus of much research. There are other topics, however. Osteoporosis, for example, has enjoyed recent attention in the press. Decrease in bone mass becomes a serious problem for one out of four white women as increasing brittleness leads to slow-to-heal fractures and bedridden status. Traditionally this condition has been pretreated by estrogen therapy following menopause. Because of the connections between estrogen use and endometrial cancer, however, this practice is being reviewed by the medical community. Exercise and calcium supplements are two alternate therapies. Women who are now elderly led relatively sedentary lives in their younger years; women who are young now lead more active lives and perhaps their habits of exercise will carry through to old age.

CAUSE OF DEATH

The leading cause of death among women is major cardiovascular disease (Map 9.4) followed by malignant neoplasms (Map 9.5) and accidents (Map 9.6). These maps are based on 1978 data compiled by the National Center for Health Statistics as part of an annual compendium of vital statistics. Causes of death follow an international classification of diseases (ICD). The variable mapped in each case is the percentage of all female deaths in a state attributed to a given disease. Of the 872,498 female deaths in 1978, 53.2% were from cardiovascular disease, 20.7% from cancer, and 3.6% from accidents. (For males these percentages were, respectively, 47.5, 20.5, and 7.0%.) Remember, of course, that these are relative values, not absolute death rates. What is geographically interesting are the areas of the country that deviate from these nationwide averages. Possible environmental factors then become part of the etiology of a disease.

Major Cardiovascular Disease

Major cardiovascular disease is a large category including various diseases of the heart of which ischemic heart disease (deficient blood supply) is only one. Cerebrovascular disease (stroke) and arteriosclerosis (blockage of arteries) are included as well. Map 9.4, therefore, represents deaths related to failures in the circulatory system, but with varying causes and body locations.

Major cardiovascular disease in the United States is concentrated in the old industrial sections of the Northeast and Midwest, suggesting the traditionally stated urban, stress-related predisposition for the disease. Since Iowa leads the nation with 57.4% of its women dying from cardiovascular disease in 1978, this hypothesized urban relationship is somewhat offset by the fact that 40% of Iowa's female population is rural. Clearly other factors may influence this distribution, including those related to the environment, such as water quality or pollution; socioeconomic conditions such as crowding, age of the population, or ethnic composition; or individual behavior, such as smoking, uncontrolled hypertension, or diet.

The state with the lowest incidence of cardiovascular problems is Alaska with only 26.6% of its women dying from this cause. Note that the exceptionally high numbers of women dying from accidents in this state tend to depress the actual prevalence of the other diseases somewhat. Other low areas of this variable include the intermontane West from Idaho to the Mexican border and Hawaii.

Cancer

Cancer presents a puzzle of map interpretation just as it has presented a puzzle to the medical researcher. This collection of diseases affecting different body sites has been collapsed into one general heading for purposes of this map (Map 9.5). Cancer, the second leading killer in the United

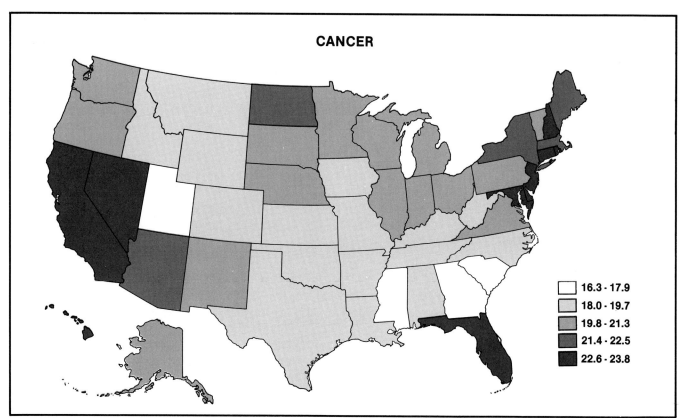

CANCER

16.3 - 17.9
18.0 - 19.7
19.8 - 21.3
21.4 - 22.5
22.6 - 23.8

Map 9.5   Cancer, as a percentage of all causes of death, 1978. U.S. average is 20.7%.

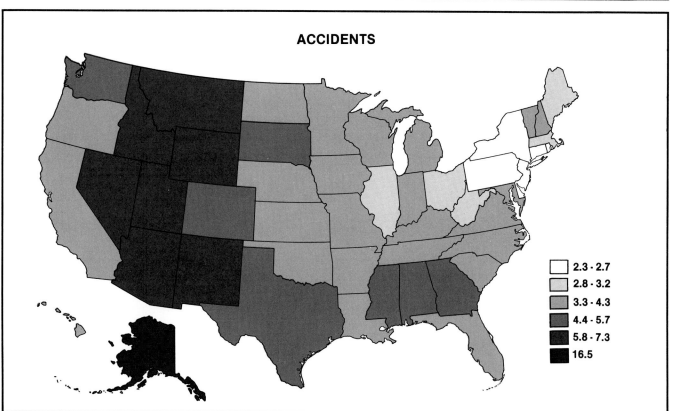

ACCIDENTS

2.3 - 2.7
2.8 - 3.2
3.3 - 4.3
4.4 - 5.7
5.8 - 7.3
16.5

Map 9.6   Accidents, as a percentage of all causes of death, 1978. U.S. average is 3.6%.

States, claimed 180,995 female lives in 1978. Cancer is a puzzle because its causes are multifactorial involving interaction among environmental, genetic, and life-style variables. It is extremely difficult to sort out causative agents for a disease that takes a long time to develop.

The map pattern of cancer is marked by coastal concentrations: specifically the California–Nevada–Hawaii, Florida, and Northeast Seaboard regions. The highest value in the nation is Hawaii with 23.8% of its deaths due to some form of cancer. Rhode Island and New Hampshire follow closely behind. Although there appears to be some association with densely settled, urban areas of the country, the generalization does not hold for all cases. There is, for example, an anomaly in North Dakota.

The area of low concentration of cancer forms a wedge running through the intermontane West from Idaho through Colorado then opening up gradually to include the whole South from Texas to Virginia (excluding Florida). The lowest value in the nation is Mississippi at 16.3%. It forms the core of a particularly low pocket in the South. Another especially low value is represented by Utah.

Utah, because of its uniquely health-conscious population, has been examined in detail by researchers. The state is 70% Mormon, a religion whose church doctrine forbids the consumption of tobacco, alcohol, coffee, and tea. Although these precepts are adhered to by perhaps only half of church followers, the concentration of nonsmokers and nonimbibers is enough to present an interesting case study for epidemiologists. In addition to the above recommendations, the church also suggests a nutritious diet with wholesome grains and fruits, moderation in the consumption of meat, and strict moral standards regarding premarital and extramarital sexual relations. Clean, straight-arrow living? Yes, but the rewards are dramatic. The state has low cancer mortality for all body sites, not just those previously tied to smoking and drinking. Mortality rates are especially low for cancers of the buccal cavity (mouth), esophagus, colon, rectum, lungs, and bladder. This suggests a life-style that produces low risks to cancer and this is what intrigues the researchers.

Cancer is uncontrolled new growth in the body that destroys living tissue. Malignant tumors are characterized by a high rate of cell growth, cells that are immature and have no body-maintenance function, and, in later stages of the disease, extension of abnormal growth to other parts of the body perhaps far removed from the original site. Chances of acquiring cancer increase with age and the highest death rate is among elderly women. Among women the leading body sites for cancer are the breast (34,329 deaths in 1978), colon and rectum (27,573), lung (24,080), uterus (10,842), and ovary (10,651). Excluding the cancers related to gender, mor-

tality rates for the remaining cancers are similar for both sexes except for lung cancer. Lung cancer is still a bigger killer for men than it is for women (almost three times as many deaths) despite increased cigarette smoking by women. Deaths from lung cancer among women have increased steadily during recent years, however. Two categories of cancer that are gender-specific will be examined later in more detail—cancer of the breast and of the ovaries and uterus.

Accidents

The third leading cause of death among women is accidents (Map 9.6); in 1978 this category was responsible for a total of 31,680 deaths or 3.6% of all female deaths. (Among men this category contributed 73,881 deaths or 7.0% of all male deaths.) Approximately half of the deaths are transport-oriented and, of these, motor-vehicle accidents accounted for 14,272 female deaths in 1978. Other major causes of accidental deaths are accidental falls with 6,509 deaths in 1978, followed by accidents caused by fire or flame (2,377 deaths), drowning or submersion (1,050), and accidental poisoning by drugs or medicine (870). Although neither are considered accidents in the ICD scheme, deaths from suicide (7,106) and homicide (4,594) add some perspective for comparison.

Accidents, as a percentage of all female deaths, dominate in the western half of the country with the exception of California, Hawaii, and Oregon. An additional region of high incidence of accidental death exists in the three contiguous southern states of Alabama, Georgia, and Mississippi. The highest value in the country by far belongs to Alaska with 16.5% of its female deaths attributed to accidents. This explains, in part, Alaska's consistently low ranking in the other diseases. The next highest value of 7.3% belongs to Wyoming.

Accidents form a low proportion of all deaths of females in the northeastern corner of the country. Rhode Island has the lowest proportion at 2.3% followed by New York.

The geography of age may contribute to an understanding of the map of accidents. The accidental death rate increases proportionally with age for women age 30 and older. Below this age, however, accidental deaths constitute the highest death rates among all causes. (Accidents are surpassed by pneumonia, however, as the leading cause of death among female babies under 1 year). Exploration, fast life-style, testing oneself, desire for independence: All these characteristics of adolescents could be equated with risk-associated situations such as fast driving, alcohol and/or drugs, limits of endurance, and confrontations with peers. In addition, increased risk-taking behavior may characterize some regions; the strong association of degree of urbanization and proportionally low accidental deaths, for example. People who spend more time outdoors for occupational or recreational reasons, as they must by choice and necessity in the rural areas of this country, are put in more life-threatening situations than someone whose main safety concern of the day is crossing the street. The West is a more hostile environment to women and accidents there have environmental connotations associated with greater physical risks.

The percentage of deaths attributed to motor-vehicle accidents (1.6% for females, 3.6% for males) creates a pattern similar to that of accidental deaths and thus explains some of the variation in the accident variable. Motor-vehicle deaths account for 45.1% of all accidental deaths of women with individual state percentages as high as 67.6 in Hawaii and 65.2 in Nevada. These two states either have notoriously bad drivers or do exceptionally well at eliminating accidental deaths from other causes to warrant such a ranking. Arizona and New Mexico have similarly bad patterns. At the other end of the scale Vermont has a low percentage of motor-vehicle deaths compared with all accidental deaths (26.7%). So does Massachusetts.

Age and Cause of Death

The death rate for all women was 778.3 per 100,000 women for the year 1978. Deaths from the major cardiovascular diseases (414.2) exceed those from malignant neoplasms (161.4). Accidents followed distantly in third place (28.3). When deaths by age categories are examined, slightly different patterns emerge, patterns that should promote caution in interpreting the preceding maps.

For the 25–29 age category, for example, the overall death rate was much lower than the average, only 72.5. The death rate for accidents (19.5) was almost twice that of cancer (9.9), the next most common cause. Among accidents, motor-vehicle deaths (13.3) were the most prominent and among malignant neoplasms, reproductive organs (1.7) were the most common site. The third leading cause of death for this age group is suicide (7.9). Note the lack of cardiovascular deaths.

Skipping 20 years to the 45–49 category, the ordering changes. With a death rate at 341.4, the most common cause of death was malignant neoplasms (135.3) with the breast (41.4) and respiratory system (24.3) leading body sites. Major cardiovascular diseases were the next leading cause (83.9) with death from actual heart attacks constituting a large part (25.0). Cerebrovascular diseases and accidents tied for third place (19.5).

Again augmenting the age category by 20 years, the death rate among women 65–69 increased to 1,685.2. Here heart problems and cancer changed order, with heart problems 1.5 times the death rate for cancer (the reverse was true in the previous age category). Deaths from major cardiovascular diseases (785.6) increased significantly as did acute myocardial infarction (286.4). Malignant neoplasms, of course, also increased (520.9), but digestive organs (143.2) became the most common cancer site. Cancers of the breast (89.9) and respiratory system (87.7) followed. Finally diabetes mellitus (50.6) became the third leading cause of death in this age category.

Among women 85 and over the death rate climbed to 13,541.2 (i.e., 13.5% of them died in 1978). Major cardiovascular diseases (9,859.2) became the dominant cause of death at 8.7 times the rate for cancer. Deaths from malignant neoplasms (1,139.3) were led by cancer of the digestive organs (459.2) and breast (157.2). The third leading cause of death in this advanced-age category was pneumonia (650.3), a side-effect of many debilitating conditions.

Diseases of Heart

When the large category of cardiovascular diseases is subdivided into diseases of the heart, cerebrovascular diseases, and arteriosclerosis, other geographical patterns of concentration emerge. This suggests, of course, that combining categories of disease according to body system obscures some of the interesting regional variations inherent in a more refined data set.

Deaths from diseases of the heart (Map 9.7) are concentrated again in the northeastern quadrant of the country, but the high-incidence area is smaller than on the previous map of major cardiovascular diseases. Rhode Island is the state with the highest proportion of women dying from this disease (43.4%). New York and Illinois follow with 42.4 and 42.2% respectively. The metropolitan corridor from New York to Philadelphia, the historical location of high death-rates from heart disease, appears to maintain its reputation, but county-level data are necessary to examine this phenomenon more closely.

The lowest value in the country for diseases of the heart is Alaska at 17.2% followed by New Mexico and Nevada. In general, the intermontane West from the Canadian border to the Mexican border represents a low trough of heart disease. Alabama and Hawaii are additional outliers.

The category of diseases represented on Map 9.7 includes rheumatic fever, hypertensive heart disease, ischemic heart disease (of which acute myocardial infarction, chronic ischemic heart disease, and angina pectoris are a part), chronic disease of the endocardium, congestive heart failure, and a catchall category of all other forms of heart disease. If a patient survives 8 weeks or more following a heart attack, the disease becomes chronic. Death within 8 weeks is classified as acute. Some inaccuracies in exact classification on death certificates may exist, depending upon the information available to the physician (autopsy and/or medical records of patient).

Heart disease is a significant killer, accounting for 38.0% of female deaths in 1978 and 37.7% of male deaths. The good news is that there are overall declines in heart-disease mortality; contributing causes include decreased smoking and dietary intake of fats, improved control of hypertension, increased physical activity, improved medical-emergency services, and better coronary-care units in hospitals. Data from the Framingham study indicate that women may have a biological protection against a major cardiovascular event through the reproductive years. Serum cholestrol levels, for example, are low for women until their later years, suggesting that this advantage lessens at the end of menopause. Women whose spouses have heart disease have double the risk of having heart disease themselves as compared with women whose husbands escaped it. Something that they do together, such as eating, must be the contributing cause.

Cerebrovascular Disease

Cerebrovascular disease (Map 9.8), another subset of major cardiovascular diseases, represents a smaller portion of female deaths—11.7% for the nation as a whole (7.0% for males). Here the map pattern deviates substantially from that on Map 9.3 with very low incidence in the populous Northeast that dominated before. Instead areas of concentration appear in the South and upper Midwest. Georgia has the highest proportion of deaths from this disease (14.9%), followed by Alabama. A lesser concentration appears in the northwestern states of Oregon and Washington.

Alaska again has the lowest proportion of this disease (6.7%). Delaware and Maryland represent other particularly low states. The weakest regions exist in the desert Southwest and the Northeast.

Cerebrovascular disease or stroke includes deaths from cerebral hemorrhage (rupture because of hypertension or defect in the blood vessel resulting in hemorrhage into the brain), cerebral thrombosis (clotting of a diseased blood vessel), and cerebral embolism (blockage by a clot or other fragment from another part of the body). Stroke is a degenerative disease especially prevalent among elderly women. It affects the central nervous system when an episode occurs and, because of its debilitating nature, may precipitate death from pneumonia.

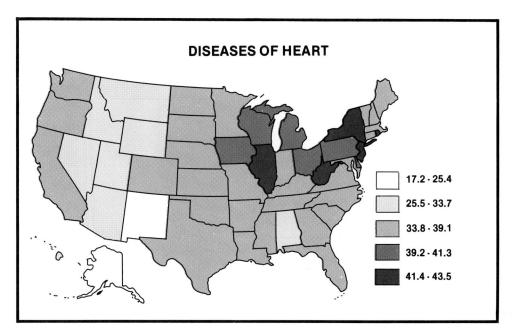

Map 9.7   Diseases of the heart, as a percentage of all causes of death, 1978. U.S. average is 38.0%.

Map 9.8   Cerebrovascular disease, as a percentage of all causes of death, 1978. U.S. average is 11.7%.

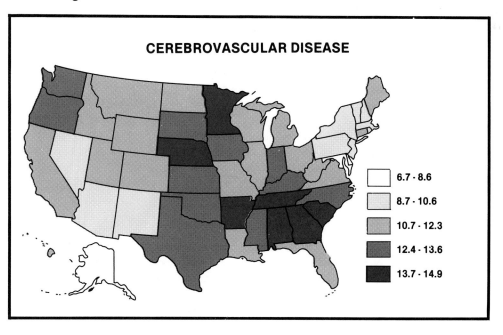

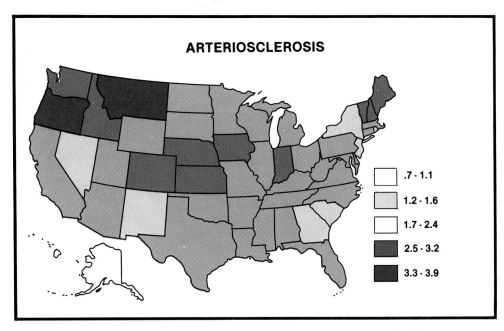

ARTERIOSCLEROSIS

	.7 - 1.1
	1.2 - 1.6
	1.7 - 2.4
	2.5 - 3.2
	3.3 - 3.9

Map 9.9   Arteriosclerosis, as a percentage of all causes of death, 1978. U.S. average is 2.0%.

Arteriosclerosis

Arteriosclerosis (Map 9.9) represents a small portion of major cardiovascular deaths—2.0% for females (1.1 for males). The state with the highest proportion of deaths is Montana at 3.9%. Oregon and New Hampshire follow. Intense areas occur in the four most northwesterly states, an assemblage of middle Plains states, and the far Northeast.

The lowest values for this disease are found in Alaska (.7%) and Hawaii (.8%). States in the next-lowest category are dispersed throughout the country.

Arteriosclerosis is a form of degeneration in the cardio-vascular system involving narrowing and blockage of arteries supplying the heart, brain, and kidneys. What starts out as decreased blood flow can eventually develop into full blockage and death. Narrowing of the arteries simply increases with age as fatty plaques are built up in the arteries. Therefore, in areas where the elderly constitute a large percentage of a population, deaths from this disease would be expected to be high as well. New evidence indicates that proper diet and exercise throughout life may retard the deposition of cholestrol deposits within arteries; hence the disease eventually may be found only among the very oldest, if we all choose to alter our personal habits.

If I lived in Iowa, I would be rather concerned about my cardiovascular health and try to find out what to do to improve it. The proportion of deaths from accidents in the state is average, the deaths from cancer are below average,

but the deaths from major cardiovascular disease are the highest in the nation. Heart problems affect above-average proportions of women in all three diseases portrayed (diseases of heart, cerebrovascular disease, and arteriosclerosis).

Breast Cancer

The focus in this chapter has been upon death, mortality from cancer, whereas it should be emphasized that people do recover from cancer, especially breast cancer, where the 5-year survival rate for localized cases is about 85% for white women and 78% for blacks. These are among the highest survival rates for all cancers in women. The fear of breast cancer, therefore, probably is not a fear of death, but a fear of disfigurement as a modified radical mastectomy (removal of breast and lymph nodes) is still the primary treatment for early symptoms.

One in 13 American women will develop breast cancer sometime in their lives. If you have had it before, your risk of having it again are high. If your mother or sister has had it, your risk is higher. (Recent research suggests that we all should look deeper into the family history for genetic connections than the close relatives of mother and sister.) If you have never given birth, your risk is higher. Nuns, for example, have high breast-cancer rates. If your diet is high in animal fats, your risk is higher. Japanese women have very low breast-cancer rates and their diets are low in animal fats. When these same women moved to the United States, however, and presumably adapted some aspects of a Western diet, their risk for breast cancer became the same as that for other American women, after two or three generations. Higher incidence of breast cancer in affluent countries and among higher economic classes point to the same dietary connection. The high correlation of breast cancer and colon cancer, a disease with a strong dietary connection to animal fat, is further evidence of the potential risk of animal fat in the diet.

Ironically, the overall mortality rate for breast cancer has not changed since the 1930s despite many advances in detection. Early detection is, of course, important in survival rates as it is important to catch the cancer before the lymph nodes become cancerous. The mortality rate has declined, however, among women under 50 whereas it has increased for women over 50. Breast cancer, just like all the diseases mentioned so far, is associated with growing older. The longer she lives, the greater a woman's risk of dying from breast cancer.

Breast cancer exhibits a similar pattern to that of cancer in general (Map 9.10). The percentage of women who died from breast cancer in 1978 is high in Hawaii, Nevada, the northern Midwest, and parts of the Northeast. The highest value in the nation belongs to Connecticut with 5.0%. Nevada follows. Note the small range in values in this map; little variation exists in mortality from breast cancer. Note especially that breast cancer is responsible for only 3.9% of female deaths.

Low areas on the map include large parts of the center of the country as well as the South, without Florida. The lowest values are found in Mississippi, West Virginia, and Wyoming, all at 2.9%.

Research has disclosed a northern predominance of breast cancer among postmenopausal women, but no explanation exists for this effect. The incidence of this disease also increases with German ethnicity and, to a smaller degree, with Scandinavian background, explaining in part the high values in North Dakota and Minnesota where both of these ethnic groups have settled in large numbers. Mortality, in general, increases with urbanization and income, and is inversely related to high birthrates. Premenopausal women with breast cancer are distributed uniformly across the country. Breast cancer in this age group is associated with ovarian cancer mortality.

Ovarian and Uterine Cancer

Cancer of reproductive organs (ovarian and uterine cancer), exhibits a strikingly different pattern from those on previous maps (Map 9.11). The 3.4% value for Alaska is considerably above the next highest value of 3.0% in New Hampshire. Since this disease has an even smaller range in values than breast cancer and represents only 2.6% of deaths, the regional variation on this map should not be overly stressed. The lowest value is in Wyoming with 1.6%, considerably below the rest of the country. Louisiana, Mississippi, Nevada, and Vermont exhibit low values as well. The remainder of the country falls in the middle category balanced about the mean. Since this category of diseases includes ovarian cancer and two main forms of uterine cancer, all with different risk factors, untangling this map becomes especially difficult.

Ovarian cancer (approximately half of the deaths in the reproductive-organ category in 1978) is three times as common among white women as it is among black women. Additional risks exist for women who have never borne a child and those with a positive family history of this type of cancer. As stated before, there is a strong association of ovarian cancer with breast cancer. Mortality from ovarian cancer is rising.

In contrast, mortality from uterine cancer is declining mostly because of the Papanicolaou test used in screening

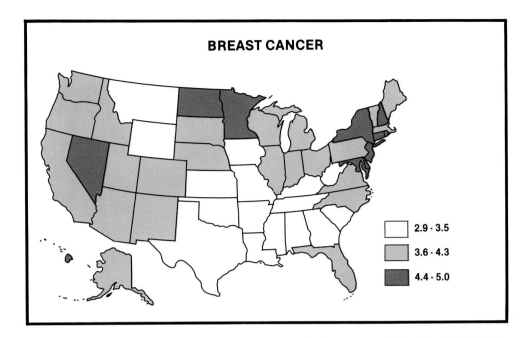

Map 9.10   Breast cancer, as a percentage of all causes of death, 1978. U.S. average is 3.9%.

Map 9.11   Cancer of reproductive organs, as a percentage of all causes of death, 1978. U.S. average is 2.6%.

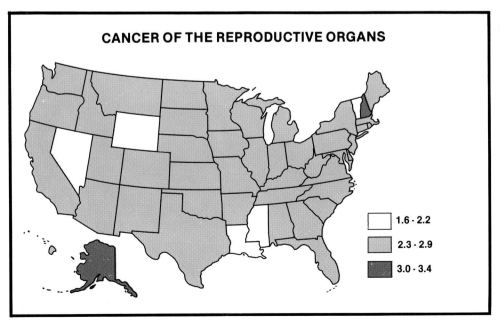

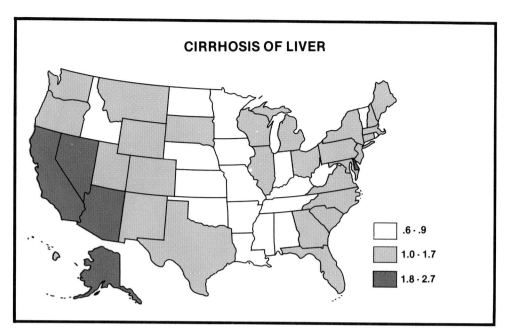

CIRRHOSIS OF LIVER

.6 - .9
1.0 - 1.7
1.8 - 2.7

Map 9.12 Cirrhosis of liver, as a percentage of all causes of death, 1978. U.S. average is 1.2%.

for cervical cancer, a subset of uterine cancer. Although there is controversy within the medical community over the recommended spacing of these tests, frequent tests are definitely recommended if a woman is taking oral contraceptives, using estrogen therapy, has multiple sexual partners, or has pelvic abnormalities. Cervical cancer is higher among American Indians, Hispanics, blacks, women in poor urban areas, and those who experienced sexual relations early or who had a number of sex partners. This particular form of cancer is low for women who never married.

Endometrial cancer, another form of uterine cancer, is uncommon among premenopausal women. Persistent estrogen secretion appears to be the predisposing factor. Such a condition arises out of late menopause, menstrual irregularities, no children, or low parity. The disease is less common among black women than whites. Estrogen-users for at least 3.5 years are more likely to develop the disease as are those women who are obese.

Cirrhosis of Liver

Cirrhosis of the liver is mapped not because it is a major killer of women (only 1.2% of all deaths), but because it is a surrogate for alcoholism (Map 9.12). The disease is degenerative and often associated with alcohol abuse. During the 1970-to-1980 period, 40% of all deaths attributed to cirrhosis of the liver were positively linked to alcohol, but it is esti-

mated that 90 to 95% of these deaths could be linked to alcohol. Not all alcoholics die of cirrhosis of the liver, of course, as alcohol abuse is a risk factor for other diseases as well.

Cirrhosis deaths are prevalent in the far southwestern part of the country with Alaska and Delaware forming additional centers. The highest value is in Nevada with 2.7% of its deaths attributed to this cause; Alaska follows with 2.5%. The lowest value of .6% belongs to Arkansas and Kansas. These states form the core of that middle-of-the-country trough of low values spatially associated with Bible Belt mentality and clean living. Variation on this map is minimal, however, and interpretation possibilities somewhat limited.

Have you ever known a female drunk? Differences in rules of alcohol usage still exist in America for males and females. It is all right for a woman to have a drink, but never to indulge in excess in public. Historically, intoxication was tied to a woman's impaired ability to care for a child, her primary role in life. It was also linked to the loss of sexual inhibitions and hence wanton public behavior. These societal attitudes are what has driven many women into being quiet drinkers in the confines of their own homes or with friends.

The reasons behind alcohol abuse are complex and addiction is even more a mystery. Women with higher socioeconomic status, more education, and jobs tend to do more drinking. Two-thirds of all women have at least an occasional drink. Drinking has strong negative sanctions among Mexican-American women, however, and thus abstainers are more likely to be found in the Southwest. Religious groups such as Mormons, Seventh-day Adventists, and Southern Baptists also promote abstinence. Of the estimated 10 million alcoholics in this country, one-third are women. This proportion is increasing especially among teen-agers. Data from a behavioral-risk study, which will be discussed later in this chapter, indicate 4.2% of women in the sample were chronic heavy drinkers whose alcoholic intake exceeded 56 drinks per month. Acute heavy drinking with five or more drinks per occasion once in the past month affected 11% of females. Drinking and driving (driving after having too much to drink at least once in the past month) involved 2.5% of the female respondents. In all three consumption situations female median values were exceeded by that of males. In addition, all of these negative drinking habits for women reach a peak for the group between 18 and 34.

What distinguishes female drinking patterns from that of males, aside from the greater prevalence of male alcoholics, is polyaddictions among women. Psychotropic drugs are often given by physicians to combat the same symptoms that led to drinking in the first place. Health-care changes in traditionally male-oriented treatment centers and outpatient services need to be made to accommodate the newly out-of-the-

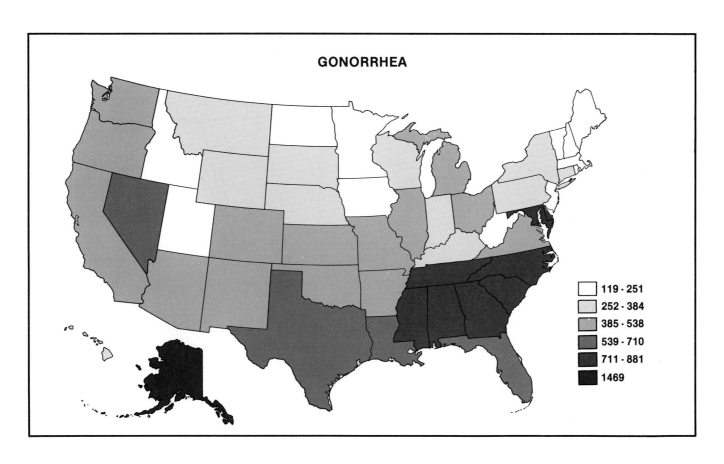

GONORRHEA

☐	119 - 251
☐	252 - 384
☐	385 - 538
☐	539 - 710
☐	711 - 881
☐	1469

Map 9.13 Gonorrhea—reported cases per 100,000 women 15 years and older, 1979. U.S. average is 452.

closet female client. Finally, the medical community has advised no drinking during pregnancy. Although the effect upon an unborn baby is not completely documented to date, the risk factors appear serious enough for the warning to be issued.

Sexually Transmitted Diseases

Gonorrhea rarely is a cause of death, so in that sense this disease does not belong in a discussion of mortality. Since it ranks first among reported communicable diseases in the United States, however, perhaps it should have special consideration. Gonorrhea is one of many forms of sexually transmitted diseases (STD), or venereal diseases. In 1979 there were 413,195 reported cases of gonorrhea among women, but only 5,692 cases of primary and secondary syphilis, another STD. Male syphilis rates are three times those for women, but male gonorrhea rates are only 1.4 times those for women. Herpes II, the subject of much recent attention, is not classified as a reported disease, and therefore, no data are collected by the Centers for Disease Control.

Gonorrhea (Map 9.13) is expressed as a rate of reported civilian cases in 1979 per 100,000 women 15 years and over. Known military cases are excluded. The CDC estimate that only half of all cases are reported, so the reader should be aware of possible underrepresentation. The state with the highest rate is Alaska at 1,469, substantially above the next highest values of 881 found in Mississippi and 873 in Alabama. The high concentration of this disease in the South is unmistakable. Border South states and Virginia are not included in the high-incidence region, but Maryland and Delaware are. Nevada is a western anomaly.

The lowest rate in the country belongs to New Hampshire (119) with Massachusetts trailing at 136 reported cases per 100,000 women. These states form the core of a distinct northeastern low area. In general, rates are low across the northern half of the country with other predominantly low rates in the northern Plains and Mormon states of Utah and Idaho.

Incidentally, the geographical pattern for syphilis is similar to that for gonorrhea. The highest rates belong to Louisiana, Mississippi, and Georgia in that order (23 to 20). The rate for Alaska, in contrast to that for gonorrhea, is quite low at 3 reported cases per 100,000 women. North Dakota and Vermont had no reported syphilis cases in 1979. Maine, Nebraska, South Dakota, and Utah had exceptionally low rates as well.

Women who live in large cities have rates for gonorrhea higher than those in small cities or rural areas. As expected, based on population, Los Angeles, New York, and Chicago have the greatest number of reported cases of the disease. Baltimore and Atlanta, however, have more reported cases than expected based upon population whereas, among the very largest cities, both San Diego and Phoenix have lower rates than expected.

The biggest problem for women contracting gonorrhea is the complications of PID (pelvic inflammatory disease). If improperly treated, permanent sterility is the result in 15 to 40% of patients. Gonorrhea has also been associated with arthritis in women.

Increases in sexual contacts as a result of our permissive society has been blamed for the high, maybe even epidemic, rates of gonorrhea, especially among adolescents. Relatively recent efforts to screen high-risk populations and encourage identification of sexual partners (both aimed at reducing the infectious reservoir) have necessarily also increased the number of reported cases among women. All of the increase cannot, therefore, be blamed on loose morals.

WELL-BEING

Women may be living longer than men, but their lives apparently are not healthier. Using standard measures of morbidity and medical-care patterns, women have more illnesses, more disabilities, make more visits to physicians, and are hospitalized at higher rates. Females, for example, averaged 5.2 physician-visits per year whereas males had 4.0 visits (based on 1981 household interviews of the noninstitutionalized population). Dental visits were 1.8 for females as opposed to 1.5 for males. Female short-stay hospital episodes accounted for 51.8% of the total. In addition, women had more restricted-activity days per year, more bed-disability days, and more workdays lost (average 5.3 per year).

Morbidity data are not as precise as mortality data, which are collected through an intricate system of local, state, and federal agencies. Death, after all, is a verifiable event, although determining the cause may be complicated. Only a few, small-sample surveys have ventured into the domain of everyday health problems and addressed such personal topics as frequency of colds or hours of sleep required. Many of the trends published in the popular literature are based, in fact, on estimates derived from small samples. Survey information, moreover, is full of bias and frustrates even the most

meticulous researcher. For example, are a woman's days off from work related to her health or to that of her children? Are more physician-visits among women a result of their greater readiness to seek health care or a result of more health problems? No country-wide data differentiated by sex exist at the state level for health variables. Both diary and recall information have limitations and large samples are needed to establish regional patterns.

Disability

One measure of health that is available at the state level is self-identified disability status. The 1980 census asked whether a person had a physical, mental, or health condition which had lasted for 6 or more months and which limited the amount or kind of work they could do at a job. Health problems can include those involving seeing, hearing, or speech, but pregnancy or a temporary health problem (such as a broken bone) are not in the definition. Map 9.14 presents the 8% of women who do not have full occupational choice because of some handicap. Only women 16 to 64 are included; institutionalized women are not. The work-disability category contains 9.0% of all males.

The highest value on the map belongs to Arkansas, where 11.8% of the women considered themselves disabled. Similar values exist in Mississippi and West Virginia. The southeastern corner of the country, with the exception of Virginia, represents a concentrated area of high disability status for women. Michigan and Oregon are additional above-average states. Low socioeconomic status may be a partial explaining variable.

Alaska has the lowest value in the nation with 5.0% of its women in this category. Hawaii, Wyoming, and North Dakota follow closely behind with other low values. The relative absence of disability status is apparent in the upper Midwest and Rocky Mountain states.

Work disability is a confounded variable that includes varying degrees of activity restrictions; analysis becomes difficult with the amount of information presented here. Regional variations are likely to exist in the perception and reporting of disability status. The success of rehabilitation programs is relevant to the area pattern as well. Although it is possible that disabled people migrate to more sensitive communities with adequate facilities (for example, the exemplary work in Berkeley, Calif.), no information exists. Oregon may represent one of these enlightened magnet states.

The census also asked which people were actually prevented from working because of a disability. This more restricted category involved 4.7% of the female population 16

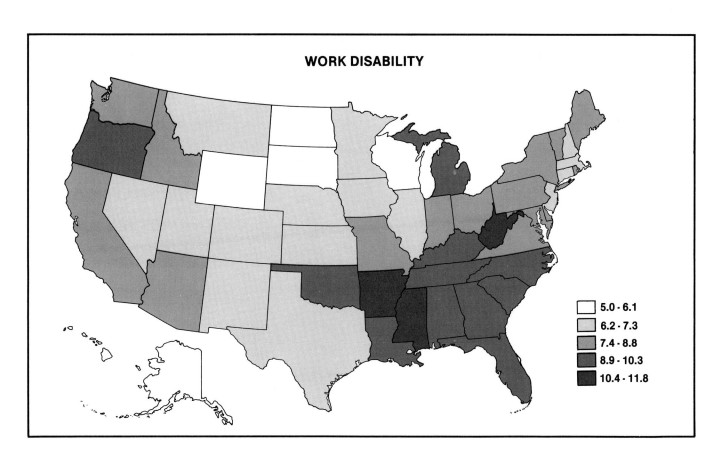

WORK DISABILITY

☐	5.0 - 6.1
☐	6.2 - 7.3
☐	7.4 - 8.8
☐	8.9 - 10.3
☐	10.4 - 11.8

Map 9.14 Work disability, as a percentage of females 16 to 64 years of age, 1980. U.S. average is 8.0%.

to 64 years of age (4.0% of the male population). The regional associations are similar: the southern and border states of Alabama, Kentucky, Louisiana, Mississippi, Tennessee, and West Virginia have the highest proportion of women in this category; the western and upper Midwestern states of Alaska, Minnesota, South Dakota, Utah, and Wyoming have the lowest proportion who were severely disabled.

Behavioral-risk Factors

Preventive health is the new watchword. This emphasis upon preventive rather than therapeutic measures to deter disease and untimely death also encompasses the assessment of personal health habits. Certain factors have been linked through research with the leading causes of death. Age, sex, and genetic background are factors that cannot be modified, but personal habits that contribute to primary diseases can.

In response to this new interest in preventive medicine, the Centers for Disease Control have recently surveyed small samples of people in selected states to determine their proclivity toward a set of behavioral-risk factors: chronic and acute

use of alcohol, drinking and driving, sedentary life-style, uncontrolled hypertension, cigarette smoking, being overweight, and use of seat belts. Sample sizes range from 456 to 5,480 respondents per state and a random digit-dialing telephone survey was used. Responses are self-reported and, hence, errors in assessment are inevitable. Three of the eight behavioral-risk factors plus a composite map are presented here. Not all states are represented because of a lack of data and variations in survey questions.

Being overweight is one of the behavioral-risk factors receiving lots of popular attention in the press. Survey respondents' reported height and weight were compared with ideal weights from the 1959 Metropolitan Life Insurance Company tables. If weight was 120% or greater than ideal weight (mid-value of medium-frame person), then that woman was placed in the overweight category. The result is Map 9.15, displaying the states arrayed around a 22.6% median value for women. The highest percentage is found in Maine with 32.3% of its female population estimated to be in the overweight category based on the sample results. Florida and the District of Columbia have similar high values. Of the states east of the Mississippi, only Delaware, New Hampshire, and Virginia do not

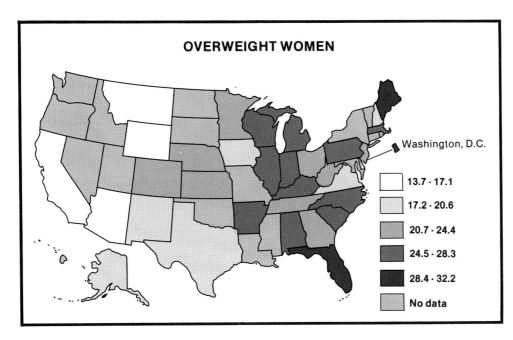

OVERWEIGHT WOMEN

Washington, D.C.

	13.7 - 17.1
	17.2 - 20.6
	20.7 - 24.4
	24.5 - 28.3
	28.4 - 32.2
	No data

Map 9.15 Overweight women—percentage of female respondents at 120% or greater of ideal weight, 1980–82. U.S. median is 22.6%.

Map 9.16 Cigarette smoking—percentage of female respondents who are currently smokers, 1980–82. U.S. median is 28.5%.

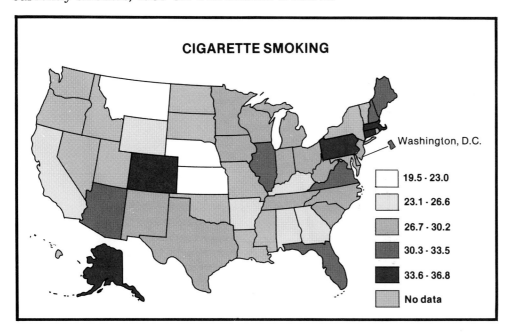

CIGARETTE SMOKING

Washington, D.C.

	19.5 - 23.0
	23.1 - 26.6
	26.7 - 30.2
	30.3 - 33.5
	33.6 - 36.8
	No data

have average or above-average percentages of their women in this category. The phenomenon, therefore, has a strong regional association with the East. In contrast, the lowest value of 13.7% represents California. Arizona has the next lowest value at 15.3%. These states are just two among many in the below-average western area.

One theory to explain the map pattern involves the growing obsession about body size and appearance among American women. Much of this movement is perpetuated by the Hollywood image and it comes as no surprise, therefore, that California with its special life-style has a low percentage of its women in this category. Possibly California is but part of a larger regional association of devotion to health, exercise, and good nutrition.

The overweight woman, among other factors, has not maintained a balance of exercise and food intake. Are there many areas of the country, therefore, especially prone to a sedentary behavior? Women who claimed a combined low level of activity from exercise, work, and recreation on the above survey were classified as having sedentary life-styles. Connecticut, with 27.9% of its women in this category, leads the nation in inactivity with Maine, Wisconsin, Minnesota, and Washington, D.C., following in that order. Long winters and, thus, seasonal lack of exercise opportunities may account for some of the variation in patterns of overweight. Calorie consumption would be another variable to examine, but appropriate dietary data do not exist by state. Research provides some additional clues. The fat woman is most likely to be in her middle years between 45 and 64, living below the poverty level, and black rather than white. Obviously the explanation of this overweight spatial pattern is complex. More information about life-styles would help; so would overweight data for more states.

Obesity is a health-risk factor because it puts extra strain on the body systems, especially the cardiovascular system, and aggravates most health conditions. Control of weight is, however, not a simple matter, and societal influences are profound. The point made here is that being overweight is perhaps more acceptable in certain eastern parts of this country just because so many of one's peers are in the same condition.

Cigarette smoking, the second of the mapped behavior-risk variables, does not display distinct spatial patterns (Map 9.16). Women who responded that they were currently cigarette smokers form a 28.5% median value for the United States. The highest percentage of smokers is found in Connecticut with 36.8% of its women in this category. Pennsylvania, Colorado, Massachusetts, and Alaska follow in that order. The lowest value in the country belongs to the women of Kansas with only 19.5%. Montana and Nebraska follow. The only continuous region, at either end of the scale, is that

Atlas of American Women

above-average area in four New England states. Possibly there are some links of cigarette smoking with stressful, urban environments.

Despite a succession of surgeon general's reports warning that cigarette smoking can lead to lung cancer, women in this country have not abandoned the habit. The percentage of men who smoke has declined faster than the percentage of women. Already the increase in deaths of women from lung cancer has been enormous. Researchers expect lung cancer soon to surpass breast and colon cancer as the leading cancer killer for women. Women are starting to smoke at younger ages and thus they become heavy smokers earlier. The adolescent smoking rate is higher for girls.

The risk is especially great among pregnant women, where cigarette smoking has been shown to retard fetal growth and increase the rate of spontaneous abortion. Women who are smokers and take oral contraceptives significantly increase their chances of heart disease. More respiratory infections, bed-disability days, dental disease, osteoporosis, and skin damage round out the list of probable results of smoking.

Have women opted for equality with men in cigarette smoking as a result of stress and tension associated with their new participation in the labor market? Has advertising by cigarette companies linking smoking to youth, beauty, and independence unfairly encouraged teen-agers to start a habit? Both questions are currently under investigation.

The evidence in favor of seat-belt use is undeniable—it saves lives in motor-vehicle accidents. Why, therefore, have 59.3% of the women in this country never used a seat-belt while riding in or driving a car? Map 9.17 indicates that the greatest offenders are the women of South Carolina of whom 85.9% have never used a seat belt. Colorado and New Hampshire follow with 73.3 and 68.2%. The most compliance is found in Connecticut and Wisconsin with 38.0 and 38.2% of its women never having buckled up. As with cigarette smoking, there are no distinguishable trends on the map. Most likely this variable is linked to state laws and prominence of state advertising campaigns. The map is presented as a curiosity for the reader interested in checking out his or her state. Perhaps it will also nudge certain legislators. Mandatory seat-belt laws in Great Britain have significantly reduced their accidental death rate.

Three behavioral-risk factors have been presented; each has substantial claims that moderation, elimination, or use (respectively) will improve health and prolong life. We all see the frequent public-service announcements in the popular press regarding these factors and some of the factual information must register in each of our guilt-ridden consciences. Why is there such a discrepancy, therefore, between belief

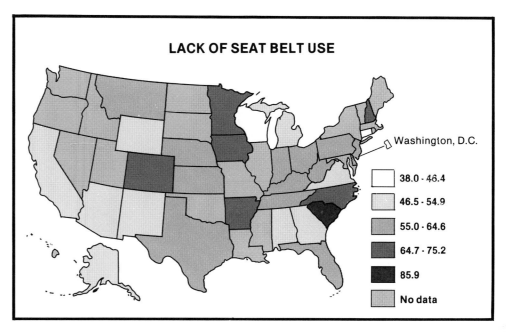

LACK OF SEAT BELT USE

Washington, D.C.

	38.0 - 46.4
	46.5 - 54.9
	55.0 - 64.6
	64.7 - 75.2
	85.9
	No data

Map 9.17. Lack of seat-belt use—percentage of female respondents who have never used a seat belt while riding or driving a car, 1980–82. U.S. median is 59.3%.

and action? What are the public-relations people doing wrong? Is there really a strong sentiment in favor of dying young, but having lived a happy life full of appropriate vices to counter the stress of living? Perhaps everyone thinks they will be the one to beat the odds. Since the American populace has not responded to reasoned arguments, maybe they will respond to money. State insurance-regulators are considering asking health insurors to charge higher rates for people who smoke, have high blood pressure, or who are overweight. They theorize that health-care costs can only be controlled when individuals take responsibility for their health. They propose, therefore, rewarding those who have minimized their risks.

Map 9.18 is a composite of all eight behavioral-risk factors. If environment and our fellow creatures truly have an influence on our behavior, this map should indicate potentially healthy and unhealthy behavior areas of the country. Maine turns out to be the worst of all possible worlds, but Massachusetts follows close behind. Colorado, Illinois, New Jersey, Pennsylvania, and South Carolina are not much better. It seems to be time for the women on the East coast to take another look at the health quality of their lives. Traditionally urban environments have been stressful; maybe it is time to make some changes. The women of Maine should focus on the overweight question; Massachusetts and Pennsylvania women need to throw away their cigarettes. Illinois women

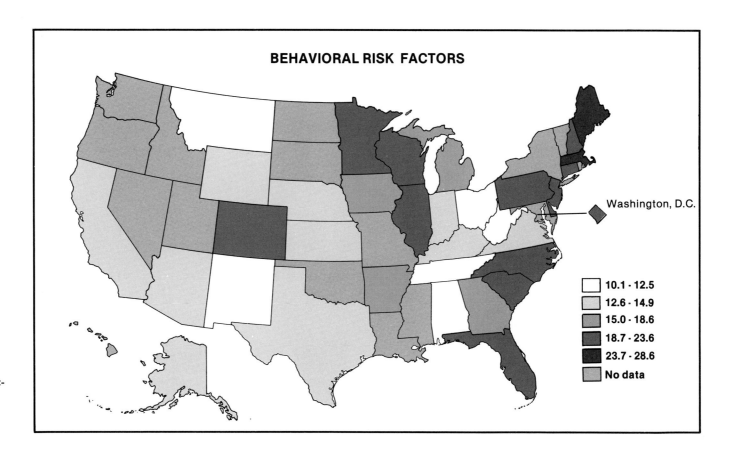

BEHAVIORAL RISK FACTORS

Washington, D.C.

	10.1 - 12.5
	12.6 - 14.9
	15.0 - 18.6
	18.7 - 23.6
	23.7 - 28.6
	No data

Map 9.18 Behavioral-risk factors—composite ranking for eight factors, 1980–82. U.S. median is 16.1.

should endeavor to arrest their uncontrolled hypertension while New Jersey women need to work on both chronic and acute excessive drinking habits. In Colorado, the primary regional anomaly, women should reduce their cigarette smoking and use seat belts more frequently. Women in South Carolina need to use seat belts more often, too.

Women in New Mexico, Ohio, and Tennessee have good prospects for a healthy, long life. So do those in Alabama, Arizona, Montana, Nebraska, and West Virginia. California, also, is relatively healthy. Life in the fast lane there is apparently tempered by good health habits. Women have no extreme problems, except for chronic heavy drinking, and they do a good job on weight and seat-belt usage.

CHAPTER TEN

CRIME

INTRODUCTION

The woman as victim and the woman as offender are considered in this chapter on crime. Women, of course, are victims of a great variety of crimes, just as men are, but not as often. The victimization rate per 1,000 people for personal crimes of violence (rape, robbery, and assault) is 46 for males and 25 for females. For personal crimes of theft (larceny without contact, purse snatching, and pocket picking) the rate for males is 91 and for females 80. Two crimes against women are mapped here—rape and wife battering. Both are deplorable evidence of a male-dominated society, and both are more rampant than the numbers would indicate. Underreporting is a problem.

The National Survey of Crime Severity, conducted in 1977, asked a nationwide sample of people to rate the severity of 204 illegal events described in scenarios. Forcible rape with the victim dying as a result of injuries ranked second behind planting a bomb in a public building. If the woman were not to die, the severity of the crime decreased to tenth position, a ranking similar to that of skyjacking. The definition of rape is complex and has varied through time. There also is variation in definition from state to state, one of many variables that influences the distribution shown. A map of the forcible-rape rate, based on the number of offenses, is followed by a map of rape-prevention and treatment resources. Next a map of shelters for battered wives serves as a surrogate for the offense itself.

Crime predominantly belongs to men. Although female participation in crime is increasing, women still constitute small proportions of those arrested, convicted, jailed, and imprisoned. Social scientists speculate on whether female crime-rates will increase in the future as a result of increased opportunity through participation in the labor force. Women as a percentage of all prisoners in state and federal facilities as well as women prisoners compared with the female population of a state are both mapped to provide two perspectives on this general issue. A map of the leading offenses of convicted female defendants in each state concludes the chapter.

VICTIMS

Because of underreporting we simply do not know the extent of forcible rape, reprehensible a crime as it is. The FBI suggests that all estimates be multiplied by 10 to come closer to what actually is happening. Since there are important differences in reporting behavior across the United States, the data presented in Map 10.1 should not inspire total confidence. For example, nonwhites are more likely to report rape to police than whites and this, of course, would affect rates in certain parts of the country. The map is made, however, with the best data available for reported rapes and, even with the above caveats, some general patterns are clear. The rapes in this map do not include sexual abuse within marriage or statutory rapes of young children.

The southern half of the country has the highest rape rate, led in 1980 by Nevada's 67.2 rapes per 100,000 inhabitants. Such a striking concentration leads to a facile environmental-temperature correlation of rape with latitude. Several striking exceptions challenge this theory. On the one hand, the second highest rate is in Alaska (62.5) and two other northern states, Michigan and Washington, also have high rates. Rape in Alaska may represent the last vestiges of frontier mentality. Possibly some associations of rape with the poor economic conditions in the other two states exist. The reverse exception is Alabama, Arkansas, and Mississippi. Relatively low rates of rape occur in the upper Midwest and Plains, the Northeast, and the border South states of Kentucky and West Virginia. The lowest rate is 9.5 for North Dakota followed by 12.5 for South Dakota and 12.9 for Maine.

Rape is disproportionately an urban crime. In 44 states the highest rape rates were in SMSAs (Standard Metropolitan Statistical Areas). Alaska, Vermont, and Wyoming do not have any urban agglomerations large enough to be classed as an SMSA. Alaska's highest rape rate, therefore, occurred in its smaller cities, but rape rates for Vermont and Wyoming as well as Hawaii, Massachusetts, and New Jersey were highest in their rural areas. Among the states with large urban concentrations, Nevada had the highest rape rate for women liv-

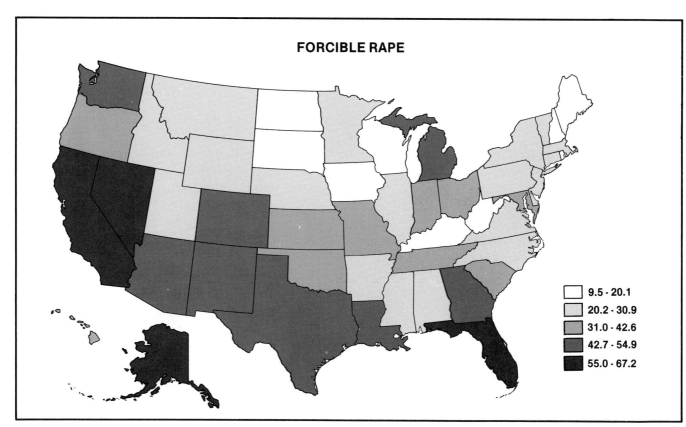

FORCIBLE RAPE

☐	9.5 - 20.1
☐	20.2 - 30.9
☐	31.0 - 42.6
☐	42.7 - 54.9
■	55.0 - 67.2

Map 10.1   Forcible rape—rate per 100,000 inhabitants, 1980. U.S. average is 36.4.

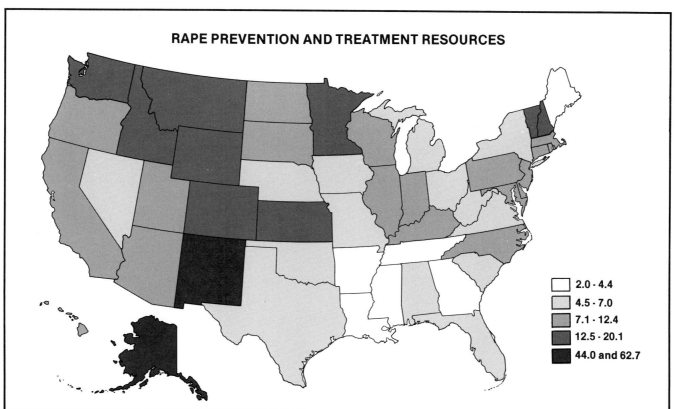

RAPE PREVENTION AND TREATMENT RESOURCES

☐	2.0 - 4.4
☐	4.5 - 7.0
☐	7.1 - 12.4
☐	12.5 - 20.1
■	44.0 and 62.7

Map 10.2   Rape-prevention and treatment resources—number of facilities per 1.0 million women 15 years and older, 1981. U.S. average is 8.4.

ing in SMSAs at 75.9 whereas North Dakota had the lowest at 15.4. The highest rate among rural areas was for the rural women in New Jersey (48.2) and the lowest was in South Dakota (1.6). Rural parts of Iowa, Minnesota, Nebraska, North Dakota, and Wisconsin are also relatively "safe" spots.

An interesting hypothesis of social scientists connects rape rates with religion. Traditionally a low religious involvement among a population has been associated with a high crime rate. Similarly, the greater the percentage of Catholics in a population, the lower the rape rate. The strict sexual regulation among Catholics with regards to birth control, premarital sex, and abortion discourages sexual deviancy. The same relationship may hold for other dogmatic groups.

No one knows how to explain rape behavior. There are models that blame the victim for sexual teasing, hitchhiking, walking in dark areas, and being out alone at night; models that attack the offenders for psychopathic deviance or character disorder; models that place the blame on a sick society that permits machismo upbringing, violence in the media, women as an oppressed class, and an ineffective justice mechanism; and models that blame environmental factors such as dark alleys, overcrowded buildings, drunkenness, and misunderstood messages. A complex statistical model with religion, unemployment, urbanization, and alcoholism all as variables still could explain only 55% of the spatial variation in rape occurrence.

Rape-victimization rates are highest for women who are divorced or separated followed by those who have never married. Women who are 16 to 19 years old are more likely to be raped than any other group with women 20 to 24 years old the next most likely. The general public considers rape a rare event, but it is not. Although victimization rates are higher for other violent crimes such as assault or robbery, such a cursory calculation does not take into account unreported rapes. A woman has about the same chance of being raped as she does of getting cancer or being divorced. The silent oppression, however, is what really infuriates women. Why should fear of a violent sexual attack have to disturb life activities so drastically?

The highest number of rapes occur among relatively homogeneous and residentially clustered groups that condone aggressive behavior. Since it is a crime of opportunity, it often takes place on the offender's turf. Most rape is intraracial (90%) and intraclass. The composite statistical profile of the rapist portrays a young man under 25, not married, and black. Black women, therefore, are more likely to be victims. The rapist has low educational attainment and holds an unskilled job or is unemployed. To use sociological jargon, he has "low social integration" and does not mix well with the rest of society. He has a low stake in family and community rela-

tions. Finally, he is most likely to commit his crime in an 8-week period between July 7 and September 8.

So what is being done about rape? Some parts of this country have extensive resources available for both the victim and the offender. Counseling services are the dominant function of these organizations, but classes in self-defense, liaison with police and medical personnel, community education, and monitoring of legislation are other examples of functions. Some are ethnically oriented and may even offer bilingual hotlines. Nearly every college town has one. Services are offered by a diverse group of organizations, including rape-crisis centers, community mental-health centers, medical facilities, and police departments. Funding is equally diverse; one source of money is federal programs administered through local government agencies.

Rape-prevention and treatment resources are the subject of Map 10.2 where the data are expressed as a rate of number of facilities per million women 15 years and older, the group at risk of being raped. Information comes from a 1981 directory of 764 centers compiled by the National Center for the Prevention and Control of Rape.

The number of resources in relation to population is so high in Alaska and New Mexico that they merit a separate category. Other high rates are in the intermontane West plus Kansas and Minnesota. The rate is particularly low in the southeastern corner of the country. Mississippi has the lowest rate of 2.0 facilities per 1 million women. Maine, Tennessee, Georgia, and Arkansas follow.

Comparison of Maps 10.1 and 10.2 is eye opening. Virtually no correspondence exists between areas with a high rape-rate and those with a high rate of rape resources. No clue allows us to interpret whether the facilities preceded the problem with an aim toward prevention or whether they are a response to a problem. Some equilibrium in supply and demand appears to exist in Alaska, Colorado, and Washington where both the rape and resource rates are above average. Maine has few rapes and few resource centers. States that appear to be undersupplied with rape resources include Florida, Georgia, Louisiana, Nevada, Tennessee, and Texas. Those that have more resources than expected based on the rape rate are Idaho, South Dakota, Montana, New Hampshire, and Minnesota.

Battered women have always been with us. Only recently, however, have this and other aspects of domestic violence such as child abuse and incest been labeled as social problems and brought out into the open. The anti-wife-beating campaign, for example, dates only from the mid-1970s. This late entry reflects the ambivalence about whether or not wife-beating is a crime. The criminal-law system has had a long-term reluctance to intrude into family problems. The women's movement, however, has forced us to look at this example of power inequality.

Although wife-beating undeniably exists and crosses social class, income level, race, and education, reliable data on battered women are nonexistent. Reports underestimate the extent of violence, mainly because it takes place behind closed doors. Only when medical treatment is necessary, law-enforcement personnel are called, or the wife leaves and takes legal action, may wife-beating be reported and recorded as such. More often, however, the battered wife stays home and tells no one. Part of the reason for not reporting an episode, of course, is a fear of retaliation from the husband. Another part is societal influences. What some communities may regard as tolerable behavior, others would judge as activity definitely prohibited by norms. It is up to the woman to decide, based on her perceptions of violence in her culture, whether she has had enough.

Incidences of wife-beating may be precipitated by alcohol abuse or stress induced by such conditions as unemployment. Difficulties with life outside the family could provoke a husband to take out his frustrations upon a wife, one of the few targets over whom he can covertly exert power in physical form. Alcohol and stress are but excuses for violent behavior, however. Something makes some men more prone to use violence than others. Studies report that men are more likely to approve of physical violence against women if they observed their fathers hitting their mothers. Living in an area of the country where cultural training condones the use of violence to exert power is another predisposition to wife-beating. Irrefutably, violence is more prevalent in some parts of this country than others. The Deep South, ghetto areas of large cities, and parts of the Wild West come immediately to mind.

One aspect of wife-beating for which data are available is the number of shelters for battered women. Map 10.3 portrays the rate per million married women 15 years or older. Shelter data are from a directory compiled by the National Clearinghouse on Domestic Violence. In 1981 a total of 465 shelters provided temporary housing for a woman and her children as well as other services such as a hotline, emergency transportation, child care, and legal aid. In the past, religious bodies and charitable organizations sponsored these facilities, but increasing numbers of houses now draw upon a variety of funding sources, including federal and state monies.

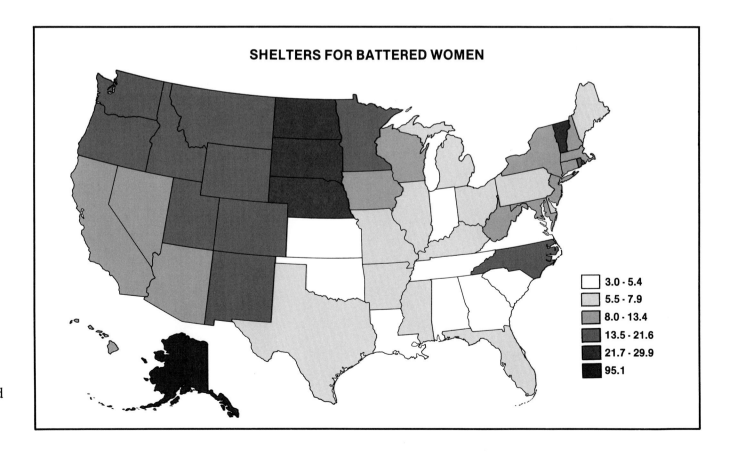

SHELTERS FOR BATTERED WOMEN

3.0 - 5.4
5.5 - 7.9
8.0 - 13.4
13.5 - 21.6
21.7 - 29.9
95.1

Map 10.3 Shelters for battered women—number of facilities per 1.0 million married women 15 years and older, 1980. U.S. average is 9.3.

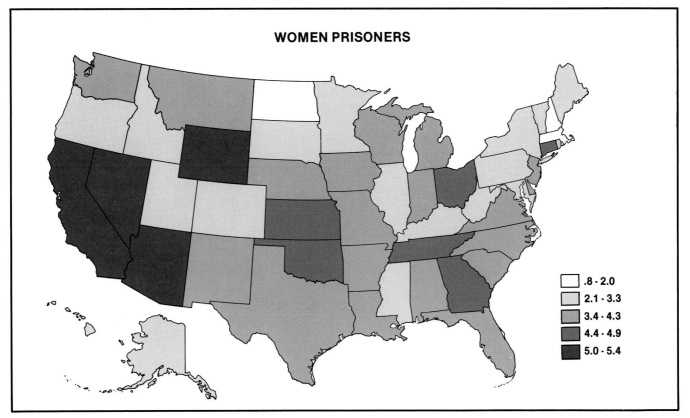

WOMEN PRISONERS

.8 - 2.0
2.1 - 3.3
3.4 - 4.3
4.4 - 4.9
5.0 - 5.4

Map 10.4   Women prisoners—percentage of all prisoners in state and federal institutions, 1980. U.S. average is 4.0%.

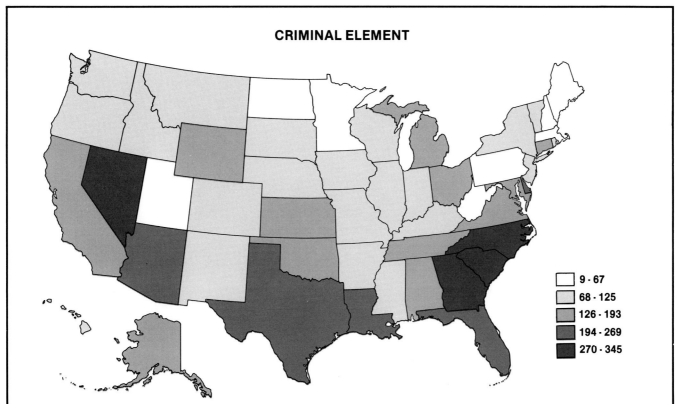

CRIMINAL ELEMENT

9 - 67
68 - 125
126 - 193
194 - 269
270 - 345

Map 10.5   Criminal element—female prisoners in state and federal facilities per 1.0 million female population 18 years and older, 1980. U.S. average is 155.

Crime

Interpretation of the patterns in Map 10.3 resurrects the old, unanswerable question of which came first. Are shelters created by socially responsible groups in anticipation of a potential problem or are they established in response to a problem? If we accept that the map pattern reflects the incidence of battering, then the West is guilty of cruelty to their women. A deep V from Washington to New Mexico to Minnesota encloses an area with a high rate of shelters to women. Alaska has an abnormally high rate, enough to warrant a separate class. A warning about literal interpretation of rates is in order. The map indicates that Alaska has 95.1 shelters per million women. Actually Alaska only has 8 shelters for its 84,127 women in this category. Nebraska is the next highest at 29.9 shelters per million women (11 total shelters).

If we accept the pattern as a sign of social consciousness, then the South has a long way to go. With the exception of North Carolina, the southeastern quadrant of the country has relatively few shelters. South Carolina's two shelters just will not suffice in an environment that has the potential for violence. In contrast, residents in Rhode Island, Vermont, and that western V may be cognizant of a potential problem and have elected to do something about it. The few shelters in Rhode Island, for example, are multiply funded from diverse state, federal, and local sources indicating that someone is hustling to bring wife-battering to the attention of the public in that state.

OFFENDERS

The number of female criminals has increased in the last 10 years along with an increase in population and the general crime rate. The percentage of criminals who are women, however, has remained fairly constant. This is one career where occupational segregation has not been eroded; the world of crime still belongs to men. With regards to arrests, 15.8% in 1980 were of women. For the same year only 4% of the prisoners in state and federal facilities were women, 7% of jail inmates, and 20% of juveniles under correctional supervision.

Maps 10.4 and 10.5 portray a limited segment of the criminal element from two different perspectives. Female prisoners are compared with the total prison population and then with the female population of a state. Prisoners in state and federal facilities are the subject of these maps; these women have committed serious crimes with incarcerations longer than 1 year.

Examination of Map 10.4 reveals little range in the percentage of prisoners who are female. The low of .8% in North Dakota is balanced at the other end of the scale by the high of 5.4% in California, Nevada, and Wyoming. In general, no strong regions are developed. Small areas of the upper Midwest and Northeast have low values whereas that far-Southwest bloc of three states has the highest value in the nation.

One interpretation of the map is that large percentages of female hard-core prisoners are a sign of increased female equality. In four states, in particular, women have made deeper inroads into an almost exclusively male bastion. Perhaps, for example, women in these states have more opportunity for crime through their employment. Economic pressures may lead to crime as well.

The presence of the female element is documented on Map 10.5, where prisoners in state and federal facilities are compared with the female population 18 and over in each state. The map is a restricted measure of regional variation in crime among women, or at least among those who have been caught and sentenced at this level. The areas of highest incidence form an intermittent Sun Belt with notable exceptions of Alabama, California, Mississippi, and New Mexico. The highest rate in the country is found in Nevada where there are 345 prisoners per million adult women. South Carolina and Georgia trail at 286 and 283 respectively. The lowest prisoner rates are in North Dakota with 9 and New Hampshire with 14. In general, the female criminal element is minor in the Frost-belt states. Most of us have had little personal contact with the serious female criminal just because they are so rare. Even in Nevada, female prisoners constitute only .03% of the female population of the state.

Of the 13,258 female prisoners in the United States in 1980, 49.4% were black. This proportion far exceeds the 10.9% of black women in the population and, inevitably, leads to inferences regarding the strong racial associations of crime. There are no black female prisoners in Maine, Montana, New Hampshire, North Dakota, South Dakota, and Vermont, states whose female black population is .1 to .3% of all females. Only in these six states, however, is the prison percentage less than the population percentage of black women. In all other states, prison percentages are higher by varying margins. The highest proportions of black female prisoners are 76.9% in Maryland and 73.7% in New Jersey. Louisiana, Alabama, and Delaware have the next highest values. Comparatively more black prisoners than expected, based on the number of black women residents of the state, may be found in New Jersey, Ohio, Connecticut, and Rhode Island. Black women are comparatively underrepresented among prison populations in Tennessee and South Carolina. Discrimination in the criminal-justice system is an unconfirmed but possible explanation of the racial disparity.

Crime is sex-typed just as other "occupations" are. Women only rarely commit crimes involving burglary, motor-vehicle theft, gambling, and weapons offenses where the

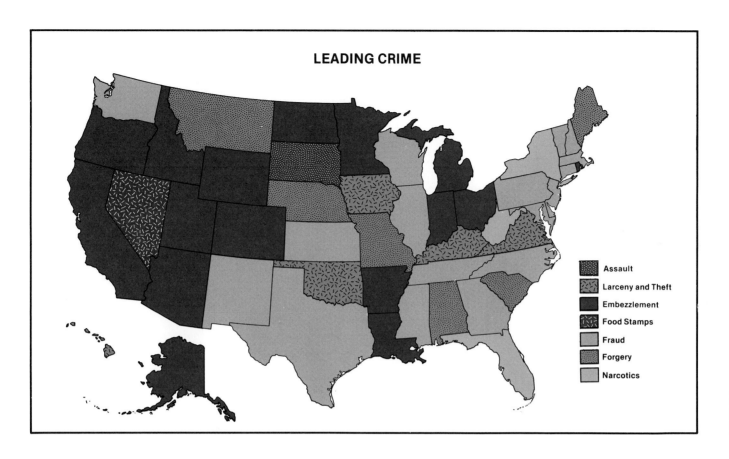

LEADING CRIME

Legend:
- Assault
- Larceny and Theft
- Embezzlement
- Food Stamps
- Fraud
- Forgery
- Narcotics

Map 10.6 Leading crime, of female convicted defendants in U.S. district courts, 1982–83.

ratio of male to female arrests is about 18 to 1. In contrast, fraud, larceny, forgery and counterfeiting, and embezzlement are more weakly sex-typed and have a ratio of 4 male arrests to 1 female arrest. In 1982, for example, women constituted only 27.6% of those arrested for serious crimes. Of these 80% were for larceny-theft, 6.8% for burglary-breaking and entering, and 7.8% for aggravated assaults.

The leading crime of female convicted defendants in U.S. district courts during a 12-month period ending in June of 1983 are presented by state in Map 10.6. Fraud, or the practice of deceit or intentional misrepresentation of fact to deprive someone of money or rights, leads in the greatest number of states. Embezzlement, the "white-collar" crime, is a close second. The predominance of embezzlement in parts of the West and fraud in parts of the Northeast form the only substantial groupings of states on the map.

CHAPTER ELEVEN

POLITICS

INTRODUCTION

Women are able to effect change in the political process in this country through their vote and their participation as politicians, volunteers, and contributors to campaign funds. In turn politics through enacted legislation has had a significant effect upon women's ability to seek equality in our society. This chapter, therefore, examines politics from the two angles: women as participants in the political process and as benefactors of the political process.

Women have majority status at the ballot box because women outnumber men of voting age in most of the states. Moreover, a higher percentage of women than men are registered to vote and, in the last two presidential elections, a higher percentage of women voted than did men. Maps of women's voting participation are presented. Although there is no reason to believe that women will vote as a gender bloc, still the potential is there to influence the outcome on issues of concern to women. Women have long been opposed to military spending, military intervention, and environmental exploitation, for example. They favor programs that assist minorities and the poor. By their vote, and hence choice of elected representatives, women can make these desires known.

Women's political participation is moving forward at the national level only slowly. More progress is evident at the state level, where women held 14.6% of the seats in state legislatures in 1985. As of the beginning of the 99th U.S. Congress in 1985, women constituted 2% of the Senate and 5% of the House of Representatives. At the current rate of progress, in 40 years women will hold only 12 percent of the seats in the House, a long way from equality. A map of the hometowns of all the congresswomen who served from 1917 to 1985 has some surprising regional gaps.

The League of Women Voters, born out of the women's suffrage movement, is one of the prominent activist organizations in this country. Many female politicians owe their start to the experience gained in this nonpartisan group. A map of league-membership strength by state confirms the tie to female legislative representation.

Almost no one will deny today that women have the basic right to determine for themselves what they want to do with their lives. Many legal obstacles exist, however, to achieving this right. Women must receive help from the law in their quest for equality because courts traditionally have regarded women as inferior to men and sought to protect them. The vote on two constitutional amendments of particular concern to women's rights are displayed. First the congressional vote on the women's suffrage resolution of 1919 and the state passage dates of full suffrage for women are presented. Next, states that never ratified the Equal Rights Amendment are singled out; in addition, an attempt is made to assess congressional support for the ERA.

ERA is only one of several "women's issues" before Congress. Using voting records on a series of issues selected by the National Women's Political Caucus, a spatial report card is presented for each state's delegation to the 1983–84 Congress. Three states clearly flunk the test.

Finally, state legislation related to women is examined and a responsiveness index is presented in map form. Some states are laggards in enacting legislation relating to role change and role equity for women whereas others have been leaders in enhancing the status of women in the eyes of the law.

VOTING PATTERNS

Women of voting age outnumber men in the American population (Map 11.1). They formed 52.3% of eligible voters in 1984 and are the majority voting group in all states except Alaska, Hawaii, Nevada, and Wyoming. Alaska has the lowest proportion with only 46.2% of its population of voting age being women. In general, percentages of women are low throughout the intermontane West. The greatest potential for women's political impact exists in the northeastern states. Here New York leads, with 53.7% of its eligible voters being female. Massachusetts and Rhode Island follow with 53.6 and 53.5% respectively. Another area of concentration occurs in parts of the South.

Potential voter figures can be deceptive. More important measures are the percentage of women who have registered to vote and then those who actually do. Map 11.2 indicates the percentage of females 18 and over who were registered

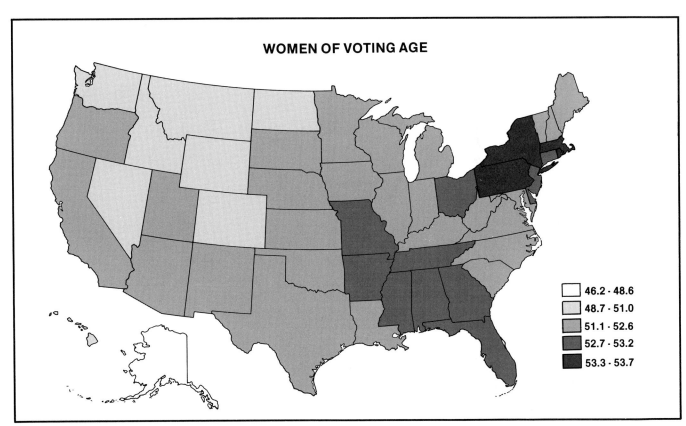

WOMEN OF VOTING AGE

	46.2 - 48.6
	48.7 - 51.0
	51.1 - 52.6
	52.7 - 53.2
	53.3 - 53.7

Map 11.1 Women of voting age, as a percentage of all eligible voters, 1984. U.S. average is 52.3%.

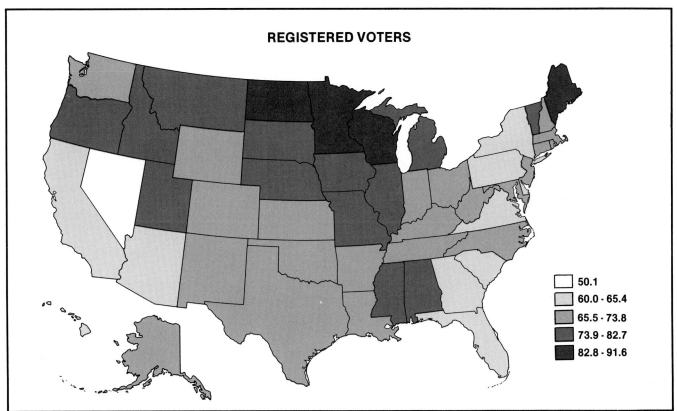

REGISTERED VOTERS

	50.1
	60.0 - 65.4
	65.5 - 73.8
	73.9 - 82.7
	82.8 - 91.6

Map 11.2 Registered voters—percentage of females 18 years and older reported registered, 1984. U.S. average is 69.3%.

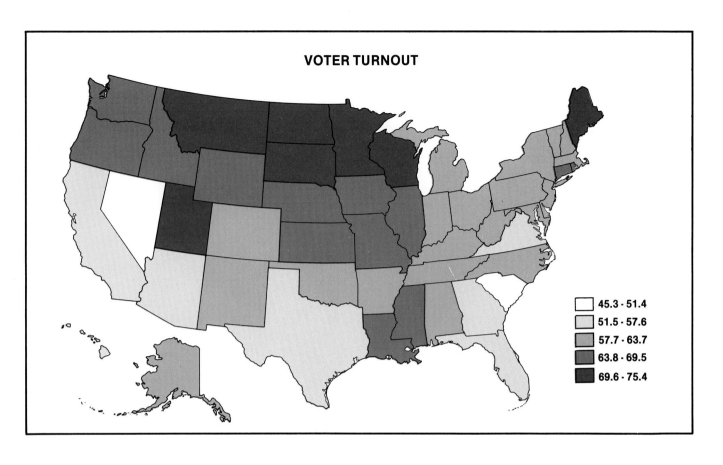

VOTER TURNOUT

☐	45.3 - 51.4
☐	51.5 - 57.6
▨	57.7 - 63.7
▨	63.8 - 69.5
▨	69.6 - 75.4

Map 11.3 Voter turnout—percentage of females 18 years and older reported voting, 1984. U.S. average is 60.8%.

in 1984. Data are based on questions asked in the Current Population Survey of the Census Bureau; sampling took place in November 1984, approximately two weeks after the presidential election.

The north central states, upholding their long tradition of voter participation, have the greatest percentage of registered voters. In North Dakota 91.6% of the eligible females are registered to vote, in Minnesota 85.5%. Maine and Wisconsin follow. A pattern of generally high voter-registration dominates the Midwest plus parts of the Northwest, two New England states, and two southern states. Unexpectedly, Mississippi is the fifth highest state with 82.6% (Alabama is the tenth with 76.6%). Recent and controversial registration drives in these latter two states have obviously been successful in overcoming traditional low voter-interest in the South.

Low political awareness can be found in the far Southwest, the far Southeast, and selected states of the Northeast. Nevada has the lowest value with only 50.1% of its female eligible voters registered. South Carolina and Hawaii follow with 60.0 and 60.2% respectively. Apathy at even this preliminary stage of the electoral process is also evident in Arizona, California, and Virginia.

The percentage of females who are registered to vote exceeds that of males by 2.0% for the country. In Nebraska and Colorado, however, the difference is as high as 7.4 and 7.2% in favor of women. Differences of 5.9, 5.8, and 5.7 are found in Kansas, Oklahoma, and Florida respectively. Compounded by the greater female population of voting age in all of these states, this means that women definitely have the potential to control the ballot box if they vote and if they vote as a bloc. The male percentage for registered voters exceeds the females' in only 11 states. In Wyoming the male rate is 3.6% higher, in Kentucky 3.5% higher, and in Tennessee 2.9% higher. Local political coalitions should endeavor to equalize the percentages in these 3 states if an equal voice for women in politics is the goal.

In 1978, the last year for which sex-differentiated election data by urban areas were published by the Census Bureau, the three leading SMSAs with high-reported voter registration for females were all in the north central states. Minneapolis–St. Paul had a 79.2% registration of eligible women, followed by Milwaukee with 76.0% and St. Louis with 73.2%. Boston, with a 72.4%, broke the regional pattern, but Detroit (68.8%) and Kansas City (66.5%) ranked next, and emphasized the north central regional component of political interest.

Of the 30 SMSAs surveyed, Houston with 51.9% had the lowest voter registration among women. New York followed with 52.3% and Miami with 52.4%. These three cities are where local voter-registration drives need to be emphasized to ensure more citizen involvement. Incidentally, Houston also had the lowest voter-registration among men. With the exception of Baltimore, all of the southern SMSAs (Atlanta, Dallas, Houston, Miami, and Washington, D.C.) were in the bottom third in registration ranking. Baltimore, a maverick in many respects, actually ranked in the top third with 64.6% registration.

Voter registration is but a preliminary to the actual voting process. Map 11.3, the percentage of eligible female voters who reported voting in 1984, is based on data from the same sampling procedure used to ascertain registered voters. Despite some limitations, the data represent a nationwide assessment of what is essentially a secret, personal act.

Voter turnout among women was highest in the north central states, duplicating the registration pattern. Montana, South Dakota, and Utah contribute to an expanded high-value category around a Minnesota–North Dakota–Wisconsin core. The greatest voter participation occurred in Minnesota, where 75.4% of eligible women voted. Utah and Wisconsin followed with 74.0 and 72.6% respectively. North Dakota and Montana were next. Adding in the next-highest category expands the intense pattern of voting to the Midwest states, the Northwest, three New England states, and two southern states, this time Louisiana and Mississippi.

Low voter-turnout was especially evident in Nevada (45.3%) and South Carolina (50.0%). The women of Georgia, Arizona, and Texas also expressed apathy with 51.6, 53.9, and 54.8% respectively. Areas of low voter-interest occurred in the Southwest, the Southeast, and Hawaii.

In 1978 Minneapolis–St. Paul had the highest percentage of women voting (60.7). Four of the top six voter participatory SMSAs were, as before, in the north central region (Detroit, Milwaukee, and St. Louis in addition to Minneapolis–St. Paul). Boston and Philadelphia were the two additional ranking metropolitan areas. The three lowest percentages among the 30 SMSAs surveyed belonged to the southern states. Houston again had the most apathetic performance with only 32.4% of its adult females voting. Atlanta and Dallas had similarly low percentages. Houston took indifference honors for men as well.

The discrepancy between registered voters and voter turnout for females is 8.5% for the entire country. For North Dakota this difference is 19.9% whereas for Alabama it is 14.5%, for Maine 14.0%, and for Mississippi 13.5%. Perhaps some of the exemplary voter-registration proportions in these states should be viewed as an empty gesture unless a concerted effort is made to get out the vote on election day. In contrast, a close correspondence between original intention (registration) and actual follow-through (the vote) exists in Delaware where the difference is only 3.4 percent. In Wyoming it is 3.8 percent.

STATE LEGISLATORS

The integration of women into state legislative bodies has progressed steadily in recent years, but, as with all political activities, more women need to be elected to move from tokenism to equality in state politics. In 1969 only 4.0% of state legislators were women. In 1985 that proportion had climbed to 14.6%. Increased representation at the state level appears to be critical for women because of recent federal policy to transfer control of many programs affecting women and children to state and local officials.

It is popularly believed that women politicians have a higher standard of ethics than men, work harder, are more human-needs oriented, and are more devoted to their constituents. If this notion is true, why are so few women elected to the chambers of power? Based on polls, voters are apparently indifferent to the sex of a candidate at the state and local levels and would vote for qualified women if nominated. Certainly a large pool of women in each state are eligible to run based on education and interest in political issues. Several researchers point to the recruitment procedures at the local level as the culprit; qualified women are passed over for nominations because of the "good old boy" system.

Several overlapping strategies appear viable to increase the representation of women in government. More women are likely to be elected if more women run. In 1985, for example, 63% of female state legislative candidates won their races. Competent women need to be encouraged to put themselves in the public arena. Perhaps the first step could be at the local level as a school-board candidate or city commissioner. If the woman has aptitude for the political game, then encourage her to seek a position at a higher level. Secondly, women need to have access to the behind-the-scenes power in partisan politics. Where unfavorable conditions exist in local politics, change is possible through pressure groups that work from the outside or infiltration of existing organizations.

Map 11.4 portrays women as a percentage of all state legislators in 1985. Two regions of success dominate the map: New England and parts of the West. Outliers occur in Florida, Maryland, and Wisconsin.

New Hampshire has the greatest participation of women in state legislatures with 33.0%, a figure far above the closest

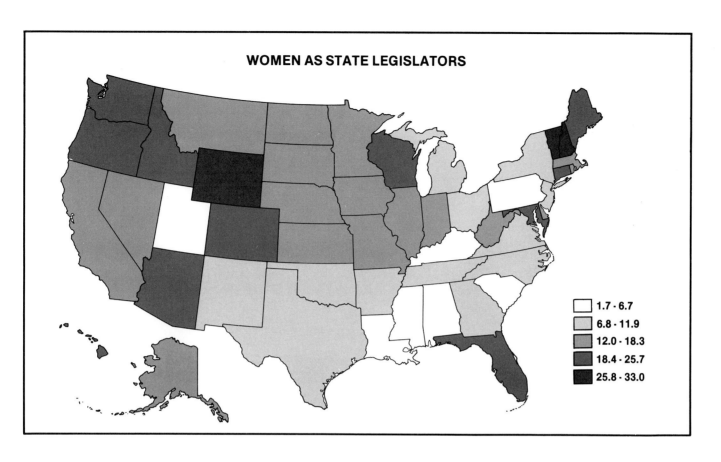

WOMEN AS STATE LEGISLATORS

☐	1.7 - 6.7
☐	6.8 - 11.9
☐	12.0 - 18.3
☐	18.4 - 25.7
■	25.8 - 33.0

Map 11.4 Women as state legislators, as a percentage of all legislators, 1985. U.S. average is 14.6%.

competitors of Vermont at 26.7% and Wyoming at 26.1%. The legislature of New Hampshire, however, is a special case. It has 400 positions in its lower chamber and 24 in the upper chamber, resulting in a uniquely high representative/constituent ratio. In addition, the state's low salary of $200 per year is no inducement to the professional. The two factors together have led to the election of a large number of older women who view legislative participation as a civic duty. Not all of New Hampshire's high rate of women legislators can be explained away by uninviting conditions, however. Neighboring states of Connecticut, Maine, and Vermont have high proportions as well. Daniel Elazar's classic descriptions of political subcultures in the United States is germane. New England, according to him, belongs to a moralistic political culture where politics are viewed as for the public good and a sensitive relationship exists between representative and the populace. As a result, there is more amateur involvement in politics.

Urbanization, high proportions of ethnic populations, and the Democratic party in Massachusetts and Rhode Island dilute the moralistic strain. Historically these situations and interest groups reflect traditional values that promote sex-role differentiation; politics are not for women. Also working-class women, a large proportion of working women in these two states, are less likely to have time to become involved in politics. Participation in civic affairs has long belonged to Republican women. In addition to the New England states, Arizona, Colorado, Oregon, and Washington also have a dominant moralistic strain. So does Utah, but here moralistic politics in regards to women are negated by the effect of the Mormon church.

Other political subcultures include the individualistic form where politics is business and best left to professionals (the dominant form in urban areas especially in the Northeast), and the traditionalistic form present in the South that is based on a hierarchy with only the elite at the top taking care of things. Both political forms inherently display antipathy to women in politics. Regions of dominance for both political cultures have low female participation in state politics. Mississippi and Louisiana, the lowest participation rates at 1.7 and 3.5% respectively, are part of the traditionalistic culture of the South. Florida, as with many other issues, is not the same political animal as the rest of the South. Here massive influxes of nonsouthern values have nationalized politics. Pennsylvania, with the third lowest participation rate of 5.1%, is part of the individualistic core.

Although a perfect correlation does not exist between Elazar's regions and the relative prominence of women in state politics, his ideas are an interesting starting point for discussion. Hawaii, Maryland, and Wyoming, for example, remain unexplained. Anomalies such as these three states only hint at the complexity of regional politics that defy simple explanations. In addition, neither of the two major parties are the same through space, with local variations in policies and adherents.

During the time period 1971 to 1985 women showed the greatest absolute increase in representation in New Hampshire (legislative positions doubled from 70 to 140), Vermont (increase of 30 positions), Maine (29), and Massachusetts (28). Kansas, Minnesota, and Washington follow. In Mississippi women actually lost three seats during the time period; in Utah two seats were lost. In more recent time (1981 to 1985) Florida, Idaho, Massachusetts, and New Hampshire have made the greatest strides with regards to number of seats. Incidentally, females in state senate seats are still a rare phenomenon. In the 1984 elections a woman finally broke into the all-male Texas senate. There are still no female senators in the legislatures of Louisiana, Mississippi, or Virginia.

CONGRESSWOMEN

At the elite level of the U.S. Congress, where the number of women is small, generalizations are difficult to make because election or appointment is such an individual event. Each congresswoman has come by her position through a unique combination of circumstances and the stories are fascinating reading. Of the 15 women who have served in the Senate, for example, only the two most recently elected (Nancy Kassebaum and Paula Hawkins) were not appointed to vacancies caused by the death of a husband or some other senator. Although several of the women senators were eventually re-elected on their own (Hattie Caraway from Arkansas, Margaret Chase Smith from Maine, and Maurine Neuberger from Oregon), initially their entry was through their husbands. A similar widow phenomenon exists in the House; succession, however, is not by courtesy appointment but a widow must be elected to the vacated post, often through a special election. The lack of automatic succession is emphasized by the fact that many widows in their bereavement had to conduct campaigns with opposition. For example, of the 31 women succeeding their husbands in the House from 1923 to 1975 all but five faced opposition in either the primary or general election. Widow succession is disappearing, how-

ever; in the 99th Congress only 5 of 22 representatives gained their initial entry by being elected to a seat vacated upon the death of a husband.

Many women, of course, have entered Congress through their own endeavors, often after hard work in the political hierarchy. Since politics is one of the societal institutions that is changing slowly, successful women who have chosen to be politicians at the national level are a scarce commodity. The power of incumbency in a male-dominated legislature has retarded change. In recent years, for example, each chamber has averaged only 15% first-termers. That is not much turnover.

The hometowns of all 118 women who have served in Congress from 1917 to 1985 are identified in Map 11.5. Members of the Senate and the House are color-coded; members of the 99th Congress have special symbols. At first glance the geographical spread in the map is impressive until additional analysis is made.

Nine states have never had a female legislator—Delaware, Iowa, Mississippi, New Hampshire, North Dakota, Vermont, Virginia, Wisconsin, and Wyoming. Congresswomen in another eight states arrived at their positions only through their own widowhood or by temporarily filling the position of a deceased congressman—Alabama, Arkansas, Louisiana, Missouri, Pennsylvania, North Carolina, South Carolina, and Tennessee. Katherine Langley of Kentucky was elected to her husband's vacant seat after he was imprisoned for bootlegging. Women who have stood for national public office entirely on their own merit are exceptions, especially in southern states. Iris Blitch of Georgia and Barbara Jordan of Texas are exceptions, and, therefore, especially worthy of note.

Women in politics past and present are clustered in the large urban areas of Baltimore, Chicago, Los Angeles, New York, and San Francisco. The remainder of the symbols are evenly dispersed with the voids noted above. Currently Maryland has the greatest female visibility in Congress with four representatives. California follows with three. Illinois, Ohio, and Connecticut have two representatives whereas Kansas has one representative and one senator.

Both of the female senators in the 99th Congress are Republican; of the 22 House members, 11 are Republicans and 11 are Democrats. From 1917 to 1985, 60.2% of female representatives were Democrats; 39.8% were Republicans. Political-party division is almost equal in the Senate with eight female Democratic senators and seven Republican senators over the same time period. As with men, incumbency has led to some long terms in the House of Representatives. Edith Rogers of Massachusetts served for 35 years, Frances Bolton of Ohio for 29, Mary Norton of New Jersey for 26, and Leonor Sullivan of Missouri for 24. Margaret Chase Smith has the

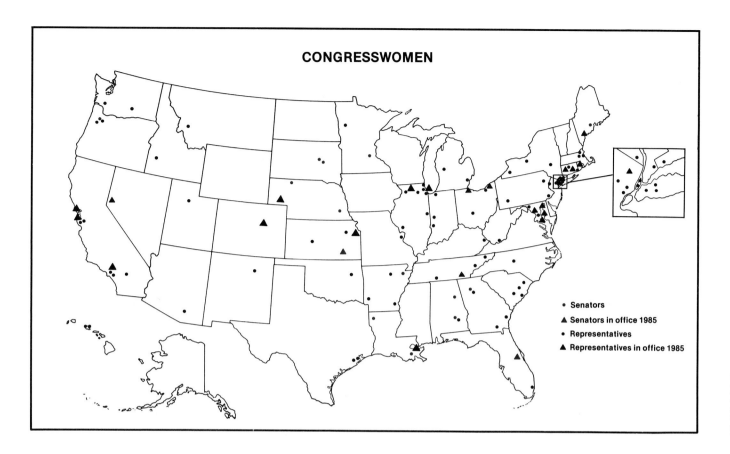

CONGRESSWOMEN

- • Senators
- ▲ Senators in office 1985
- • Representatives
- ▲ Representatives in office 1985

Map 11.5 Congresswomen—hometowns of women serving in the U.S. Congress from 1917 to 1985.

longest term in the Senate with 24 years. The number of women in the Senate has never exceeded the three in the 83rd Congress, 1953–55. The House now stands at its maximum of 22 women.

LEAGUE OF WOMEN VOTERS

Many women legislators at state and national levels include membership in the League of Women Voters among their affiliations. Examining public-policy issues through the league often has been the training ground for later legislative endeavors. In addition to inadvertently feeding the political process with candidates, the league also performs a nonpartisan role in community politics. Examining the regions of membership strength by state reveals how active women are in the local political process.

The League of Women Voters was founded in 1920, just before the Nineteenth Amendment to the Constitution was ratified, to educate the citizenship about political issues. Women's issues were not the only focus. The group lobbies

for passage of socially beneficial legislation and encourages more participation in the electoral process. Nonpartisan candidate forums, for example, are one of the more visible activities of the league. Registering voters is another.

League membership is open to any citizen over 18, male or female. Membership data for January 1985 provided by the national office do not indicate gender. The organization, however, still has a largely female membership and, for purposes of the mapping process, it has been assumed that all 106,970 state members are female. Number of members per state are presented as a rate per 1,000 resident women 18 or over (based on population estimate for 1984). The average membership is 1.175 League members for every 1,000 eligible females (Map 11.6).

The greatest strength in league participation exists in Massachusetts with a rate of 3.360. The next highest value of 2.805 belongs to Connecticut. Minnesota and Wyoming follow at 1.960 and 1.949 respectively. In general, the highest relative memberships are found in New England and mid-Atlantic states. Other highly rated states are scattered across the northern half of the country—Alaska, Colorado, Minnesota, Oregon, and Wyoming. The state with the highest num-

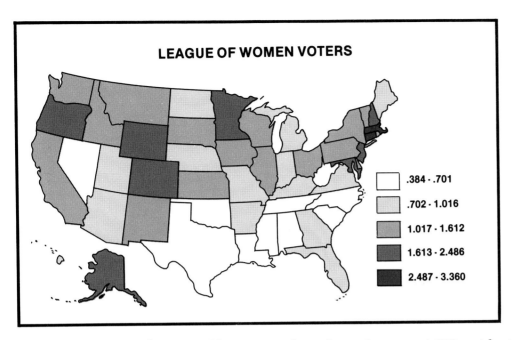

LEAGUE OF WOMEN VOTERS

.384 - .701
.702 - 1.016
1.017 - 1.612
1.613 - 2.486
2.487 - 3.360

Map 11.6   League of Women Voters—number of members per 1,000 resident women 18 years and older, 1985. U.S. average is 1.175.

ber of members is California with 12,092. After adjustment for the large female population, however, this state has only an average membership rate.

Many of the same states with high league participation are ones with a high percentage of women state legislators. In Colorado, Connecticut, Maryland, New Hampshire, Oregon, and Wyoming the relationship is especially strong. Similarly, areas with low league participation have low female involvement in the state legislative process. Many southern states and Michigan are examples.

Mississippi has the lowest participation rate in the league with a rate of .384. Nevada, Tennessee, and Alabama follow with .512, .562, and .570 respectively. Although the South forms the largest area of political apathy, scattered other states in the Southwest and Midwest display similar low values. Factors such as educational background, level of participation in volunteer organizations, and amount of free time also explain part of the map patterns.

SUFFRAGE

Women's suffrage for presidential elections followed a long and controversial fight that ironically met with bandwagon congressional support in the end. The 72-year campaign began at the first national women's assembly in Seneca

Falls, N.Y., in 1848. Formal attempts to attain voting rights started with a 1867 roll-call vote in the 39th Congress on a resolution to amend the Constitution. Congressmen defeated the measure at that time with 56 votes for and 105 votes against. In a series of votes from 1914 through 1919 Republicans supported suffrage for women more consistently than their Democratic counterparts, but Republicans never controlled enough seats to ensure passage. Republican and women's common affiliation with Prohibition perhaps led to the voting marriage. Intense education efforts finally led to passage in 1919. On a joint resolution proposing an amendment to the Constitution extending the right of suffrage to women the 66th Congress voted 308 yeas, 92 nays, and 35 not voting.

The voting on this resolution is displayed by state on Map 11.7. Exclusively affirmative voters dominate the western half of the country plus Illinois and Indiana, West Virginia, Delaware, and three New England states. Six additional states had affirmative votes with some members not voting for one reason or another. These two categories together show the strong western regional support for the Nineteenth Amendment.

Seven representatives from South Carolina voted unequivocally no on the resolution; Mississippi representatives also voted no but with two members of the congressional delegation assuming a wavering "no vote" stance. Of the states that had mixed voting, Alabama, Georgia, Louisiana, North Carolina, and Virginia all had more nays than yeas. Connecticut, Florida, Kentucky, Massachusetts, Michigan, New Jersey, New York, Ohio, Pennsylvania, Tennessee, Texas, and Wisconsin had predominantly affirmative votes. Only in Maryland was there a tied decision.

Part of the western affirmation can be explained by what was happening in individual states with regards to suffrage for women (Map 11.8). Congressional representatives, in general, reflected individual state action on suffrage. As early as 1869 Wyoming had granted full suffrage to women, enabling them to vote in presidential elections. Utah responded in kind in 1870 although the move was later rescinded by the federal government and then reinstated with statehood in 1896. Colorado and Idaho had joined the exclusive group with amendments to their state constitutions. During the next 15 years 8 other states were added, and all except for Illinois were in the western half of the country. Through 1919 when the climactic voting was taking place in Congress, 15 other states joined the list, though in some, women were granted only partial suffrage. All remaining 21 states received full suffrage by default on August 26, 1920 when the amendment was ratified by the necessary three-fourths of the states. Alabama, Delaware, Florida, Georgia, Louisiana, Maryland, Mississippi, North Carolina, South Carolina, and Virginia never

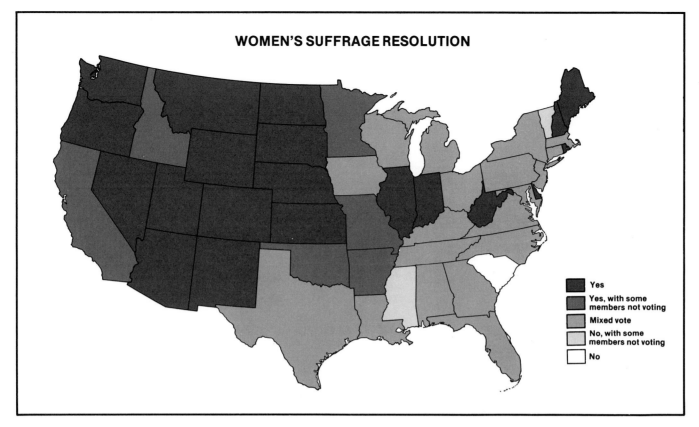

WOMEN'S SUFFRAGE RESOLUTION

Legend:
- Yes
- Yes, with some members not voting
- Mixed vote
- No, with some members not voting
- No

Map 11.7 Women's Suffrage Resolution—congressional voting, 1919, 66th Congress, 1st Session.

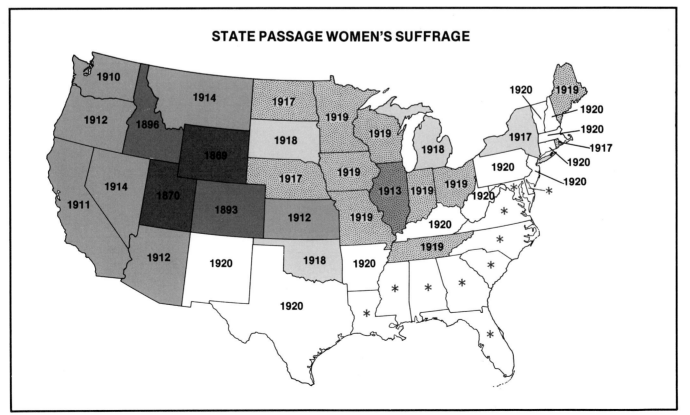

STATE PASSAGE WOMEN'S SUFFRAGE

Legislation passed
- by 1875
- 1876–1900
- 1901–1915
- 1916–1919
- 1920, granted by constitutional amendment
- Partial suffrage (allowed to vote for presidential electors)
- * Never ratified constitutional amendment

Map 11.8 State passage of full women's suffrage—ratification of constitutional amendment, 1869–1919.

ratified it. The diffusion of state support for women's suffrage, therefore, originated in the West and spread first west and then east from a central core.

ERA

"Equality of rights under the law shall not be denied or abridged by the United States or by any state on account of sex." Such a simple statement, the proposed Equal-rights Amendment to the Constitution, produced an unexpected outpouring of animosity in the country during the late 1970s and early 1980s. Commonsense suggests that the amendment eventually will be passed as governmental control at all levels transfers to more enlightened, younger politicians. Besides, women's newfound political savvy will assure passage the next time around, just as the suffragists learned how to communicate and push the right power buttons. Legislative sleight-of-hand on the part of a few state legislators has been duly noted.

ERA legislation was drafted to eliminate discriminatory practices in employment such as those imposed by protective labor-standard laws. Protective laws had become restrictive laws as more women entered the labor force. Marital property rights were another specific target of the legislation. One way to assure no sex discrimination under the law on such issues is to rely upon Supreme Court rulings under the Fifth and Fourteenth amendments on cases of discrimination. The court repeatedly, however, has been reluctant to consider equal-rights cases. Another approach is to work for equal-rights legislation through state legislative action, but this laborious statute-by-statute process assures no uniform code.

The history of the ERA has been just as tangled and political as suffrage for women was. The National Women's Party saw to it that an ERA resolution was introduced in every Congress from 1923 until 1972. In the Senate it was actually passed three times during that time period, but the action was killed by a rider. The ERA resolution never made it out of the House, partly because Emanuel Celler's Judiciary Committee sat on the legislation until 1970. At that time a parliamentary move by Representative Martha Griffiths of Michigan forced consideration on the floor of the House in that and subsequent years. The House approved the resolution, 265 to 87, on October 12, 1971. On March 22, 1972, the Senate, led by Senators Bayh and Cook, voted, 84 to 8, to approve. Within three months, 19 state legislatures had ratified the ERA, Hawaii and Pennsylvania being among the first. By 1975 the total was 35 states, 3 short of the necessary 38 to pass. ERA supporters petitioned for an extension that was granted

until June 30, 1982, but no additional states were added in the extended time period. Idaho, Nebraska, and Tennessee actually rescinded their votes of approval, Kentucky attempted to do the same, and South Dakota declared its original ratification void if the amendment was not approved by the original 1979 deadline.

The states that never ratified the Equal-rights Amendment are indicated on Map 11.9. Most of these are the same southern states that opposed suffrage for women. If the Deep South is ignored as a lost cause, probable states for future ratification, based on regional politics, include Illinois and Florida. Anti-ERA Illinois, an especially early sponsor of suffrage for women, should hang its head. States with a high number of female state legislators are places of possible success. Arizona is the best bet here. This outlined strategy assumes, of course, that the rest of the states will ratify again as they did before.

In order to be ratified, the next ERA resolution has to be approved first by the Congress before it is submitted for ratification by the states. Map 11.10 is concerned with the strength of congressional support for the ERA and is based on two measures. House voting on an ERA resolution on November 15, 1983 (where the measure was voted down, 278 for and 147 against, 6 votes short of the two-thirds majority required for passage) is used for part of the state delegation assessment. Senators who were sponsors of HJR-1, a reintroduced Equal-rights Amendment in 1983, also are included in the value. The map reflects the percentage of each state delegation that was supportive of the ERA during the 98th Congress. Every 2 years slight changes in the composition of this body may be expected; new voting alignments could result in modifications to the map.

Unanimous support for ERA is seen in a total of 10 states scattered across the northern half of the country, plus Alaska and Hawaii. The most concentrated regional grouping is present in four New England states. High-support states can be found intermixed among the previous unanimous states with the pattern extending intermittently across the northern states; extensions southward are represented by California and Oklahoma.

States where there is no support among the congressional delegation are Idaho, Nevada, Utah, and Wyoming. All four are Mormon-influenced. Other low-value states are found scattered through the interior West and Plains, and in parts of the South plus Indiana.

One purpose of looking at congressional support spatially is to target those states that are anomalies in the general pattern and can be the focus for future endeavors. Oklahoma, for example, sticks out like a sore thumb. This is a state that did not ratify the ERA in the first ratification round, yet all

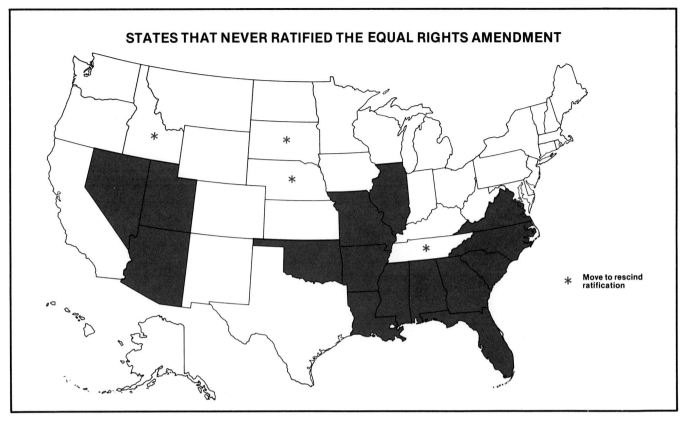

STATES THAT NEVER RATIFIED THE EQUAL RIGHTS AMENDMENT

* Move to rescind
ratification

Map 11.9 States that never ratified ERA, 1972–82.

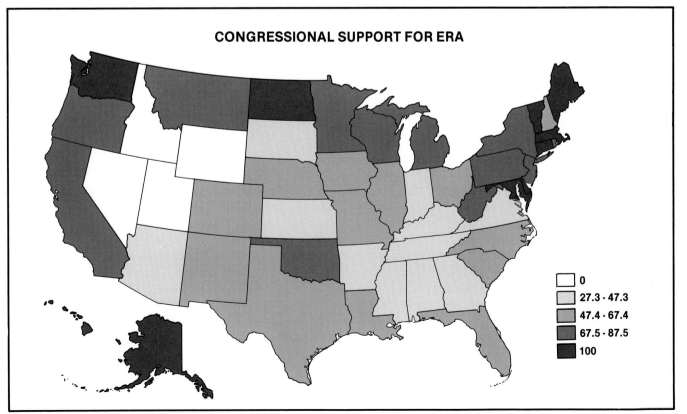

CONGRESSIONAL SUPPORT FOR ERA

☐	0
☐	27.3 - 47.3
☐	47.4 - 67.4
☐	67.5 - 87.5
■	100

Map 11.10 Congressional support for ERA—percentage of state's delegation in favor of ERA, 1983.

Politics

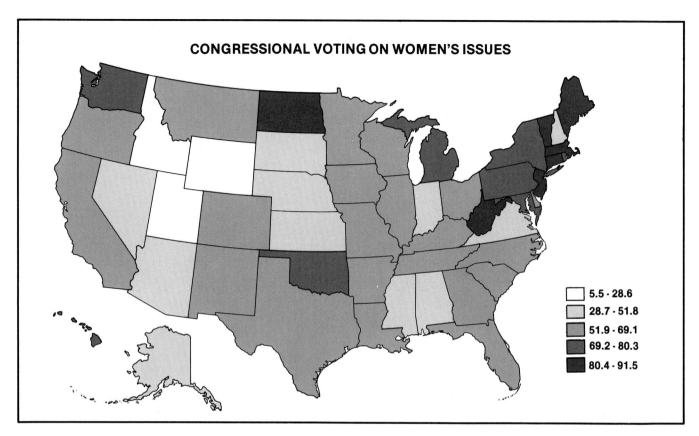

CONGRESSIONAL VOTING ON WOMEN'S ISSUES

Legend:
- 5.5 - 28.6
- 28.7 - 51.8
- 51.9 - 69.1
- 69.2 - 80.3
- 80.4 - 91.5

Map 11.11   Congressional voting on women's issues, 1983–84 Congress. U.S. average index value is 63.5.

but one Republican senator and one Republican representative were behind the ERA in 1983. Surely Oklahoma will yield in the next ratification round. On the other hand, congressmen from several states need to be reminded that they are not representing the wishes of their constituents. New Hampshire appears as a regional anomaly, not being as liberally supportive as its neighbors. New Hampshire's two Republican senators were not responsive. The two Republican senators from Indiana behaved similarly. Three Republican representatives and one Republican senator from Kansas needed to be reminded of their responsibilities; so did two Republican senators from South Dakota.

Conservative Republicans have dragged their heels. In the 1983 reintroduced ERA, 37 of the sponsoring senators were Democrats; 19 were Republicans. Eight of the remaining 10 nonsponsoring Democrats were southerners, a breed apart from the rest of the party when it comes to sex discrimination. The other two recalcitrant Democrats were both from Nebraska. President Reagan opposed the ERA, and thus provided the party cue for voting behavior on an issue that should follow conscience, not party lines.

Congresswomen's support for the ERA is divided and does not follow partisan lines. The two Republican senators are on opposite sides of the issue. Eight Republican representatives are for the ERA; so are 11 Democratic representatives. One Democratic and one Republican representative voted against the ERA resolution in 1983.

WOMEN'S ISSUES

The ERA is not the only women's issue acted on by Congress. For the 1983–84 Congress the National Women's Political Caucus selected 11 key votes for the Senate and nine for the House to measure how representatives in Washington added up. Using these data, Map 11.11 is a "report card" on each state's legislative delegation with regards to women's issues. The index that is mapped represents the average legislative score for that state. If congressional voting truly does represent constituents' opinions, then the map is a rough indicator of state attitudes toward women's status across our country. Readers should remember that an anti-NWPC position vote could be a reaction to other concerns in some cases, such as a poorly drafted bill, budget reduction, or dislike of government intervention in private affairs. In addition, many of the issues affect interest groups other than women. The 11- and 9-vote sample for the chambers, however, gives a fair measure of a legislator's general stance.

Senate issues included the Hatch amendment on abortion; abortion for federal employees under health insurance; before- and after-school child-care programs; spending cuts in education, nutrition, and job training; deficit reduction on health care; divorced military-spouse benefits; Wilkensen nomination; and Civil Rights Act regarding Grove City decision (twice). House of Representatives issues were the U.S. Commission of Civil Rights membership; Equal-rights amendment; abortion costs; Civil Rights Act of 1984; federal pay equity; child nutrition; domestic spending; education, nutrition, and job-training fund restoration; and hunger relief.

The most liberal legislative voting on issues concerning women was done by delegations from the far northeastern corner of this country, plus North Dakota and West Virginia. West Virginia had the highest pro-NWPC voting pattern with a composite 91.5 score. Connecticut followed with 90.3; then Maine with 87.8 and New Jersey with 87.5. The Northeast appears as a prominent supporter of women's issues, with New Hampshire as the regional exception. As with ERA voting, Oklahoma displays a uniquely liberal attitude for its section of the country.

Conservative positions in the West are assumed by the Mormon triumvirate of Idaho, Utah, and Wyoming. Idaho has the lowest score with only 5.5% of its congressional delegation votes being for women. The two senators and one of the representatives did not favor any of the NWPC positions. The remaining representative voted in favor of two issues. Utah had a score of 10.2 and Wyoming's was 15.7. These three states ranked far below the rest of the country. Voting records for the 23 legislators completely opposed to the NWPC stance (score of zero) all belong to Republicans. Six of these negative votes came from southern states, 7 from the Midwest, and 10 from the West. As expected, none came from the Northeast, although one senator from New Hampshire came close to putting himself on the failing-grade list.

Just because a congresswoman is a woman does not mean she will always vote positively for women's issues; the average score for the 23 women in the 98th Congress of 1983–84 was 75.1. The 2 female senators, both of whom were Republicans, had an average score of 40.5; the 21 representatives averaged 78.4. Subdividing the House by party, the 9 Republican members had an average value of 65.4, and the 12 Democrats 88.1.

State legislators have voted on a variety of issues related to women just as have lawmakers at the federal level. Using

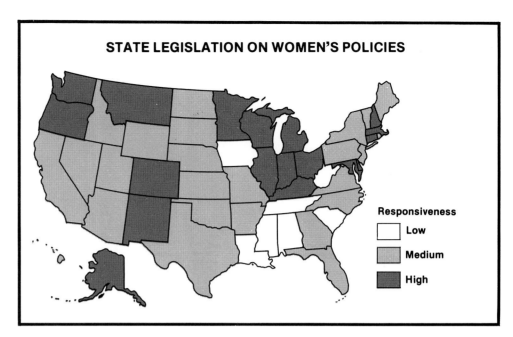

Map 11.12   State legislation on women's policies, 1976.

as a measure whether or not a state had passed a specific law related to women by 1976, Blair and Savage developed an evaluation of the states. They selected 88 measures related to equal rights, including specific laws on suffrage, work conditions, employment practices, spousal and child support, worker's compensation, credit, housing, prostitution, and rape. By synthesizing their results, Map 11.12 indicates three levels of responsiveness to women's legal status in policies of role change and role equity, factors of immediate concern to those interested in changing the status of women in the eyes of the law.

States that exhibited high responsiveness as of 1976 are found in parts of New England, the mid-Atlantic region, the industrial Midwest, the Northwest including Alaska, and in two states of the Southwest. Colorado had the highest index value, followed by Montana and Washington. Kentucky and Maryland appear at the next highest level.

States that exhibited low responsiveness to women's policies are clustered in parts of the South plus Iowa and West Virginia. South Carolina had the lowest index value, followed by Alabama and Mississippi. Iowa, Louisiana, Tennessee, and West Virginia appear in the next lowest level of this category.

Such map patterns reinforce many of the previous findings in this set of maps dealing with the effects of politics on women. The South is behind the rest of the country in the formulation of laws designed to assure that women are treated as equals with men. Several of the southern states, however, show more liberal attitudes toward social justice. Florida, as expected, is in the more liberal corner, but Arkansas, Georgia, North Carolina, Texas, and Virginia are there, too. Kentucky is the major regional exception with its high responsiveness rating. Kentucky, North Carolina, and Virginia, for example, lead the nation in the formulation of family partnership laws; Arkansas and Texas are leaders in credit equity.

High responsiveness occurs across the northern half of the country, but with slightly different shifts in locale from previous maps. Iowa is the odd state in the midwestern con-centration; slow reactions to credit and political equity are responsible for its low score. Since the West was the core of early suffrage passage, one could expect the same positive reaction to women's rights issues, but this is not the case. Idaho, South Dakota, and Wyoming are laggards in family-partnership laws, for example, and Nebraska, South Dakota, and Utah are laggards in credit equity.

It is unfortunate that this map represents laws passed by 1976 because since then, of course, additional changes in state laws have occurred. Comparing state laws is difficult, but we need a study updating the Blair and Savage survey.

DATA SOURCES

(**Note:** Population census materials are from the U.S. Department of Commerce, Bureau of the Census. Citations below are in a shortened form.)

Chapter One—DEMOGRAPHICS

Maps 1 to 2, 4 to 6, 15, Table 1
1980 Census of Population, Chap. B, U.S. Summary, May 1983. Table 67. Persons by age, race, Spanish origin, and sex, for states.

Map 3
1980 Census of Population, Chap. D, state volumes, various dates. Table 205. Marital status, presence of spouse, and marital history for persons 15 years and over, by race, Spanish origin, sex and age.

Map 7
1980 Census of Population, Chap. B, state volumes, various dates. Table 19. Persons by age, race, Spanish origin, and sex.

Map 8
1980 Census of Population, Chap. B, state volumes, various dates. Table 17. Race by sex: 1900 to 1980.

Map 9
1980 Census of Population, Chap. D, state volumes, various dates. Table 200. Residence in 1975 by age, sex, race, and Spanish origin.

Map 10
Quinn, Bernard, Herman Anderson, Martin Bradley, Paul Goetting, and Peggy Shriver. *Churches and Church Membership in the United States, 1980.* Atlanta: Glenmary Research Center, 1982.

Maps 11 to 14
1980 Census of Population, Chap. B, U.S. Summary, May 1983. Table 62. Persons by race and sex for regions, divisions, and states.

Map 16
1980 Census of Population, Chap. D, state volumes, various dates. Table 196. Selected social and economic characteristics by nativity, year of immigration, and country of birth.

Figure 1
1980 Census of Population, Chap. B, U.S. Summary, May 1983. Table 43. Persons by age, race, Spanish origin, and sex.

Table 2
1980 Census of Population, Chap. B, C, and D, U.S. Summary, May 1983, December 1983, and March 1984. Table 46. Household and family characteristics by race and Spanish origin; Table 74. Race by sex; Table 75. Persons by Spanish origin, race, and sex; Table 259. Residence in 1975 by age, sex, race, and Spanish origin; Table 262. Years of school completed for persons 15 years old and over by age, sex, race, and Spanish origin; Table 270. Children ever born and marital status of women by age, race, and Spanish origin; Table 272. Labor force status by age, race, Spanish origin, and sex; Table 296. Income in 1979 of persons 18 years and over by years of school completed, age, race, Spanish origin, and sex; and Table 304. Persons below specified poverty level in 1979 by relationship, age, sex, race, and Spanish origin.

Table 3
1980 Census of Population, Chap. B, U.S. Summary, May 1983. Table 69. Persons by race and sex for areas and places.

Table 4
1980 Census of Population, Chap. B, U.S. Summary, May 1983. Table 70. Total persons and Spanish origin persons by type of Spanish origin, race, and sex, for areas and places.

Chapter Two—LABOR FORCE

Maps 1 to 5, Table 1
U.S. Department of Labor, Bureau of Labor Statistics. "Geographic Profile of Employment and Unemployment, 1982." Bulletin 2170, May 1983.

Figure 1
U.S. Department of Commerce, Bureau of the Census. *Statistical Abstract of the United States, 1982–1983.* 103rd edition, 1982. Table 639. Marital status of women in the civilian labor force: 1940–1981.

Maps 6 to 8
1980 Census of Population, Chap. C, U.S. Summary, December 1983. Table 240. Labor force characteristics for divisions and states.

Figure 2
U.S. Department of Labor, Bureau of Labor Statistics. "Marital and Family Patterns of Workers: An Update." Bulletin 2163, May 1983.

Map 9
1980 Census of Population, Chap. C, state volumes, various dates. Table 61. Selected social and economic characteristics by race.

Table 2
U.S. Department of Labor, Bureau of Labor Statistics. "Geographic Profile of Employment and Unemployment, 1984." Bulletin 2234, May 1985.

Chapter Three—EARNINGS/INCOME

Maps 1 to 2
1980 Census of Population, Chap. C, state volumes, various dates. Table 71. Income characteristics in 1979.

Maps 3 to 5
U.S. Department of Labor, Bureau of Labor Statistics, Wage and Industrial Relations. *Area Wage Surveys.* Bulletins 3015–3 through 3020–14, February 1982 to May 1983.

Map 6
1980 Census of Population, Chap. D, state volumes, various dates. Table 231. Industry of the experienced civilian labor force by earnings in 1979.

Map 7
"The Forbes Four Hundred." *Forbes 400,* 134 (October 1, 1984): 72–162.

Table 1
1980 Census of Population, Chap. C, state volumes, various dates. Table 124. Income characteristics in 1979 for areas and places.

Chapter Four—OCCUPATIONS

Maps 1 to 5, Table 1
1980 Census of Population, Chap. D, state volumes, various dates. Table 230. Industry of employed persons by age and sex.

Table 2
1980 Census of Population, Chap. D, U.S. Summary, March 1984. Table 276. Detailed occupation of the experienced labor force and employed persons by sex: 1980 and 1970; and Nancy F. Rytina. "Earnings of Men and Women: A Look at Specific Occupations." *Monthly Labor Review,* 105 (April 1982):25–31.

Maps 6 to 13
1980 Census of Population, Chap. D, state volumes, various dates. Table 217. Detailed occupation of the experienced civilian labor force and employed persons by sex: 1980 and 1970.

Chapter Five—EDUCATION

Maps 1 to 3
1980 Census of Population, Chap. C, state volumes, various dates. Table 66. Educational characteristics.

Table 1
U.S. Department of Commerce, Bureau of the Census. "Educational Attainment in the United States: March 1975." Ser. P-20, no. 295, June 1976; and *Statistical Abstract of the United States, 1981.* 102nd ed., 1980.

Maps 4 to 5
National Center for Education Statistics. "Increases Noted in Degrees Conferred for 1979–80." *Bulletin,* Washington, D.C., August 14, 1981.

Maps 6 to 9, Table 3
Office for Civil Rights. "Data on Earned Degrees Conferred by Institutions of Higher Education by Race, Ethnicity, and Sex: Academic Year 1976–77." Vols. 1 and 2, U.S. Department of Health, Education, and Welfare, Washington, D.C., 1979.

Map 10
"Women's Colleges and Universities in the United States." Listing from Women's College Coalition, Washington, D.C., 1983.

Map 11
Women's Studies Quarterly, 9 (1981):25–35.

Table 2
1980 Census of Population, Chap. C, state volumes, various dates. Table 119. Educational characteristics for areas and places.

Chapter Six—SPORTS

Maps 1 to 9, Table 1
National Federation of State High School Associations. *National Federation Handbook 1984–85.* Kansas City, Mo., 1984.

Maps 10 to 15
Barry Green and Alan Green. *The Directory of Athletic Scholarships.* New York: G. P. Putnam's Sons, 1981; and "1985 Scholarship Guide," *Women's Sports and Fitness,* 7 (January/February 1985): 31–45.

Map 16
New York Times, February 5, 1984, sect. 5, p. 5; *Los Angeles Times,* July 27, 1984, pt. 8, pp. 20–32.

Map 17
Women's International Bowling Congress. *1983–84 Annual Report.* Greendale, Wis., 1984.

Chapter Seven—RELATIONSHIPS

Maps 1 to 5, 8 to 9, Table 1
U.S. Department of Commerce, Bureau of the Census. "Provisional Estimates of Social, Economic, and Housing Characteristics." 1980 Census of Population and Housing, supplementary report, March 1982, Table P-1. General, family, and fertility characteristics.

Maps 6 to 7
Bureau of the Census. *State and Metropolitan Area Data Book, 1982.* U.S. Government Printing Office, 1982. Table C. Marriages, divorces, and registered aliens.

Maps 10 to 11
U.S. Department of Commerce, Bureau of the Census. "Provisional Estimates of Social, Economic, and Housing Characteristics." 1980 Census of Population and Housing, supplementary report, March 1982, Table P-4. Income and poverty status in 1979.

Chapter Eight—PREGNANCY

Maps 1, 3 to 5
1980 Census of Population, Chap. D, state volumes, various dates. Table 211. Children ever born and marital status of women by age, race, and Spanish origin.

Map 2
Bureau of the Census. *State and Metropolitan Data Book, 1982.* U.S. Government Printing Office, 1982. Table C. Births and deaths.

Map 6
Aida Torres and Jacqueline D. Forrest. "Family Planning Clinic Services in the United States, 1981." *Family Planning Perspectives,* 15 (November/December 1983):274.

Map 7
Stanley K. Henshaw and Kevin O'Reilly. "Characteristics of Abortion Patients in the United States, 1979 and 1980." *Family Planning Perspectives,* 15 (January/February 1983):12.

Map 8
U.S. Department of Commerce, Bureau of the Census. *Statistical Abstract of the United States, 1982–83.* 103rd edition, 1982. Table 104. Legal abortions.

Chapter Nine—HEALTH

Map 1
Bureau of the Census. *State and Metropolitan Data Book, 1982.* U.S. Government Printing Office, 1982. Table C. Death rates by cause, average lifetime, and marriages.

Maps 2 to 12
U.S. Department of Health and Human Services. National Center for Health Statistics. *Vital Statistics of the United States, 1978.* Vol. 2—Mortality, pt. B, sec. 7. Geographic detail for mortality, 1981.

Map 13
U.S. Department of Health and Human Services. Centers for Disease Control. "Sexually Transmitted Disease Fact Sheet," Edition 35, Atlanta, 1981.

Map 14
1980 Census of Population, Chap. C, state volumes, various dates. Table 70. Labor force status in 1979 and disability and veteran status.

Maps 15 to 18
M. Kirsten Bradstock, James S. Marks, Michelle Forman, Eileen M. Gentry, Gary C. Hogelin, and Frederich L. Trowbridge. "Behavioral Risk Factor Surveillance, 1981–1983." *CDC Surveillance Summaries,* 33, 1SS (1984): 1–4; Centers for Disease Control, "Annual Summary 1982: Reported Morbidity and Mortality in the United States." *Morbidity and Mortality Weekly Report,* 31, 54 (1983):127–31; Centers for Disease Control. "Behavioral Risk Factors Prevalence Survey—United States, Fourth Quarter 1982." *Morbidity and Mortality Weekly Report,* 33, 18 (1984):247–49; Gary C. Hogelin. "Behavioral Risk Factor Surveillance—Selected States." *CDC Surveillance Summaries,* 32, 1SS (1983):11–17; Craig A. Lambert, David R. Netherton, Lorenz J. Finison, James N. Hyde. "Risk Factors and Life Style: A Statewide Health-Interview Survey." *New England Journal of Medicine,* 306 (April 29, 1982):1048–51.

Chapter Ten—CRIME

Map 1
Timothy J. Flanagan and Maureen McLeod, eds. *Sourcebook of Criminal Justice Statistics—1982.* U.S. Department of Justice, Bureau of Justice Statistics. Washington, D.C.: U.S. Government Printing Office, 1983.

Map 2
National Center for the Prevention and Control of Rape. *National Directory: Rape Prevention and Treatment Resources.* Washington, D.C.: National Institute of Mental Health, 1981.

Map 3
Center for Women Policy Studies. *Programs Providing Services to Battered Women.* Washington, D.C.: Resource Center on Family Violence, 1980.

Maps 4 to 5
Office of Justice Assistance, Research and Statistics. *National Prisoner Statistics: Prisoners in State and Federal Institutions on December 31, 1980.* Washington, D.C.: Department of Justice, 1982.

Map 6
Administrative Office of the United States Courts. *Federal Offenders in the United States Courts 1983.* Washington, D.C.: Government Printing Office, 1984.

Chapter Eleven—POLITICS

Map 1
Donald E. Starsinic. "Projections of the Population of Voting Age for States: November 1984." Bureau of the Census, Current Population Reports, ser. P-25, no. 948, 1984.

Maps 2 to 3
Bureau of the Census. "Voting and Registration in the Election of November 1984 (Advance Report)." Current Population Reports, ser. P-20. no. 397, 1985.

Map 4
"Number of Women in State Legislatures," *Women's Political Times,* 10 (January/February 1985):7.

Map 5
Biographical Directory of the American Congress, 1774–1971. Senate Document no. 92-B, Washington, D.C.: Government Printing Office, 1971: *Congressional Directory.* Washington, D.C.: Government Printing Office, 65th Congress, 1st Session, April 1917 through 99th Congress, 1st Session, 1985.

Map 6

Communication from Faye Pritchard, Membership and Development, National Office of League of Women Voters of the United States, May 30, 1985.

Maps 7 to 8

Charles O. Paullin. *Atlas of Historical Geography of the United States.* Carnegie Institution of Washington and American Geographical Society of New York, 1932. Table 41 and Plates 126C to 128A.

Map 9

"ERA Dies Three States Short of Ratification." *1982 Congressional Quarterly Almanac,* 97th Congress, 2nd Session, 1982, pp. 377–78. Congressional Quarterly, 1983.

Map 10

"ERA Analysis—U.S. Senate—1983–1984." *National NOW Times,* 16 (March 1983): 2; and "Roll-Call Vote on the Equal Rights Amendment." *Women's Political Times,* 8 (November/December 1983): 16.

Map 11

"1983–84 Congressional Voting Record: How do Your Representatives in Washington Add Up?" *Women's Political Times,* 9 (October 1984):6–10.

Map 12

Diane D. Blair and Robert L. Savage. "Dimensions of Responsiveness to Women's Policies in the Fifty States." *Women and Politics,* 4 (Summer 1984):49–68.

BIBLIOGRAPHY

CHAPTER ONE— DEMOGRAPHICS

Acosta-Belén, Edna, ed. *The Puerto Rican Woman.* New York: Praeger, 1979.

Allen, James P. "Changes in the American Propensity to Migrate." *Annals of the Association of American Geographers,* 67 (1977):577–87.

Allen, Walter R. "The Social and Economic Statuses of Black Women in the United States." *Phylon,* 42 (1981):26–40.

Boulding, Elise, Shirley A. Nuss, Dorothy Lee Carson, Michael A. Greenstein. *Handbook of International Data on Women.* New York: Sage Publications, 1976.

Bouvier, Leon F., and Cary B. Davis. "The Future Racial Composition of the United States." *The Mankind Quarterly,* 23 (1983):299–327.

Bureau of the Census. "A Statistical Portrait of Women in the United States: 1978." Current Population Reports, ser. P-23, no. 100, 1980.

Cooney, Rosemary Santana, and Vilma Ortiz. "Nativity, National Origin, and Hispanic Female Participation in the Labor Force." *Social Science Quarterly,* 64 (1983):510–23.

de Vaus, David A. "The Impact of Children on Sex Related Differences in Church Attendance." *Sociological Analysis,* 43 (1982):145–54.

_____. "Workforce Participation and Sex Differences in Church Attendance." *Review of Religious Research,* 25 (1984):247–56.

Easterlin, Richard A., David Ward, William S. Bernard, and Reed Veda. *Immigration.* Cambridge, Mass.: Belknap Press, 1982.

Ferriss, Abbott L. *Indicators of Trends in the Status of American Women.* New York: Russell Sage Foundation, 1971.

Fuchs, Victor R. *How We Live: An Economic Perspective on Americans from Birth to Death.* Cambridge, Mass.: Harvard University Press, 1983.

Glenn, Evelyn Nakano. "Split Household, Small Producer and Dual Wage Earner: An Analysis of Chinese-American Family Strategies." *Journal of Marriage and the Family,* 45 (1983):35–46.

Graff, Thomas O., and Robert F. Wiseman. "Changing Concentrations of Older Americans." *The Geographical Review,* 68 (1978):379–93.

Guttentag, Marcia, and Paul F. Secord. *Too Many Women? The Sex Ratio Question.* Beverly Hills, Calif.: Sage, 1983.

Haber, Barbara, ed. *The Women's Annual, 1980: The Year in Review.* Boston: G.K. Hall, 1981.

_____, ed. *The Women's Annual, 1981: The Year in Review.* Boston: G.K. Hall, 1982.

_____, ed. *The Women's Annual, 1982–83.* Boston: G. K. Hall, 1983.

Infomap. *Atlas of Demographics: U.S. by County.* Boulder, Colo.: Infomap, 1982.

Jones, Barbara A.P. "The Economic Status of Black Women." In *The State of Black America 1983,* edited by James D. Williams, 115–54. New York: National Urban League, 1983.

Joseph, Gloria I., and Jill Lewis. *Common Differences: Conflicts in Black and White Feminist Perspectives.* New York: Doubleday-Anchor, 1981.

Long, Larry, and Diana De Are. "Repopulating the Countryside: A 1980 Census Trend." *Science,* 217 (1982):1111–16.

Markson, Elizabeth W. *Older Women.* Lexington, Mass.: Lexington Books, 1983.

Mazey, Mary Ellen, and David R. Lee. *Her Space, Her Place: A Geography of Women.* Washington, D.C.: Association of American Geographers, 1983.

McKee, Jesse O., ed. *Ethnicity in Contemporary America: A Geographical Appraisal.* Dubuque, Iowa: Kendall/Hunt, 1985.

McKinney, William, and Wade Clark Roof. "A Social Profile of American Religious Groups," in *Yearbook of American and Canadian Churches 1982.* Nashville: Abingdon Press, 1982, pp. 267–73.

Melville, Margarita B., ed. *Twice a Minority: Mexican American Women.* St. Louis: C. V. Mosby, 1980.

Mirandé, Alfredo, and Evangelina Enriquez. *La Chicana: The Mexican-American Woman.* Chicago: University of Chicago Press, 1979.

Momeni, Jamshid A. *Demography of Racial and Ethnic Minorities in the United States: An Annotated Bibliography with a Review Essay.* Westport, Conn.: Greenwood Press, 1984.

_____. *Demography of the Black Population in the United States: An Annotated Bibliography with a Review Essay.* Westport, Conn.: Greenwood Press, 1983.

Pritchard, Sarah M., ed. *The Women's Annual, 1983–1984.* Boston: G. K. Hall, 1984.

Rodgers-Rose, La Frances, ed. *The Black Woman.* Beverly Hills, Calif.: Sage, 1980.

Shortridge, James R. "The Pattern of American Catholicism, 1971." *Journal of Geography,* 77 (1978):56–60.

_____. "Patterns of Religion in the United States." *The Geographical Review,* 66 (1976):420–34.

Siegel, Jacob S., and Maria Davidson. "Demographic and Socioeconomic Aspects of Aging in the United States." Bureau of the Census, Current Population Reports, ser. P-23, no. 138, 1984.

Sivard, Ruth Leger. *Women . . . a World Survey.* Washington, D.C.: World Priorities, 1985.

Taeuber, Cynthia M. "America in Transition: An Aging Society." Bureau of the Census, Current Population Reports, ser. P-23, no. 128, 1983.

CHAPTER TWO— LABOR FORCE

Brown, David L., and Jeanne M. O'Leary. "Labor Force Activity of Women in Metropolitan and Nonmetropolitan America." U.S. Department of Agriculture, Economics, Statistics, and Cooperatives Service, Rural Development Research Report no. 15, 1979.

Bureau of Labor Statistics, U.S. Department of Labor. "Children of Working Mothers." Bulletin 2158, March 1983.

Carliner, Geoffrey. "Female Labor Force Participation Rates for Nine Ethnic Groups." *Journal of Human Resources,* 16 (1981):286–93.

Chorvinsky, Milton. "Preprimary Enrollment 1980." National Center for Education Statistics, 1982.

Cooney, Rosemary Santana. "Intercity Variations in Puerto Rican Female Participation." *Journal of Human Resources,* 14 (1979):222–35.

Hayghe, Howard. "Perspectives on Working Women: A Databook." U.S. Department of Labor, Bureau of Labor Statistics, Bulletin 2080, 1980.

Marcum, John P., and Mary Radosh. "Religious Affiliation, Labor Force Participation and Fertility." *Sociological Analysis,* 42 (1981):353–62.

Mott, Frank L. *Women, Work, and Family: Dimensions of Change in American Society.* Lexington, Mass.: Lexington Books, 1978.

Nollen, Stanley D. *New Work Schedules in Practice: Managing Time in a Changing Society.* New York: Van Nostrand Reinhold, 1982.

O'Connell, Martin, and Carolyn C. Rogers. "Child Care Arrangements of Working Mothers: June 1982." Bureau of the Census, Current Population Reports, ser. P-23, no. 129, 1983.

Oppenheimer, Valerie Kincade. *Work and the Family: A Study in Social Demography.* New York: Academic Press, 1982.

Presser, Harriet B., and Virginia S. Cain. "Shift Work among Dual-Earner Couples with Children." *Science,* 219 (1983):876–79.

Schwartz, Judith I. "Reconciling Women's Changing Status with Children's Enduring Needs." *Educational Horizons,* 59 (Fall 1980):15–21.

Smith, Ralph E. *The Subtle Revolution: Women at Work.* Washington, D.C.: The Urban Institute, 1979.

Stromberg, Ann H., and Shirley Harkess. *Women Working: Theories and Facts in Perspective.* Palo Alto, Calif.: Mayfield, 1978.

U.S. Commission on Civil Rights. "Child Care and Equal Opportunity for Women." Clearinghouse Publication no. 67, June 1981.

Waite, Linda J. "U.S. Women at Work." *Population Bulletin,* 36 (May 1981).

Waldman, Elizabeth, Allyson Sherman Grossman, Howard Hayghe, and Beverly L. Johnson. "Working Mothers in the 1970's: A Look at the Statistics." *Monthly Labor Review,* 102 (October 1979):39–49.

Yohalem, Alice M. *Women Returning to Work: Policies and Progress in Five Countries.* Montclair, N.J.: Allanheld, Osman, 1980.

CHAPTER THREE— EARNINGS/INCOME

Blaxall, Martha, and Barbara Reagan. *Women and the Workplace: The Implications of Occupational Segregation.* Chicago: University of Chicago Press, 1976.

Bureau of Labor Statistics, U.S. Department of Labor. "Earnings Gap." *Monthly Labor Review,* 105 (November 1982):2.

Chesler, Phyllis, and Emily Jane Goodman. *Women, Money & Power.* New York: William Morrow, 1976.

Lewin, Tamar. "A New Push to Raise Women's Pay." *New York Times,* January 1, 1984, sec. 3–1.

Rytina, Nancy F. "Earnings of Men and Women: A Look at Specific Occupations." *Monthly Labor Review,* 105 (April 1982):25–31.

Selden, Catherine et al. *Equal Pay for Work of Comparable Worth: An Annotated Bibliography.* Chicago: American Library Association, Office for Library Personnel Resources, 1982.

Trieman, Donald J., and Heidi I. Hartmann, eds. *Women, Work, and Wages: Equal Pay for Jobs of Equal Value.* Washington, D.C.: National Academy Press, 1981.

CHAPTER FOUR— OCCUPATIONS

Braslow, Judith B., and Marilyn Heins. "Women in Medical Education: A Decade of Change." *The New England Journal of Medicine,* 304 (1981):1129–35.

Carter, Michael J., and Susan Boslego Carter. "Women's Recent Progress in the Professions or, Women Get a Ticket to Ride after the Gravy Train Has Left the Station." *Feminist Studies,* 7 (1981):477–501.

Epstein, Cynthia Fuchs. *Women in Law.* New York: Basic Books, 1981.

Howe, Louise Kapp. *Pink Collar Workers: Inside the World of Women's Work.* New York: G. P. Putnam's Sons, 1977.

Kalbacher, Judith Z. *Women Farmers in America.* U.S. Department of Agriculture, Economic Research Service, publication no. 679, 1982.

Katzman, David M. *Seven Days a Week: Women and Domestic Service in Industrializing America.* New York: Oxford University Press, 1978.

Kessler-Harris, Alice. *Out to Work: A History of Wage-Earning Women in the United States.* New York: Oxford University Press, 1982.

Mandelbaum, Dorothy Rosenthal. "Why Women Want to Work: A Look at Career Persistence." *Journal of National Association for Women Deans, Administrators, and Counselors,* 46 (1983):11–17.

Martorelli, Debra. "Is Teaching a Female Ghetto?" *Instructor,* 92 (September 1982):30–34.

Marwell, Gerald, Rachel Rosenfeld, and Seymour Spilerman. "Geographic Constraints on Women's Careers in Academia." *Science,* 205 (1979):1225–31.

Melosh, Barbara. *"The Physician's Hand:" Work Culture and Conflict in American Nursing.* Philadelphia: Temple University Press, 1982.

Nelson, Jill. "I'm Not Your Girl! Household Workers Organize." *Essence,* (November 1980):99.

Rossiter, Margaret W. *Women Scientists in America: Struggles and Strategies to 1940.* Baltimore: Johns Hopkins University Press, 1982.

Royle, Marjorie H. "Women Pastors: What Happens after Placement?" *Review of Religious Research,* 24 (1982):116–26.

Rytina, Nancy F., and Suzanne M. Bianchi. "Occupational Reclassification and Changes in Distribution by Gender." *Monthly Labor Review,* 107 (March 1984)11–17.

Sachs, Carolyn E. *The Invisible Farmers: Women in Agricultural Production.* Totowa, N.J.: Rowman & Allanheld, 1983.

Urquhart, Michael. "The Employment Shift to Services: Where Did It Come from?" *Monthly Labor Review,* 107 (April 1984):15–22.

Walsh, Mary Roth. "The Rediscovery of the Need for a Feminist Medical Education." *Harvard Educational Review,* 49 (1979):447–66.

CHAPTER FIVE— EDUCATION

Bales, S. N., and M. Sharp. "Women's Colleges—Weathering a Difficult Era with Success and Stamina." *Change,* 13 (1981):53–56.

Boxer, M. J. "For and About Women: The Theory and Practice of Women's Studies in the United States." *Signs,* 7 (1982):661–95.

Brown, George H. "Degree Awards to Women: An Update, January 1979." Washington, D.C.: National Center for Education Statistics, 1979.

Bureau of the Census. "Educational Attainment in the United States: March 1979 and 1978." Current Population Reports, ser. P-20, no. 356, 1980.

Chamberlain, M. "Period of Remarkable Growth: Women's Studies Research Centers." Change, 14 (1982):24–29.

Glenn, Norval D., and Charles N. Weaver. "Education's Effects on Psychological Well-Being." Public Opinion Quarterly, 45 (1981):22–39.

Graham, Patricia Albjerg. "Expansion and Exclusion: A History of Women in American Higher Education." Signs, 3 (1978):759–73.

Hearn, James C., and Susan Olzak. "Sex Differences in the Implications of the Links Between Major Departments and the Occupational Structure." In The Undergraduate Woman: Issues in Educational Equity, edited by Pamela J. Perun. Lexington, Mass.: Lexington Books, 1982.

Heyns, Barbara, and Joyce Adair Bird. "Recent Trends in the Higher Education of Women." In The Undergraduate Woman: Issues in Educational Equity, edited by Pamela J. Perun. Lexington, Mass.: Lexington Books, 1982.

Howe, Florence. "Introduction: The First Decade of Women's Studies." Harvard Educational Review, 49 (1979):413–21.

Hunter, Carman St. John, and David Harman. Adult Illiteracy in the United States. New York: McGraw-Hill, 1979.

Kendall, Elaine. "Peculiar Institutions": An Informal History of the Seven Sisters Colleges. New York: G. P. Putnam's Sons, 1975.

Keniston, Kenneth, and the Carnegie Council on Children. All Our Children: The American Family Under Pressure. New York: Harcourt Brace Jovanovich, 1978.

McCarthy, Abigail. "A Threatened Resource: Leadership and Catholic Women's Colleges." Commonweal, 110 (1983):357–58.

National Center for Education Statistics. Digest of Education Statistics, 1982. Washington, D.C., 1982.

_____. "Public High School Graduates, 1980–81." Washington, D.C., 1983.

Plisko, Valena White, ed. The Condition of Education. 1983 ed. Washington, D.C.: National Center for Education Statistics, 1983.

Polachek, Solomon William. "Sex Differences in College Major." Industrial and Labor Relations Review, 31 (1978):498–508.

Randour, Mary Lou, Georgia L. Strasburg, and Jean Lipman-Blumen. "Women in Higher Education: Trends in Enrollments and Degrees Earned." Harvard Educational Review, 52 (1982):189–202.

Reuben, Elaine, and Mary Jo Boehm Strauss. "Women's Studies Graduates." Washington, D.C.: National Institute of Education, 1980.

Wellborn, S. N. "A Nation of Illiterates?" U.S. News and World Report, 92 (May 17, 1982):53–57.

Women's College Coalition. "A Second Profile of Women's Colleges." Washington, D.C., 1981.

Wood, Donna S. "Academic Women's Studies Programs." Journal of Higher Education, 52 (1981):155–72.

CHAPTER SIX— SPORTS

Beezley, William H., and Joseph P. Hobbs. "'Nice Girls Don't Sweat': Women in American Sports." Journal of Popular Culture, 16 (1983):42–53.

Davenport, Joanna. "The Eastern Legacy: The Early History of Physical Education for Women." Quest (National Association for Physical Education in Higher Education), 32 (1980):226–36.

Emery, Lynne. "Women's Participation in the Olympic Games: A Historical Perspective." Journal of Physical Education, Recreation, and Dance, 55 (1984):62–63.

Marsden, Peter V., John Shelton Reed, Michael D. Kennedy, and Kandi M. Stinson. "American Regional Cultures and Differences in Leisure Time Activities." Social Forces, 60 (1982):1023–49.

Miller, David, and Lauren Doyle. "Geographical Variation in Sport Participation for High School Boys and Girls." Abstracts of Research Papers: 1981 AAHPERD Convention, (1981):75.

Miller Brewing Company. Miller Lite Report on American Attitudes Toward Sports. Milwaukee, Wis., 1983.

National Advisory Council on Women's Educational Programs. Title IX: The Half Full, Half Empty Glass. Washington, D.C.: Government Printing Office, 1981.

Nielsen, Linda. "Putting Away the Pom-Poms: An Educational Psychologist's View of Females and Sports." In Women, Philosophy, and Sport: A Collection of New Essays, edited by Betsy C. Postow. Metuchen, N.J.: Scarecrow Press, 1983.

Rooney, John F., Jr. *A Geography of American Sport: From Cabin Creek to Anaheim.* Reading, Mass.: Addison-Wesley, 1974.

Snyder, Eldon E., and Elmer Sprietzer. "Change and Variation in the Social Acceptance of Female Participation in Sports." *Journal of Sport Behavior,* 6 (1983):3–8.

Spears, Betty. "The Transformation of Women's Collegiate Sport." *National Forum,* 62 (1982):24–25.

Twin, Stephanie L. *Out of the Bleachers: Writings on Women and Sport.* Old Westbury, N.Y.: Feminist Press, 1979.

Westkott, Marcia, and Jay J. Coakley. "Women in Sport: Modalities of Feminist Social Change." *Journal of Sport and Social Issues,* 5 (1981):32–45.

CHAPTER SEVEN— RELATIONSHIPS

Bequaert, Lucia H. *Single Women, Alone and Together.* Boston: Beacon Press, 1976.

Bernard, Jessie. "Facing the Future." *Society,* 18 (1981):53–59.

Bureau of the Census. "American Families and Living Arrangements." Current Population Reports, ser. P-23, no. 104, 1980.

_____. "Households, Families, Marital Status, and Living Arrangements: March 1983." Current Population Reports, ser. P-20, no. 382, 1983.

Cherlin, Andrew J. *Marriage, Divorce, Remarriage.* Cambridge, Mass.: Harvard University Press, 1981.

Espenshade, Thomas J. "The Economic Consequences of Divorce." *Journal of Marriage and the Family,* 41 (1979):615–26.

Gerson, Kathleen, "Changing Family Structure and the Position of Women." *Journal of the American Planning Association,* 49 (1983):138–48.

Hyman, Herbert H. *Of Time and Widowhood: Nationwide Studies of Enduring Effects.* Durham, N.C.: Duke Press Policy Studies, 1983.

Kitagawa, Evelyn M. "New Life-Styles: Marriage Patterns, Living Arrangements, and Fertility Outside of Marriage." *Annals of the American Academy of Political and Social Science,* 453 (1981):1–17.

Levitan, Sar A., and Richard S. Belous. *What's Happening to the American Family?* Baltimore: Johns Hopkins University Press, 1981.

_____. "Working Wives and Mothers: What Happens to Family Life." *Monthly Labor Review,* 104 (1981):26–30.

Macklin, Eleanor. "Nontraditional Family Forms: A Decade of Research." *Journal of Marriage and the Family,* 42 (1980):905–22.

Price-Bonham, Sharon, and Jack O. Balswick. "The Noninstitutions: Divorce, Desertion, and Remarriage." *Journal of Marriage and the Family* 42 (1980):959–72.

Rawlings, Steve W. "Families Maintained by Female Householders 1970–79." Bureau of the Census, Current Population Reports, ser. P-23, no. 107, 1980.

_____. "Households and Family Characteristics: March 1982." Bureau of the Census, Current Population Reports, ser. P-20, no. 381, 1983.

Saluter, Arlene F. "Marital Status and Living Arrangements: March 1982." Bureau of the Census, Current Population Reports, ser. P-20, no. 380, 1983.

Spanier, Graham B. "Married and Unmarried Cohabitation in the United States: 1980." *Journal of Marriage and the Family,* 45 (1983):277–88.

Weiss, Robert S. *Going It Alone: The Family Life and Social Situation of the Single Parent.* New York: Basic Books, 1979.

CHAPTER EIGHT— PREGNANCY

Alan Guttmacher Institute. *Teenage Pregnancy: The Problem That Hasn't Gone Away.* New York: Alan Guttmacher Institute, 1981.

Bush, Diane. "Fertility-Related State Laws Enacted in 1982." *Family Planning Perspectives,* 15 (1983):111–16.

Centers for Disease Control. "Abortion Surveillance, Annual Summary, 1979–80." Washington, D.C.: U.S. Department of Health and Human Services, 1983.

Clark, Samuel D., Laurie S. Zabia, and Janet B. Hardy. "Sex, Contraception and Parenthood: Experience and Attitudes Among Urban Black Young Men." *Family Planning Perspectives,* 16 (1984):77–82.

Henry, Norah F. "Regional Dimensions of Abortion-Facility Services." *Professional Geographer,* 34 (1982):65–70.

Henshaw, Stanley K., Jacqueline Darroch Forrest, Ellen Sullivan, and Christopher Tietze. "Abortion Services in the U.S., 1979–80." *Family Planning Perspectives,* 14 (1982):5–15.

Henshaw, Stanley K., and Kevin O'Reilly. "Characteristics of Abortion Patients in the U.S., 1979–80." *Family Planning Perspectives,* 15 (1983):5–16.

Laslett, Peter, Karla Oosterveen, and Richard M. Smith, eds. *Bastardy and Its Comparative History.* Cambridge, Mass.: Harvard University Press, 1980.

Nestor, Barry. "Public Funding of Contraceptive Services, 1980–82." *Family Planning Perspectives,* 14 (1982):198–203.

Orr, Margaret Terry. "Private Physicians and the Provision of Contraceptives to Adolescents." *Family Planning Perspectives,* 16 (1984):83–86.

Phipps-Yonas, Susan. "Teenage Pregnancy and Motherhood: A Review of the Literature." *American Journal of Orthopsychiatry,* 50 (1980):403–31.

Tietze, Christopher. *Induced Abortion: 1979.* 3rd ed. New York: Population Council, 1979.

Torres, Aida, and Jacqueline D. Forrest. "Family Planning Clinic Services in the U.S., 1981." *Family Planning Perspectives,* 15 (1983):272–78.

Ventura, Stephanie J. "Births of Hispanic Parentage, 1980." *Monthly Vital Statistics Report,* National Center for Health Statistics, 32 (September 1983).

Vinorskis, M. A. "An Epidemic of Adolescent Pregnancy? Some Historical Considerations." *Journal of Family History,* 6 (1981):205–30.

Wilkie, Jane R. "The Trend Toward Delayed Parenthood." *Journal of Marriage and the Family,* 43 (1981):583–91.

CHAPTER NINE—
HEALTH

Apfel, Roberta J. "How Are Women Sicker than Men? An Overview of Psychosomatic Problems in Women." *Psychotherapy and Psychosomatics,* 37 (1982):106–18.

Blot, William J., Joseph F. Fraumeni, Jr., and B. J. Stone. "Geographic Patterns of Breast Cancer in the United States." *Journal of the National Cancer Institute,* 59 (1977):1407–11.

Cohen, Judith Blackfield, and Jacob A. Brody. "The Epidemiological Importance of Psychosocial Factors in Longevity." *American Journal of Epidemiology,* 114 (1981):451–61.

Edinburg, Golda M. "Women and Aging." In *The Woman Patient,* Vol. 2, *Concepts of Femininity and the Life Cycle,* edited by Carol C. Nadelson and Malkah T. Notman. New York: Plenum Press, 1982.

Enstrom, James E. "Cancer Mortality Among Mormons." *Cancer,* 36 (1975):825–41.

Fabsitz, R., and M. Feinleib. "Geographic Patterns in County Mortality Rates from Cardiovascular Diseases." *American Journal of Epidemiology,* 111 (1980):315–28.

Fingerhut, Lois A. "Changes in Mortality Among the Elderly, United States, 1940–78, Supplement to 1980." Analytical and Epidemiological Studies, Vital and Health Statistics, ser. 3. Hyattsville, Md.: National Center for Health Statistics, 1984.

Glick, Barry J. "The Spatial Organization of Cancer Mortality." *Annals of the Association of American Geographers,* 72 (1982):471–81.

Gomberg, Edith S. Lisansky. "Historical and Political Perspective: Women and Drug Use." *Journal of Social Issues,* 38 (1982):9–23.

Greenwald, Edith D., and Edward S. Greenwald. *Cancer Epidemiology.* Medical Examination Publishing Co., 1983.

Harwood, Alan, ed. *Ethnicity and Medical Care.* Cambridge, Mass.: Harvard University Press, 1981.

Hing, Esther, Mary Grace Kovar, and Dorothy P. Rice. "Sex Differences in Health and Use of Medical Care, U.S., 1979." Analytical and Epidemiological Studies: Vital and Health Statistics ser. 3. Hyattsville, Md.: National Center for Health Statistics, 1983.

Hubbard, Ruth, Mary Sue Henifin, and Barbara Fried, eds. *Biological Woman—The Convenient Myth.* Cambridge, Mass.: Schenkman, 1982.

Markides, Kyriakos S. "Mortality Among Minority Populations: A Review of Recent Patterns and Trends." *Public Health Reports,* 98 (1983):252–60.

Mason, Thomas J., Joseph F. Fraumeni, Jr., Robert Hoover, William J. Blot. *An Atlas of Mortality from Selected Diseases.* Washington, D.C.: U.S. Department of Health and Human Services, 1981.

Mason, Thomas J., Frank W. McKay, Robert Hoover, William J. Blot, and Joseph F. Fraumeni, Jr. *Atlas of Cancer Mortality for U.S. Counties: 1950–1969.* Washington, D.C.: U.S. Department of Health, Education, and Welfare, 1975.

_____. *Atlas of Cancer Mortality Among U.S. Nonwhites: 1950–1969.* Washington, D.C.: U.S. Department of Health, Education, and Welfare, 1976.

McBride, Angela Barron, and William Leon McBride. "Theoretical Underpinnings for Women's Health." *Women & Health,* 6 (1981):37–55.

Moore, Emily C. "Women and Health, United States, 1980." *Public Health Reports,* supplement to September/October 1980 issue.

Nathanson, Constance A. "Social Roles and Health Status Among Women: The Significance of Employment." *Social Science and Medicine,* 14A (1980):463–71.

Pyle, Gerald F. *Applied Medical Geography.* Washington, D.C.: V. H. Winston & Sons, 1979.

Rice, Dorothy P., Esther Hing, Mary Grace Kovar, and Kate Prager. "Sex Differences in Disease Risk." In *The Changing Risk of Disease in Women: An Epidemiological Approach,* edited by Ellen Gold. Lexington, Mass.: D. C. Heath, 1984, pp. 1–24.

Sandelowski, Margarete. *Women, Health, and Choice.* Englewood Cliffs, N.J.: Prentice-Hall, 1981.

Sauer, Herbert I. "Geographic Patterns in the Risk of Dying and Associated Factors, Ages 35–74 Years, U.S., 1968–72." Hyattsville, Md.: National Center for Health Statistics, 1980.

Verbrugge, Lois M. "Female Illness Rates and Illness Behavior: Testing Hypotheses about Sex Differences in Health." *Women & Health,* 4 (1979):61–79.

———. "Sex Differentials in Health." *Public Health Reports,* 97 (1982):417–37.

West, D. W., J. L. Lyon, and J. W. Gardner. "Cancer Risk Factors: An Analysis of Utah Mormons and Non-Mormons." *Journal of the National Cancer Institute,* 65 (1980):1083–95.

Ziegenfus, Robert C., and Wilbert M. Gesler. "Geographical Patterns of Heart Disease in the Northeastern United States." *Social Science and Medicine,* 18 (1984):63–72.

CHAPTER TEN— CRIME

Austin, Ray L. "Women's Liberation and Increases in Minor, Major, and Occupational Offenses." *Criminology,* 20 (1982):407–30.

Bowker, Lee H. *Women, Crime, and the Criminal Justice System.* Lexington Mass.: Lexington Books, 1978.

Breines, Wini, and Linda Gordon. "The New Scholarship on Family Violence." *Signs,* 8 (1983):490–531.

Bureau of Justice Statistics. *Criminal Victimization in the United States, 1981, a National Crime Survey Report.* Washington, D.C.: U.S. Department of Justice, 1983.

_____. *Report to the Nation on Crime and Justice: The Data.* Washington, D.C.: U.S. Department of Justice, 1983.

Costa, Joseph J. *Abuse of Women: Legislation, Reporting, and Prevention.* Lexington, Mass.: Lexington Books, 1983.

Dobash, R. Emerson, and Russell Dobash. *Violence Against Wives: A Case Against the Patriarchy.* New York: Free Press, 1979.

Federal Bureau of Investigation. *Crime in the United States.* Uniform Crime Report, Washington, D.C.: U.S. Department of Justice, 1984.

Hill, Gary D., and Anthony R. Harris. "Changes in the Gender Patterning of Crime, 1953–77: Opportunity vs. Identity." *Social Science Quarterly,* 62 (1981):658–71.

Johnson, Allan Griswold. "On the Prevalence of Rape in the United States." *Signs,* 6 (1980):136–46.

Michael, Richard P., and Doris Zumpe. "Sexual Violence in the United States and the Role of Season." *American Journal of Psychiatry,* 140 (1983):883–86.

Schechter, Susan. *Women and Male Violence: The Visions and Struggles of the Battered Women's Movement.* Boston: South End Press, 1982.

Simon, Rita James. *Women and Crime.* Lexington, Mass.: Lexington Books, 1975.

Stark, Steven, and Mary Jeanne Kanary. "The Effect of Religion on Forcible Rape: A Structural Analysis." *Journal for the Scientific Study of Religion,* 22 (1983):67–74.

Straus, Murray A., Richard J. Gelles, and Suzanne K. Steinmetz. *Behind Closed Doors: Violence in the American Family.* Garden City, N.Y.: Anchor Books, 1980.

U.S. Commission on Civil Rights. *Under the Rule of Thumb: Battered Women and the Administration of Justice.* Washington, D.C., 1982.

Williams, Joyce E., and Karen A. Holmes. "In Judgment of Victims: The Social Context of Rape." *Journal of Sociology and Social Welfare,* 9 (1982):154–69.

Wilson, Carolyn F. *Violence Against Women: Causes and Prevention* (A Literature Search and Annotated Bibliography),

2nd ed. Women's Education Resources, University of Wisconsin-Extension, 1980.

Yllo, Kersti. "Sexual Equality and Violence Against Wives in American States." *Journal of Comparative Family Studies,* 14 (1983):67–86.

CHAPTER ELEVEN— POLITICS

Alexander, Shana. *State-by-State Guide to Women's Legal Rights.* Los Angeles: Wollstonecraft, 1975.

Andersen, Kristi, and Stuart J. Thorson. "Congressional Turnover and the Election of Women." *Western Political Quarterly,* 37 (1984):143–56.

Baxter, Sandra, and Marjorie Lansing. *Women and Politics: The Visible Majority.* Rev. ed. Ann Arbor, Mich.: University of Michigan Press, 1983.

Boulding, Elise. "Focus On: The Gender Gap." *Journal of Peace Research,* 21 (1984):1–3.

Brown, Barbara A., Ann E. Freedman, Harriet N. Katz, and Alice M. Price. *Women's Rights and the Law: The Impact of the ERA on State Laws.* New York: Praeger, 1977.

Bureau of the Census. "Voting and Registration in the Election of November 1978." Current Population Reports, ser. P-20, no. 344, 1979.

Carroll, Kathleen M. "The Age Difference Between Men and Women Politicians." *Social Science Quarterly,* 64 (1983):332–39.

Daynes, Byron W., and Raymond Tatalovich. "Religious Influence and Congressional Voting on Abortion." *Journal for the Scientific Study of Religion,* 23 (1984):197–200.

Diamond, Irene. *Sex Roles in the State House.* New Haven, Conn.: Yale University Press, 1977.

Elazar, Daniel J. *American Federalism: A View from the States,* 2nd ed. New York: Thomas Y. Crowell Company, 1972.

Flammang, Janet A., ed. *Political Women: Current Roles in State and Local Government.* Beverly Hills, Calif.: Sage, 1984.

Gruberg, Martin. "From Nowhere to Where? Women in State and Local Politics." *Social Science Journal,* 21 (1984):5–11.

Hill, David B. "Women State Legislators and Party Voting on the ERA." *Social Science Quarterly,* 64 (1983):318–26.

Houghton, Mary. "Women Gain State Seats." *Women's Political Times,* 9 (November/December 1984): 3.

Kincaid, Diane D. "Over His Dead Body: A Positive Perspective on Widows in the U.S. Congress." *Western Political Quarterly,* 31 (1978):96–104.

Monk-Turner, Elizabeth. "Sex and Voting Behavior in the United States of America." *Journal of Social, Political and Economic Studies,* 7 (1982):369–76.

Robinson, Joan. *An American Legal Almanac: Law in All States.* Chap. 8, "Women and the Law." Dobbs Ferry, N.Y.: Oceana Publications, 1978.

Rossi, Alice S. "Beyond the Gender Gap: Women's Bid for Political Power," *Social Science Quarterly,* 64 (1983):718–33.

Sapiro, Virginia. *The Political Integration of Women: Roles, Socialization, and Politics.* Urbana: University of Illinois Press, 1983.

Stineman, Esther. *American Political Women.* Littleton, Colo.: Libraries Unlimited, 1980.

Tinker, Irene, ed. *Women in Washington: Advocates for Public Policy.* Beverly Hills, Calif.: Sage, 1983.

INDEX

Rhode Island, 3, 4, 9, 10, 13, 19, 27, 29, 31, 33, 45, 48, 51, 53, 59, 64, 74, 83, 87, 89, 97, 99, 100, 103, 104, 109, 113, 114, 130, 133, 137
Richmond, Virginia, 36
Rochester, New York, 16
Rocky Mountain states. *See* West
Rogers, Edith, 138
Rural, 4, 8–9, 9*m.*, 33, 35, 125–27
Rwanda, 24

S

Saginaw, Michigan, 36
San Antonio, Texas, 19, 21, 33, 36, 59
San Diego, California, 36, 120
San Francisco, California, 16, 19, 33, 36, 40, 45, 67, 138
San Jose, California, 17, 33
Sarasota County, Florida, 7
Saudi Arabia, 24, 97
Sculptors, 55–56
Seat-belt use, 123, 123*m.*
Seattle, Washington, 17, 59
Secretaries, 47*m.*, 48
Sedentary lifestyles, 122
Senators, 138–39
Separated women, 83, 85*m.*, 86, 87, 127
Servants, 52*m.*, 53
Service sector, 41, 42
Sex education, 101
Sex ratios. *See* Male/female ratio
Sexually transmitted diseases, 119–20
Shelters for battered women, 128–30, 128*m.*
Single parent (female) families, 89, 90*t.*, 91*m.*, 92–93
Single women, 83, 84*m.*, 87, 89, 127
Smith, Margaret Chase, 138
SMSAs (Standard Metropolitan Statistical Areas), 9, 17, 19, 24, 33, 59, 89, 125, 135, 136
Soccer, 70, 74–75, 74*m.*, 77–78, 78*m.*
Social sciences majors, 65
Softball (fast pitch), 70, 71, 74, 74*m.*, 77, 77*m.*
Softball (slow pitch), 71, 74
South, 4, 6, 8, 9, 13, 16, 19, 21, 22, 26, 27, 28, 33, 45, 46, 48, 50, 51, 53, 55, 56, 59, 62, 63, 65, 67, 70, 72, 73, 74, 77, 78, 81, 87, 89, 95, 99, 103, 107, 113, 115, 117, 119, 120, 127, 130, 133, 135, 136, 137, 140, 142, 145
South America, 21
South Asia, 4, 8
South Carolina, 15, 16, 17, 23, 24, 27, 29, 31, 45, 51, 53, 55, 57, 59, 67, 70, 75, 83, 87, 89, 97, 98, 100, 101, 107, 123, 124, 130, 135, 136, 138, 140, 145
South Dakota, 4, 6, 8, 9, 13, 17, 19, 27, 30, 31, 33, 35, 39, 48, 53, 61, 63, 70, 73, 86, 87, 93, 95, 97, 103, 104, 109, 120, 121, 125, 127, 130, 136, 142, 144, 146
Southeast. *See* South
Southern Baptist Convention, 13, 87, 118

Southwest, 13, 21, 26, 27, 48, 50, 72, 74, 100, 115, 118, 130, 135, 136, 140, 145
Sports, 69–81
Sports participation, 70–72, 70*m.*, 71*t.*
St. Louis, Missouri, 16, 78, 135, 136
Starr County, Texas, 59
State Legislators, 133, 136–38, 137*m.*, 140
Suffrage, 140–42, 141*m.*
Suicide, 113, 114
Sullivan, Leonor, 138
Summit County, Colorado, 59
Sun Valley, Idaho, 59
Sunbelt, 3, 25, 86
Sweden, 8, 97
Switzerland, 97
Syphilis, 119

T

Taliaferro County, Georgia, 59
Teachers, elementary, 48–50, 49*m.*
Teenagers, 69–75, 98–101, 113–14, 118, 123
   fertility, 99–101, 99*m.*
   marriage, 100
   out-of-wedlock births, 99, 100–101, 100*m.*
   pregnancy, 98–101
Tennessee, 19, 21, 22, 27, 29, 31, 51, 57, 100, 111, 121, 124, 127, 130, 135, 138, 140, 142, 145
Tennis, 70, 71, 72
Texas, 1, 7, 9, 10, 16, 19, 21, 22, 25, 27, 33, 35, 40, 51, 55, 59, 67, 77, 80, 86, 87, 89, 97, 101, 103, 127, 136, 138, 140, 146
Title IX, 69, 72, 75–76
Track and field, outdoor, 70, 71, 72*m.*, 73, 76*m.*, 77, 78
Trenton, New Jersey, 9
Tulsa, Oklahoma, 19

U

Unemployment, 26–27, 26*m.*, 48, 51, 52, 53, 56
United Methodist Church, 13
Urban, 4, 8–9, 33, 33–35, 89, 118, 125
U.S.S.R., 24
Utah, 6, 7, 8, 13, 15, 24, 26, 27, 29, 31, 35, 36, 48, 53, 57, 62, 70, 71, 83, 86, 89, 95, 97, 98, 99, 100, 101, 103, 109, 113, 119, 120, 121, 136, 137, 138, 140, 142, 145, 146
Uterine cancer, 113, 117–18, 117*m.*

V

Venereal diseases. *See* Sexually transmitted diseases
Vermont, 9, 10, 14, 17, 19, 27, 29, 31, 35, 45, 50, 51, 55, 56, 59, 63, 67, 73, 74, 75, 78, 98, 99, 100, 101, 102, 109, 114, 117, 120, 125, 130, 137, 138
Victims of crimes, 125–30
Vietnamese, 17, 19, 22

Virginia, 8, 10, 19, 22, 23, 27, 29, 33, 53, 59, 61, 64, 109, 121, 135, 138, 140, 146
Volleyball, 70, 71, 73–74, 73*m.*, 77, 77*m.*, 80
Voter turnout, 135*m.*, 136
Voting patterns, 133–36, 134*m.*

W

Waitresses, 51–52, 52*m.*
Washington, 13, 17, 19, 27, 33, 48, 57, 61, 80, 86, 101, 103, 115, 125, 127, 137, 138, 145
Washington, D.C., 8, 10, 17, 24, 33, 36, 48, 61, 104, 121, 122, 136
Wealth, 37–40, 38*m.*, 39*m.*
Well-being, 120–24
West, 4, 7, 9, 14, 17, 21, 24, 26, 27, 29, 30, 37, 45, 48, 50, 51, 55, 59, 63, 64, 73, 74, 77, 78, 83, 86, 89, 92, 95, 97, 98, 102, 103, 107, 109, 111, 113, 114, 120, 127, 130, 131, 136, 140, 142, 145
West coast. *See* West
West Germany, 97
West Virginia, 9, 10, 13, 14, 17, 19, 22, 23, 24, 28, 30, 35, 45, 46, 55, 56, 57, 67, 74, 86, 87, 95, 97, 100, 101, 103, 104, 109, 117, 120, 121, 124, 125, 140, 145
Western Europe, 105
White women, 4, 12, 14–15, 14*m.*, 27, 48, 51, 52, 53, 95–97, 102, 109, 111, 116, 117, 118
Wholesale trade, 39, 40
Widowed women, 6, 12, 83, 85*m.*, 86, 87
Wife beating. *See* Battered women
Wilmington, Delaware, 9
Wisconsin, 13, 19, 23, 25, 27, 71, 81, 87, 97, 122, 123, 127, 135, 136, 138, 140
Wolfe County, Kentucky, 59
Women's colleges, 66*m.*, 67
Women's International Bowling Congress, 80*m.*, 81
Women's studies, 66*m.*, 67
Worcester, Massachusetts, 37
Work disability, 120, 121*m.*
Working mothers, 27–29, 29*m.*
Wyoming, 4, 9, 10, 13, 23, 26, 29, 35, 45, 48, 53, 56, 57, 59, 65, 67, 83, 87, 89, 97, 98, 100, 101, 104, 113, 117, 120, 121, 125, 130, 133, 135, 136, 137, 138, 139, 140, 142, 145

Y

Years
   1940; 111
   1950; 6
   1960; 6
   1970; 6, 14, 48, 50, 51, 53, 56
   1990; 6
   2000; 8
   2020; 6
Yemen, 8

Z

Zavala County, Texas, 59